Fantasy and Mimesis

KATHRYN HUME

Fantasy and Mimesis

RESPONSES TO REALITY
IN WESTERN LITERATURE

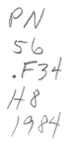
METHUEN
New York and London

First published in 1984 by
Methuen, Inc.
733 Third Avenue, New York, NY 10017

Published in Great Britain by
Methuen & Co. Ltd
11 New Fetter Lane
London EC4P 4EE

Phototypeset by Saxon Printing Ltd, Derby
Printed in Great Britain at the University Printing House, Cambridge

Library of Congress Cataloging in Publication Data

Hume, Kathryn, 1945–
    Fantasy and mimesis.
    Includes index.
    1. Fantastic literature—History and criticism.
    2. Fantasy in literature.   3. Mimesis in literature.
    I. Title
PN56.F34H8   1984   809.3'876   84-1054

ISBN 0-416-38010-7
ISBN 0-416-38020-4 (pbk.)

British Library Cataloguing in Publication Data

Hume, Kathryn.
    Fantasy and mimesis
    1. Fantastic literature—History and criticism
    I. Title
    809'.915   PN56.F34

    ISBN 0-416-38010-7
    ISBN 0-416-38020-4 Pbk

For
Fredna T. Irvine
and
John W. Irvine, Jr.

Contents

Acknowledgments

Many friends and colleagues have read this manuscript, and I am deeply indebted to them for their criticisms. Among those who brought their special expertise to bear on my arguments are W. R. Irwin and T. A. Shippey (fantasy), Judith Van Herik (psychology), and Peter Malekin (Plato). James Merod attacked my critical clichés, and Robert Secor my sense of an ending. Wilma Ebbitt edited the entire manuscript for consistency and clarity. To these and to the others, my heartfelt thanks. Doubtless my alterations are not as thorough as they would have preferred – and they should not be held responsible for the remaining shortcomings in my arguments – but the book is immeasurably better for their generous advice and suggestions. My thanks also to Janice Price and Merrilyn Julian of Methuen for their generous encouragement and expert assistance in seeing the manuscript through the press.

Preface

Western literature is traditionally discussed as representing reality, even though we know mimesis to have limitations. Authors must take a set of complex actions that occupy the three dimensions of space and the fourth of time, and transform them into a linear sequence of words, so the mimetic process is selective. It is subject to stylization and convention. Its reality is special, for the feelings, actions, ideas, people, and places need not *be* real; they only need to seem so. Although western writers through the centuries have presented very different renditions of reality, most of them have ostensibly aimed to produce something "like life".

Textual surface and analysis of the work-in-itself have occupied much of modern scholarship, but when critics do look up from their magnifying glasses to consider broader issues of audience, world, and even author, the idea of imitating reality has usually controlled their critical assumptions, despite its manifest inadequacy. Much literature does present lifelike actions and describe objects in the world we know. People, actions, and settings can be integrated in ways that we recognize as signifying or resembling what we consider reality. But literature has always been more than such a representation. Moreover, numerous works, past and present, deliberately depart from the norms of what can be called consensus reality, the reality we depend on for everyday action. We agree that food, oxygen, and liquid are necessary for life; that bodies fall; that stones are solid and hard; that humans die. This book examines the artistic motives for literary departures even from such basic realities as these, the techniques which such fantasy uses, and readers' reasons for accepting such contradictions of their experience.

For many readers, my references to mimesis will call to mind Auerbach's *Mimesis*. His panoramic survey of the styles and conventions for rendering reality makes plain just how impossible it is ever to achieve colorless imitation. Many of the authors Auerbach discusses thought of themselves as imitating reality, yet their renderings are based on such different assumptions and selections that one man's realistic imitation is another's stilted stylization. Although Auerbach thus reveals the weakness of any claim to absolute realism, he shares the western cultural bias in favor of imitation, and remains largely silent about deliberate departures from reality. My study owes much to his, but of necessity it operates in a different fashion. If the non-real is your focus, you have no stable point of reference, and the individuality of each departure from reality, each creation of something new, renders chronology largely irrelevant. Hence, I have preferred non-chronological classifications. This lets me discuss Homer's *Odyssey* along with Vonnegut's *Breakfast of Champions* if their fantasies and their assumptions about what is significant reality shed light on each other. I can also compare fantasies and mimetic works as examples of some particular response to reality. Whereas other critics writing on fantasy try to identify it as a genre or mode, I have tried *not* to isolate fantasy from the rest of literature. It is truer to literary practice to admit that fantasy is not a separate or indeed a separable strain, but rather an impulse as significant as the mimetic impulse, and to recognize that both are involved in the creation of most literature.

By fantasy I mean the deliberate departure from the limits of what is usually accepted as real and normal. The works covered range from the trivial escapes of pastoral and adventure stories to the religious visions of Langland and Dante. This does not mean that I am trying to relabel all western masterpieces "fantasy", but fantasy *is an element* in nearly all kinds of literature, especially the narrative, the most important exceptions being realistic novels and some satiric and picaresque works. Fantasy may take the additive form of deliberate distortion and departure; it may also take the subtractive form of omission and erasure. Random or radical selection can produce a fantastic chaos of the sort we see in absurdist drama or Barthelme's *Snow White*. Departure from reality does not preclude comment upon it: indeed, this is one of fantasy's primary functions. Hemingway, in mimetic terms, says "this is what life is like". In the metaphoric manner permitted by their fantasies, so do Kafka and Lewis Carroll.

In Orwell's *1984*, one of the creators of Newspeak gloats that the rapidly narrowing vocabulary of the language will soon make thoughtcrime impossible because there will be no words to express subversive ideas. Trying to talk about fantasy is practically as difficult as wordless thoughtcrime. We do not have the analytic vocabulary to frame our inquiries. Classical philosophers tore a hole in western critical consciousness when they established their negative attitude toward their traditional mythology, which hardened through changes in culture to a general distrust of fantasy. Only in the last century or so, in the work of psychologists, anthropologists, philosophers, and students of myth and religion have we even become aware that this blind spot exists. Much remains to be done before its fields of perception can be integrated into our thinking.

This book attempts to help us recover materials lost in this critical void, and it sets about the task by approaching fantasy from several angles. These fall into three groups corresponding to the book's three parts. The first explores the nature of fantasy. Chapter one surveys recent, mostly exclusive, definitions and lays out the inclusive definition I shall use. Chapter two analyzes western literary history in terms of concepts of reality, the changing functions of literature, the functions of fantasy, and the shifts in philosophy and science which accompany these changes. What I say in these chapters focuses, of necessity, on only the most essential ideas and broadest developments. To refine and solidify this material would require many books.

Part II presents the four basic possible literary responses to reality. Chapter three explores escapism, the literature of illusion. Many popular forms of literature offer the reader the chance to relax in hospitable and flattering realms: pastorals, mysteries, and pornography are some of the kinds of escapes explored.

Chapter four analyzes expressive literature, or the literature of vision. Works of this sort present the reader with a new interpretation of reality and offer the pleasures of emotional engagement with such a new world. Such realities, whether positive or negative, are "richer" than the shopworn and lackluster reality of our everyday lives. The realities may invite repulsion (Kafka's *Metamorphosis*) or effervescing delectation (Calvino's *Cosmicomics*); they may show us meaninglessness (Beckett's *Waiting for Godot*), or startle us with their detailed presentation of a realm normally closed to us, the mind of another person (Joyce's *Ulysses*). Expressive literature is a kind of mean between escapist and didactic literature: the author does not force his interpretation on us intellectually or morally, nor does he flatter us into agreement with attractive fairy tales. He engages our emotions and tries to persuade us at least to consider his interpretation of reality, however different from our own it may be.

Chapter five describes didactic literature, the literature of revision. Like expressive literature, this calls attention to a new interpretation of reality, but in addition, the author tries to force the readers to accept the proffered interpretation of reality and to revise their lives and their worlds to fit this interpretation. The author offers at least a token program for reform, and tries to cajole or coerce agreement to this line of action. Bunyan's *Pilgrim's Progress* is a Christian example of the didactic impulse. So, in a more novelistic vein, is Miller's *Canticle for Leibowitz*. Social and political didacticism inform the spirit of Steinbeck's *The Grapes of Wrath*. Although fantasy appears in all these categories based on the intended response to the author's reality, fantasy is particularly common in the didactic group because it can sugar-coat the pill of restraint and abnegation.

A writer can invite the reader to escape reality; or to acknowledge the possibility of a different reality; or to accept and live by the author's moral explanation of reality. These are the basic possible responses to a reality whose existence you believe in. Chapter six looks at another possible response: in the literature of disillusion, reality is declared unknowable. Authors living with this frightening conviction may try to shake readers into awareness of the possibility by proving to them that their senses are liars and their assumptions unfounded. Burroughs' *Naked Lunch* shows perceptions of reality to be chemical, and, as such, alterable. Calvino's *Castle of Crossed Destinies* shows communication by means of symbols to be so ambiguous that we cannot prove anything about external reality by checking with another witness, for we cannot prove that the other person understands our query, or we the answer. In *The House of Assignation*, Robbe-Grillet placidly superimposes possible, mutually contradictory, realities and defies us to make sense of them, although each alone seems plausible. Such authors batter our assurance, undercut our confidence, and mock our lack of sophistication. Like didactic literature, this literature of disillusionment attempts to force the reader's acquiescence but, unlike the didactic, it offers no program of action. We are left to face uncertainty as best we can. Such works can also be called perspectivist, because they insist that our perception of reality is a function of our perspective and vantage point.

Part III of *Fantasy and Mimesis* turns specifically to the literary and psychological influences on the creation of fantasy. Chapter seven explores fantasy as a function of literary form, and tries to analyze the literary impulses that demand from authors such departures from consensus reality. Chapter eight asks questions about the human need for fantasy, and about the psychological compulsions of authors and readers which foster its creation. This final chapter brings together various reasons for reading fantasy and sums up fantasy's role as a means of giving value to life and literary experiences.

Very early in this undertaking, I discovered the immense importance of being Ernst. In one three-month period, it seemed that all the theorists I was reading – Kris, Auerbach, Becker, Gombrich, Neumann, Kahler, Fischer, Cassirer, Curtius, Klinger – were named Ernst or Erich, and even those who slipped by the font as Johann, Karl, or Arthur were luminaries in the Germanic and European tradition: all were trained in classical languages, in philosophy, in western literature and art, some even in science. They always had Husserl and Heidegger up their sleeves, and inevitably trotted Kant out whenever they wanted irrefutable support for any argument they were presenting. I envy their truly formidable and admirable learning, and acknowledge the temerity of my skipping from

Plato to Poulet, and from Carpentier to Kafka and Calvino. My education as a medievalist lets me read the Latin, French, German, Scandinavian, and English texts in the original, but leaves me regrettably ignorant of other languages. Thus, though I have read in Icelandic about one oppressed people's stumblebum hero in Laxness' *The Bell of Iceland* trilogy, I must rely on translation for Hašek's *Good Soldier Schweik*. This should make no great difference, for my concern is the story, not the wording, but I apologize for any instances in which I miss the subtleties of the original, and for the unevenness of my knowledge of recent critical disputes. I know those surrounding *Beowulf* better than those concerning *Madame Bovary*, but since fantasy is rarely discussed in such controversies, this limitation should not matter.

Any treatise taking western literature as its realm is bound to reflect the idiosyncratic reading of its author, and this one is no exception. Although I have tried to keep my major examples diversified as to country and century, certain English and American works receive special attention, if only because I have taught them often. And in the area of minor illustrations and allusions, Anglo-American examples predominate, because that is the tradition I know in greatest detail. Throughout, however, the points I make are analytical and theoretical, not historical or national, so readers may make their own lists of equivalent works from other national traditions; the arguments I put forward should remain valid. Likewise, I stress narrative literature rather than dramatic or lyric, because that is my speciality. Readers specializing in drama can substitute their own examples, and those concerned with poetry may be able to apply my ideas to the symbolic modes of their form.

Since this is a critical overview, not detailed scholarship in a narrow area, I give all quotations in English. I have also reduced notes to only the most essential kinds of documentation and acknowledgment of indebtedness. If the number of notes seems small, it is because few critics have approached literature with its orientation toward reality as their chief concern, and of those few, only a handful have thought in terms of fantasy rather than mimesis. Critically, fantasy is all but uncharted territory. This book and the other recent studies of fantasy are equivalent to reports from the first explorers in new territory. Like those travelers, we pay great attention to the dragons and wonders we think we glimpse, and some of the Northwest Passages we have drawn boldly onto our maps may prove dead ends. One of the great pleasures of such exploration, however, is the chance to see well-known works from a new perspective. What you once thought you knew suddenly proves to be strange, intriguing, and exciting. The *Odyssey*, when analyzed with the nature of its fantasy in mind, reveals vistas not visible to those following traditional approaches. Teachers of any conventional literary speciality will find their perspectives altered after they focus on the roles played by fantasy within their area.

To many thinkers, fantasy has seemed a silly self-indulgence, even a perversion. Plato so viewed it when he was in a prescriptive mood. Although he himself used richly mythic fantasy to communicate complex ideas, his animadversions on mythology in *Phaedrus* are echoed by writer after writer down the centuries. Plato – through "Socrates" – was trying to exclude traditional myths from the phenomena which rational enquiry must explain:

> for my part, Phaedrus, I find that sort of thing pretty enough, yet consider such interpretations rather an artificial and tedious business, and do not envy him who indulges in it. For he will necessarily have to account for centaurs and the chimaera, too, and will find himself overwhelmed by a very multitude of such creatures, gorgons and pegasuses and countless other strange monsters. And whoever discredits all these wonderful beings and tackles them with the intention of reducing them each to some probability, will have to devote a great deal of time to this bootless sort of wisdom. But I have no leisure at all for such pastimes, and the reason, my dear friend, is that as yet I cannot, as the Delphic precept has it, know myself. So it seems absurd to me that, as long as I am in ignorance of myself, I should concern myself about extraneous matters. Therefore I let all such things be as they may, and think not of them, but of myself – whether I be, indeed, a creature more complex and monstrous than Typhon, or whether perchance I be a gentler and simpler animal, whose nature contains a divine and noble essence. (*Phaedrus*, 229D ff., Cassirer's translation in *Language and Myth*)

Socrates' refusal to rationalize chimeras was eminently sensible, especially given the crude methods available prior to Romantic myth-study and psychoanalysis. However, critics following his lead generalized these specific and limited objections into moral imperatives, and thunderingly decried any literary use of chimeras, pegasuses, and gorgons. Even granting that Socrates' objections were misused and misunderstood, and hence that he should not be held responsible for subsequent developments, we would now argue that he creates a false emphasis when dividing the monstrous from the divine within himself and preferring to concentrate on his diviner part. Since Freud, we feel that one can know oneself only if one recognizes the monsters inhabiting the fastnesses of the unconscious. Some of those inner monsters, like the Gorgons, are destructive and hideous. Others, like Pegasus, beggar description, and leave in their wake dissatisfied dreams of loveliness unpossessed. These denizens of the mental landscape cast long shadows on literature, so this book, by exploring these shadows, is not so far from obeying the oracle as the words of Socrates suggest.

Kathryn Hume
The Pennsylvania State University

Part I

Literature and the
representation of reality:
a new approach
to fantasy and mimesis

Introduction

Like M. Jourdain, who discovered that he had been speaking prose all his life, readers of this book may find they have been reading fantasy, teaching it, and writing about it without ever having brought their critical consciousness to bear on the fantastic elements. To many academics, after all, "fantasy" is a subliterature in lurid covers sold in drugstores; or it is a morbid manifestation of the romantic spirit found in the works of Hoffmann, Poe, and less reputable gothic writers. Or fantasy means Tolkien and his ilk – nineteenth- and twentieth-century authors whose *œuvres* are not part of traditional literature courses. But fantasy encompasses far more than these phenomena. It informs the spirit of all but a small part of western literature. We are curiously blind to its presence because our traditional approaches to literature are based on mimetic assumptions. Philosophy and Christianity have denigrated the non-real on various grounds, with the result that we have never developed an analytic vocabulary for exploring and understanding fantasy. Even now, we can form ideas about it only with difficulty, and must struggle to wrest our insights from the inchoate imprecision of wordlessness.

Part I of *Fantasy and Mimesis* will briefly examine what has been done to remedy our lack of critical understanding. Chapter one analyzes definitions of fantasy that have emerged in the last two decades and shows how they relate to one another. Chapter two sketches the history of fantasy as a literary phenomenon. When has it been most common? Why did it fall into disrepute? Why is it reappearing so frequently in contemporary writing? Only when we have become sensitized to the prevalence of fantasy can we go on in Part II to study literary responses to reality, both fantastic and mimetic. These responses are complexly varied. Imitation and imaginative transformation, metaphor and allegory, whimsy and myth interact in such elaborate patterns that creating divisions for critical purposes may seem as impracticable as separating the dancer from the dance.

But one can enjoy watching the dance the better for knowing the steps, can better appreciate the grace with which figures are executed for understanding how difficult they are. Recognizing and responding to the fantasy element in literature requires such knowledge. Part I will attempt to supply the foundation on which such knowledge can be built.

1

Critical approaches to fantasy

The doctrine of mimesis was the foundation of the Greek aesthetic; it is probably the best foundation for any aesthetic. (John Crowe Ransom, "The Mimetic Principle", *The World's Body*, 1938)

The disenfranchisement of fantasy

Today, Ransom's naive statement leaves much to be desired as a critical dictum, given our belated recognition that texts cannot transcribe reality, and indeed mostly refer to other linguistic conventions. Barthes' *S/Z* exposes some of the insufficiencies of mimetic assumptions even when those assumptions are applied to literature we think of as realistic. Robbe-Grillet insists that although description of things "once claimed to reproduce a pre-existing reality. . . . Now it seems to destroy them, as if its intention to discuss them aimed only at blurring their contours, at making them incomprehensible."[1] The extreme position posits that there is no discussable relationship between literature and reality but, in practical terms, most words in any normal narrative refer to the commonalities of human experience, and few readers can be persuaded to relinquish all expectation of meaning in a text. They will put the book down rather than try to respond to words which are being offered only as aesthetic squiggles or melodic sounds or even as infinite interplay of signifiers. Literature bears an inescapable resemblance to reality, and the more the work tells a story, the more necessary the presence of the real. Nonetheless, it is an astonishing tribute to the eloquence and rigor of Plato and Aristotle as originators of western critical theory that most subsequent critics have assumed mimetic representation to be the essential relationship between text and the real world.

The tribute, though deserved, is not altogether a happy one. We might rather say that Plato and Aristotle between them tore a large and ragged hole in western consciousness. Ever since their day, our critical perceptions have been marred by this blind spot, and our views of literature curiously distorted. To both philosophers, literature was mimetic, and they analyzed only its mimetic components. Moreover, insofar as their assumptions allowed them to recognize fantasy at all, they distrusted and disparaged it. Aristotle judged literature according to how probable its events and characters were; realistic plays he held to be better than those using fantastic gimmicks like the *deus ex machina*. Although Plato frequently used fantastic myths to clarify his more mystical arguments, he too tended to insist on the mimetic nature of literature. He banned it from the Republic because this essential feature made it a shadow of a shadow and because the object of the mimesis was too often unworthy emotion. In the *Phaedrus*, moreover, he seems unenthusiastic about the fantastic elements in traditional myths. He certainly derides attempts to rescue them through rationalization, and does not seem well disposed to the mythic monsters taken at face value.

In truth, the passage from the *Phaedrus* quoted in the preface has cast a long shadow on literary theory. Plato may have approved fantasy in some guises, since he entrusted important ideas to its images, but his negative views are the ones to have influenced later generations. Its mythic avatars, the winged horse and the chimera, leave their trail throughout later expressions of disdain for fantasy. Tasso, for instance, mentions flying horses, along with enchanted rings and ships turned into nymphs, as permissible for the ancients, but a breach of decorum for his contemporaries. Hobbes concedes that impenetrable armor, enchanted castles, and flying horses were apparently not as displeasing to the ancients as they should be to men of good sense in his own day. George Granville's "Essay on Unnatural Flights in Poetry" (1701) admits Parnassus, Pegasus, the muses, and the chimera to be acceptable poetic fictions, but condemns dwarves and giants as extravagant. David Hume disparages literary fantasy as a threat to sanity: romances, he claims, deal with nothing but "winged horses, fiery dragons, and monstrous giants", and he fears that "every chimera of the brain is as vivid and intense as any of those inferences, which we formerly dignify'd with the name of conclusions concerning matters of fact, and sometimes as the present impressions of the senses".[2]

Christianity unconcernedly perpetuated mimetic assumptions, and at the same time it further muddled critical perceptions of fantasy. The seductive attractions of classical literature included fantastic creatures and deities of an alien faith, so early Fathers of the Church developed a rhetoric of rejection that debarred these fantasies and, by implication, did the same to other fantasies as well. To many earnest Christians, literary fantasy has seemed a species of lie. The enemies of poetry addressed by Boccaccio and Sir Philip Sidney evidently numbered such literalists in their ranks; the Plymouth Brethren parents of Edmund Gosse considered all fiction whatever to be reprehensible lies. We see the secularization of this literalmindedness, and its extension as a mingling of Protestant and scientific seriousness, in *Hard Times*. Dickens is sensitive to the irreducible issue of fact versus non-fact, and he choreographs an elaborate battle between the two. An instructor expounds the literalist position to the hapless pupils:

> You are to be in all things regulated and governed . . . by fact. We hope to have before long, a board of fact, composed of commissioners of fact, who will force the people to be a people of fact, and of nothing but fact. You must discard the word Fancy altogether. You have nothing to do with it. You are not to have, in any object of use or ornament, what would be a contradiction in fact. You don't walk upon flowers in fact; you cannot be allowed to walk upon flowers in carpets. You don't find that foreign birds and butterflies come and perch upon your crockery; you cannot be permitted to paint foreign birds and butterflies upon your crockery.[3]

However, more sophisticated Christians throughout the ages have contented themselves with dismissing popular fantasy as a frivolity and therefore not deserving of serious notice. Moreover, despite hostility to the fantastic, Christianity did not quickly give rise to a realistic literary tradition, partly because it was also hostile to our fallen world and therefore could not consider realistic representations desirable or enlightening; partly, too, because it fostered allegory and other forms of fantasy deemed compatible with Christian morality. Marie de France can claim in the prologue to her *lais* that the fantastic adventures she describes conceal significant moral messages. Acceptable fantasy appears in the miracles stuffed into saints' lives. Bede, who wrote the sober and realistic *Lives of the Abbots*, adds miracles to his source for his *Life of Cuthbert*, composing this fanciful story *juxta morem*, or according to the custom, of that particular literary form.[4]

Christian fantasy encouraged the non-real, but did not sharpen critical awareness of the phenomenon because fantasy, if it served the cause of morality, became "true" and therefore ethically distinct from the lies of fable. Even today, the *vitae* of the fictitious Saints George and Christopher are held to contain moral truth, despite their unhistoricality. Christianity did nothing to redress the balance between fantasy and mimesis, although Christian poets made much use of fantasy in allegory and romance and pious tale. At most, acknowledged fantasy was tolerated as nugatory entertainment, but it received no separate, positive status, with the result that fantasy continued to seem a fringe phenomenon.

Socrates' repudiation of chimeras and pegasuses directed the attention of his successors away from fantasy's richness as a literary impulse. He also deflected inquiry away from the relationship between fantasy and the unconscious, thus discouraging systematic analysis in that direction until psychoanalysis. Now, as we focus on the psychological validity and artistic effectiveness of fantasy, we must struggle to correct our distorted perceptions and invent the requisite critical vocabulary. Since our terms evolved to meet the needs of mimetic assumptions, only the mimetic elements in literature have hitherto worn faces. However, as we finally begin to recognize the presence of this faceless, silent partner, its form gradually grows more perceptible.

In the rest of this chapter, I will discuss the theories of fantasy which have recently been put forward, their strengths, their weaknesses, and the ways in which the theories complement or challenge each other. Then, when readers have had a chance to weigh the advantages of an inclusive definition against those of exclusive definitions, I will look more closely at the idea of fantasy as literary impulse, and will spell out the assumptions I make about the nature of literature. Throughout the present chapter, from different angles, I am trying to offer answers to the question "What is fantasy?" When we have some answers, we will be in a better position to consider the questions that inspire Parts II and III, namely, "How is fantasy used?" and "Why use it?"

Exclusive definitions

Ultimately, I shall argue that recent theories of fantasy work from faulty assumptions about the nature of literature, so let me outline what these premises seem to be. The recent theorists assume, along with Plato and Aristotle, that the essential impulse behind literature is mimetic, and that fantasy is therefore a separable, peripheral phenomenon. Viewing fantasy as separable and secondary has led these critics to try to create *exclusive* definitions. They assume that fantasy is a pure phenomenon, that a few clear rules will delimit it, and that the result will be a genre or form which can be called fantasy. They frame their definitions in such a way as to exclude as many works as possible. What remains, for most of these critics, is a small corpus of texts, all fairly uniform in their uses of departure from consensus reality, and this small corpus is duly declared to be "fantasy" – with little thought given to all the works that have departures from reality which somehow fail to fit the rules. The resulting definitions do delineate various minor strains in literature, but are incapable of telling us much about the larger problem of departures from consensus reality: their nature, their aims, their effects. We can be grateful for these many insights, but I feel we need to take a broader view. If we are to unify various disparate subfields of fantasy, we shall need an inclusive definition. But first let us see what contributions the exclusive definitions can make.

Comparing the explicit and implicit definitions of fantasy put forward by three such diverse critics as Harold Bloom, J.R.R. Tolkien, and Eric Rabkin is like trying to compare interferon, saffron, and platinum. All the substances are valuable, but we need a common standard against which to measure them, some kind of framework that will highlight their similarities and differences.

The framework I would like to offer is a diagrammatic model of literature in its context. Something like this scheme is propounded by M.H. Abrams in *The Mirror and the Lamp*:

UNIVERSE

WORK

Figure 1   ARTIST   AUDIENCE

Work, artist, and audience are self-explanatory. Universe is Abrams' term for "nature", or "people and actions, ideas and feelings, material things and events, or super-sensible essences". This universe lies within the fictive work. Abrams uses his scheme to compare critical theories of literature. As he points out, "Although any reasonably adequate theory takes some account of all four elements, almost all theories . . . exhibit a discernible orientation toward one only."[5]

Author, work, and audience, as I shall call those same elements in my diagram, seem unexceptionable – they are necessary units in any communication situation – but "universe" is an oversimplification. First causes and final effects of a piece of literature are not confined to its author and audience. In addition to the universe within the work, we have to keep track of two other *cosmoi* in which those first and final effects are worked out – namely, the world surrounding the author (world-1) and that enfolding the reader (world-2). World-1 is everything outside the author that impinges upon him, consciously or unconsciously. It both reflects and shapes his scale of values. The elements an author creates with come from world-1. If the literature is especially successful, it makes its mark not just on members of the audience but, through them, on world-2, everything that impinges on the lives of members of the audience. These worlds of experience, world-1 and world-2, differ even if the artist and reader are contemporaries; world-2 indeed differs for each member of the audience. If artist and audience are separated by time, language, religion, culture, or class, the amount of shared reality may be small. The nature of what each considers significant reality will overlap even less. The universe or world within the work differs yet again. In order to compare theories of fantasy and see how they operate, we need first to be clear on the network of reciprocal relationships surrounding any work of literature. Hence, I propose the following diagram of a *text* surrounded by its successive contexts:

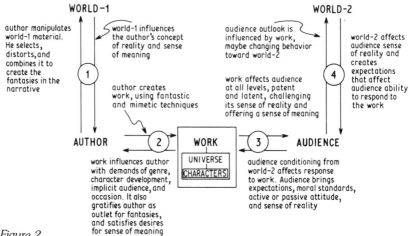

Figure 2

The descriptions labeling each arrow reflect my concern with fantasy, but the diagram is usable for discussing any critical orientation. Solid arrows indicate material covered by the critical theory; dotted arrows, as seen in figure 3 below, are areas that are lightly covered or only implicit; no arrow or parentheses around a blank indicate that the theory pays little or no attention to that part of the total system. The orientation of the arrows simply alludes to the direction of the relationship being discussed: "author←work" refers to the demands made on the author by the work through its generic conventions, and through the needs of the developing personalities of the characters. Within the work, I have labeled the third world "universe", Abrams' term for it, in order to reduce the confusion with worlds -1 and -2. Characters I treat as a sub-category within the fictive universe. They are part of that fictive universe, but some theories of fantasy make a distinction between the characters and their universe, so I mark them as separable.

One can use this scheme, for instance, to characterize the concerns of schools of criticism and thereby establish grounds for comparison. The characteristic configuration of the patristic or Robertsonian approach to medieval literature might be diagrammed as follows:

Figure 3

The individuality of the author is for all practical purposes denied. Any literary work is assumed to reflect the same set of world-1 realities, and the medieval audience supposedly brought essentially uniform and predictable assumptions to the literary experience. If the message of charity is effective, there should be a change in the audience's relationship to world-2; hence the dotted arrow. By way of contrast, New Criticism leaves worlds -1 and -2 and the author out of its field of focus. It assumes a response identical to the critic's, and concentrates on work and audience:

Figure 4

A critic treating a heavily didactic work will often implicitly set the work aside and concentrate on the flow of moral ideas which moves from author to audience:

Figure 5

Though few critical theorists pay much attention to the effect of literature on world-2, that relationship is stressed by moralists who wish to ban the sale of pornography, and by Marxists interested in social change.

The misguidedness of thinking fantasy to be a pure phenomenon relevant to a small portion of literature becomes apparent as we look at the various ways that fantasy can enter the picture through the contexts surrounding the work of literature. Let me explain the complete framework shown in figure 2, paying special attention to the reciprocal relationships numbered one through four, and to the ways in which fantasy can enter the picture.

If we think about world-1 at all in relation to the author, we normally picture world-1 as influencing the author (world-1→author), and it does indeed provide his sense of what is real and what a departure from reality. But the relationship also works in the other direction; the author manipulates and distorts the givens from world-1 (world-1←author), at least in his mind, and from its purely realistic phenomena he can create fantasy – a classical example of this process being the fantastic centaur made by joining the realistic givens of man and horse. In contemporary literature, the author may also alter his world-1 reality with drugs, or he may work with association and metaphor: Borges transforms a library into a universe; Barth makes a university the universe; Blish creates one of his universes out of a shallow pond. The author's own perceptions may incline him to see reality in terms other than the consensus; the result may be insight or insanity, mysticism or muddle, but what comes into the text will seem fantastic to readers.

In the relationship numbered 2, we tend to think only of the author as creating the work and hence as inserting fantasy into it, consciously or unconsciously; but the work also exerts an influence on the author, and calls fantasy into being. A romance needs marvels; satire calls for caricature and distortion; a saint's life demands miracles; science fiction needs galactic travel or other pseudo-scientific novelties. Fantasy may thus enter as an expression of authorial vision and psychology, or because of the demands of the genre.

Fantasy enters the third numbered relationship as something which is seen in the work by the audience; it flows from work to audience. We know surprisingly little about the effect it has on readers' outlook and behavior. Does escapist fantasy refresh readers and send them back to their real world renewed? Or does it make their real world less tolerable? Or does it undercut the readers' abilities to act – as Marxists feel? But the audience can also take some credit for calling it forth. The science fiction fans reinforce what the author feels as the demands of genre through their power as the buying public. Readers' interpretation of the nature of fantasy is also crucial. If the story goes too far beyond readers' sense of what is permissible, they may well reject the work, as many readers did Coover's *The Public Burning* on account of what the readers considered fantastic distortions of history. Readers may also introduce one kind of fantasy that is uncontrollable by the author; what the author meant literally may be interpreted as fantasy by readers of different backgrounds and eras: the monsters in *Beowulf* may be a case in point.

Finally, in the fourth numbered relationship, we see how world-2 provides the audience with its standards of what is real and what fantastic, but the effects of fantasy may be felt in the reciprocal relationship too: as C.S. Lewis points out, reading about an enchanted forest can make all subsequent woods in the real world seem a bit enchanted to the susceptible and sensitive reader.[6] If the text encourages one to look for angels dancing in a sunbeam, one may indeed see them. And if readers try to realize the fantasy in world-2, they may sometimes believe they succeed – as we can see in religious matters – and for some kinds of fantasy they can theoretically succeed if they bring a utopian community or some scientific breakthrough into being.

Theories of fantasy can be characterized by what portion of the contextual system they emphasize, and by the amount of the system they encompass. These variables, location and inclusiveness, bring out the contrasts between the theories quite sharply. Naturally, the theorists mention all of the elements in the diagram at one time or another. My identifying the focus with a limited portion of the scheme is an oversimplification, but I agree with Abrams that one can validly talk about a discernible orientation in any of these theories, and this is what I am trying to do. Since inclusiveness seems to correlate with the theory's capacity to answer basic questions, I shall discuss the authors, starting with those who focus narrowly on one element of the diagram, and ending with those who more or less encompass the entire scheme.

One-element definitions

Some critics exclude from consideration all elements but the work and its component parts, universe and characters. Two one-element, work-oriented definitions are those by Louis Vax and Brian Attebery. Vax, in *L'art et la littérature fantastiques*, despairs of defining fantasy formally, and settles for a definition based on subject matter.[7] Fantasy is that literature which deals with werewolves; vampires; portions of the human body which become detached and autonomously active; personality troubles, especially of an extravagantly sexual sort; the invisible; changes in causality, space, and time; and human degeneration – quite a grab-bag that encompasses *le roman noir*, his main concern, but would also embrace such later works as Gogol's "The Nose" and Roth's *The Breast*, and such science fiction stories as abrogate the limits of space and time. A more formal definition confining itself to the work is that of Brian Attebery.[8] His initial rule is very flexible, being based on W.R. Irwin's "overt violation of what is generally accepted as possibility", but he concentrates on the gradual advances achieved by American authors as they strove to assemble an American equivalent to the European realm of Faerie. Fantasy for Attebery is thus signalled by the presence of a vividly-realized secondary creation which gives readers the sense of its having a history beyond the fragments presented in the tale: Baum's land of Oz and Le Guin's Earthsea are such magic realms for Attebery.

Erik Rabkin also concentrates on the work, but he subdivides his material into the work's universe and its characters. Fantasy, for him, appears where "the perspectives enforced by the ground rules of the narrative world must be diametrically contradicted".[9] The changing of the ground rules must be recognized by the character as such. Carroll's Alice books offer especially clear examples. Alice realizes that her norms have been reversed when she cannot reach the garden by walking toward it, so she very intelligently walks in the opposite direction and reaches her destination. She knows that her slow fall down the rabbit hole is a fantastic reversal. She knows that when you run, you should get someplace. She thus knows that the ground rules have been changed on her. For Rabkin, much popular literature generally called fantasy does not qualify because the characters themselves accept the fantasy as normality. They are unaware of any reversal. Other works he considers true fantasy are Cortázar's "The Continuity of Parks", and Moorcock's *The Warlord of the Air*.

Two-element definitions

Critics whose definitions rely on only two elements in the framework are Tzvetan Todorov and Christine Brooke-Rose. Since Brooke-Rose adopts Todorov's definition, I shall concentrate on this, which concerns the two elements of work and audience:

> The fantastic requires the fulfillment of three conditions. First, the text must oblige the reader to consider the world of the characters as a world of living persons and to hesitate between a natural and a supernatural explanation of the events described. Second, this hesitation may also be experienced by a character . . . and at the same time the hesitation is represented, it becomes one of the themes of the work. . . . Third, the reader must adopt a certain attitude with regard to the text: he will reject allegorical as well as "poetic" interpretations. . . . The first and the third actually constitute the genre; the second may not be fulfilled.[10]

Doubt in the reader's mind about the fictive events and refusal on the reader's part to allegorize them: these are what matter. Author satisfactions or aims are irrelevant; even the characters' attitudes towards events are secondary. Fantasy is defined by the relationship between reader and work. Works that fit Todorov's definition are Jan Potocki's *Saragossa Manuscript*, Cazotte's *Le Diable Amoureux*, and I would add James' *Turn of the Screw* and Pynchon's *The Crying of Lot 49*. One inescapable drawback of Todorov's definition is that many works conform to it up until their last pages, at which point they either explain the mystery (thus becoming merely uncanny), or affirm the reality of the supernatural event and thus become examples of the marvelous.

Three-element definitions

One critic, Harold Bloom, focuses on an unusual selection of elements, namely on world-1$\longleftrightarrow$author$\rightarrow$work:

> *fantasy, as a belated version of romance, promises an absolute freedom from belatedness, from the anxieties of literary influence and origination, yet this promise is shadowed always by a psychic over-determination in the form itself of fantasy, that puts the stances of freedom into severe question.* What promises to be the least anxious of literary modes becomes much the most anxious, and this anxiety specifically relates to anterior powers, that is, to what we might call the genealogy of the imagination. The cosmos of fantasy, of the pleasure/pain principle, is revealed in the shape of nightmare, and not of hallucinatory wish-fulfillment.[11]

In other words, fantasy should free the writer from his sense of being a dwarf following after giants, although, paradoxically, the promised freedom from the ever-threatening oedipal predecessors usually elicits extreme anxiety from the author. Notice that the right side of the diagram hardly exists for Bloom: literature is the product of an author's dialogue with his predecessors (world-1) and its significance lies in the degree to which the author can assert himself. Bloom's chief example is David Lindsay's *A Voyage to Arcturus*, but he also talks about E.T.A. Hoffmann, Blake, Kafka, and his own gnostic fantasy, *The Flight to Lucifer*.

More conventional theories to rely on three of the framework's elements are those by W.R. Irwin, Marcel Schneider, and Ann Swinfen, all of whom draw on the communication sequence of author→work→audience. Irwin's definition works in two stages, the first being text-centered:

> Whatever the material, extravagant or seemingly commonplace, a narrative is a fantasy if it presents the persuasive establishment and development of an impossibility, an arbitrary construct of the mind with all under the control of logic and rhetoric. This is the central formal requisite. Without it, even the most bizarre material may be mobilized to produce something other than fantasy.

The second stage involves author and audience:

> To repeat, narrative sophistry, conducted . . . to make nonfact appear as fact, is essential to fantasy. In this effort, writer and reader knowingly enter upon a conspiracy of intellectual subversiveness, that is, upon a game. Moreover, this game, led by the writer prompting participation by the reader, must be continuous and coherent.[12]

Examples of fantasy according to this definition are Kafka's *The Metamorphosis*, Garnett's *Lady into Fox*, Bruller's *Sylva*, and Walter de la Mare's *Memoirs of a Midget*.

Marcel Schneider, like other French theorists, stresses themes, but he also makes a most welcome, if melodramatic, allusion to the relationship between fantasy and the psychological desires of both authors and audience:

> The fantastic lives on illusion, on delirium sometimes, always on hope and above all on the hope of salvation. For each of us hopes to be saved, and not only in another world but from now on, here below, thanks to the assurance that serves at the same time as talisman, secret, and recourse to the invisible powers.[13]

He mentions as the concerns of fantasy such subjects as time, destiny, the hereafter, the countenance of God, salvation, and love. He goes on to say that both author and audience may be "interested in the nocturnal portion of our existence, in dreams, daydreams, misgivings, intuitions, frenzies, phantasms, chimeras; in non-rational manifestations, portents, presages, auguries, etc., rather than in that which we do in all reason and consciousness". Schneider discusses a wide variety of authors, some of whom are Beckford, Potocki, Poe, Hoffmann, Nodier, Nerval, and Gautier.

Swinfen hardly defines fantasy at all, but she emphasizes themes (e.g., talking beasts, secondary worlds), and authorial desire to communicate ideals – religious, philosophic, social, political – to the audience. Her focus on works published since 1945 is unusual and welcome.[14]

Four-element definitions

Darko Suvin is defining science fiction, so he is somewhat outside of my direct concerns here, but he shows an unusual four-element orientation, stretching from world-1 to audience: "*SF is, then, a literary genre whose necessary and sufficient conditions are the presence and interaction of estrangement and cognition, and whose main formal device is an imaginative framework alternative to the author's empirical environment.*"[15] For the audience, the defining criteria are cognition and estrangement – the latter term including the effects of both Shklovsky's *ostraneniye* (defamiliarization) and Brecht's *Verfremdung*; for the author, the defining feature is that the work's imaginative realm be an alternative to the author's empirical environment. Suvin stresses this role of fantasy-work as comment on the author's world-1 when he analyzes the political subtexts in fantasies by Wells, Bellamy, and Verne.

Five-element definitions

Finally, we find approaches that embrace the entire, five-element framework in the Christian and Marxist theories of J.R.R. Tolkien and Rosemary Jackson, respectively. Tolkien is discussing fairy stories, so his primary emphasis is on the creation of Faerie within the text, but he is heavily concerned with justifying the form. This causes him to include a definition of fantasy and a description of what his fairytale texts should do, which prompts him to touch not just on author and audience but on world-1 and world-2 as well. He defines fantasy as "a natural human activity" which, he points out, "does not either blunt the appetite for, nor obscure the perception of, scientific verity". "For creative Fantasy is founded upon the hard recognition that things are so in the world as it appears under the sun; on a recognition of fact, but not a slavery to it. . . . If men really could not distinguish between frogs and men, fairy-stories about frog-kings would not have arisen."[16]

Fantasy as a natural human activity engages both writer and reader. For the writer, the attraction is the act of creating a secondary world. He must know reality, but he must also know what readers desire, and create out of his knowledge of these two. For the audience, the rewards of the fairy story are the fantasy for its own sake, and the experiences that the story gives us of recovery, escape, and consolation, all adding up to joy. By recovery, Tolkien meant the refreshing effect of defamiliarization, the newness available to us only after we have freed ourselves from our sense of possessing the familiar. Escape from the ugliness of industrial life and from death is for Tolkien one of the legitimate gifts of literature. The consolation offered by fairy stories is the assurance of a happy ending both for the story and for ourselves. Tolkien draws an extended comparison between fairy stories and the Gospel, stressing the spiritual impact that effective fantasy can have on the audience, and he acknowledges that fantasy can affect the audience's subsequent interaction with world-2.

Very different from Tolkien's religious sense of fairytale fantasy is Rosemary Jackson's Marxist and Freudian approach. She speaks of fantasy as:

> . . . a literature of desire, which seeks that which is experienced as absence and loss.
>
> In expressing desire, fantasy can operate in two ways (according to the different meanings of 'express'): it can *tell of*, manifest or show desire (expression in the sense of portrayal, representation, manifestation, linguistic utterance, mention, description), or it can *expel* desire, when this desire is a disturbing element which threatens cultural order and continuity (expression in the sense of pressing out, squeezing, expulsion, getting rid of something by force). In many cases fantastic literature fulfils both functions at once, for desire can be 'expelled' through having been 'told of' and thus vicariously experienced by author and reader. In this way fantastic literature points to or suggests the basis upon which cultural order rests, for it opens up, for a brief moment, on to disorder, on to illegality, on to that which lies outside the law, that which is outside dominant value systems. The fantastic traces the unsaid and the unseen of culture: that which has been silenced, made invisible, covered over and made 'absent'.[17]

Whereas Todorov emphasizes hesitation, Tolkien joy, and Irwin game, Jackson stresses fantasy as subversion and as a means for dealing with that which has been repressed and hence is inexpressible:

> The fantastic is predicated on the category of the 'real', and it introduces areas which can be conceptualized only by negative terms according to the categories of nineteenth-century realism: thus, the im-possible, the un-real, the nameless, formless, shapeless, un-known, in-visible. What could be termed a 'bourgeois' category of the real is under attack. It is this *negative relationality* which constitutes the meaning of the modern fantastic. (ibid., p. 26)

Fantasy within the text, Jackson defines as a kind of oxymoron holding together contradictions and sustaining "them in an impossible unity, without progressing towards synthesis" (p. 21). Like Tolkien but on different grounds, Jackson expresses the belief that fantasy, because of its subversive qualities, "may lead to real social transformation" (p. 10). In other words, it may affect world-2. Some of her texts are *Frankenstein*, *Melmoth the Wanderer*, *Dr Jekyll and Mr Hyde*, and *Dracula*. Although she focuses on the nineteenth-century English tradition, she also comments on later works from Europe and America, including some by authors like Kafka and Pynchon.

Let us sum up the characteristics of the various definitions, using figure 6 to aid comparisons.[18] Critics who have concentrated on work (itself consisting of fictive world and characters) include Vax, Attebery, and Rabkin:

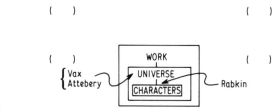

Figure 6

Todorov's definition is simple:

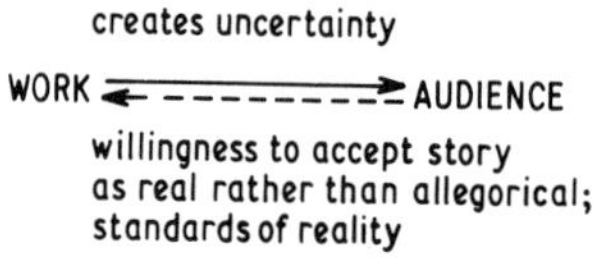

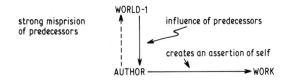

Figure 7

At the level of inclusiveness represented by three elements, we find different selections of elements. Bloom concentrates on the authorial side of the diagram:

Figure 8

W.R. Irwin and Marcel Schneider pay attention to the three elements basic to a communication situation – author, work, and audience:

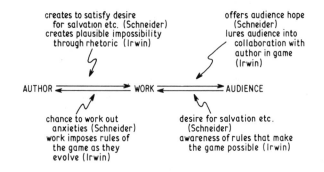

Figure 9

Suvin's array of four elements looks as follows:

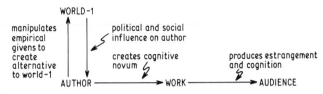

WORLD-1

Figure 10

And in Tolkien and Jackson we find yet more inclusive attempts which manage to say something, at least in passing, about world-1 and world-2 as well:

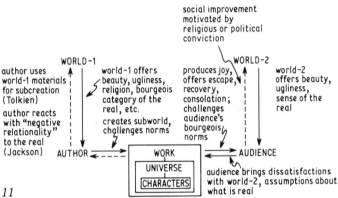

Figure 11

This collection of definitions of fantasy irresistibly reminds one of the blind men describing an elephant. Each observation is accurate for that part of the whole to which it applies, but none can stand as a description for the entire beast.

My evaluation of these definitions corresponds roughly to their inclusiveness. Those that embrace more of the contextual system are more readily usable. One can at least think of works that fit their criteria, whereas one is hard put to scrape up examples of the one- and two-element definitions. But ultimately, all of these are *exclusive*. And note, too, the relative unimportance or eccentricity or peripherality of so many of the texts these definitions confine themselves to. I am not denying that exclusive definitions can be useful. They do sensitize us to particular strains in literature and help us understand the conventions of those delimited forms. But the insights remain fragmented. They do not lend themselves to integration with the broader concerns of literary theory. Nor do most of them have much to offer as answers to such major questions as "Why use fantasy?" "What do audiences get from it?" "What good is it to authors?" "Why was fantasy displaced from the mainstream by the realistic novel in the nineteenth century?" The approaches best able to tackle some of these questions are those of Tolkien and Jackson, but overall, exclusive definitions seem to me a dead end. They will always be inadequate to the full range of non-realistic phenomena in literature. They make themselves insufficient through self-limitation.

Inclusive definition

I suggest that any major improvement in our ability to handle fantasy critically will not come from refining any of the approaches just described. It will not come from any sort of exclusive definition, nor from trying to isolate fantasy as a genre or form. The limitations of that paradigm should now be clear. *Il faut reculer pour mieux sauter*: we need to go back and rethink the original assumptions, those being (1) that the essential impulse behind literature is mimesis; (2) that fantasy is a separable and peripheral phenomenon; and (3) that, because separable, it is pure and best defined by exclusion.

I propose a different basic formulation, namely, that literature is the product of two impulses. These are *mimesis*, felt as the desire to imitate, to describe events, people, situations, and objects with such verisimilitude that others can share your experience; and *fantasy*, the desire to change givens and alter reality – out of boredom, play, vision, longing for something lacking, or need for metaphoric images that will bypass the audience's verbal defences. We need not try to claim a work as a fantasy any more than we identify a work as a mimesis. Rather, we have many genres and forms, each with a characteristic blend or range of blends of the two impulses. Tolkien's identification of fantasy as a "human activity" seems pertinent. It is necessary and useful both to the author and to the audience. Its manifestations in the text serve several purposes: relieving authorial tensions or giving voice to authorial vision; manipulating and releasing audience tensions; shocking, enchanting, and comforting. Above all, fantasy helps activate whatever it is in our minds that gives us the sense that something is meaningful.

I would like to propose a working definition of fantasy whose aim is to be as inclusive and as flexible as possible. Far from trying to avoid other definitions, it will be successful to the extent that it overlaps and includes their specifications, and makes a place for as many of their insights as possible. I shall try to analyze a wide and varied range of fantastic elements in literature, rather than extract a short list of uniform texts to be identified as a separate genre. Too frequently, studies based on exclusive definitions rouse a sense of frustration, for most stories generally called fantasy simply do not fit their definitions. If we look at western literature historically, we find all sorts of departures from consensus reality throughout its span, in the works of such major authors as Homer and Virgil; Chaucer,

Shakespeare, and Pynchon; Crétien de Troyes and Rabelais; Gottfried of Strassburg, Thomas Mann, and Kafka; Dante and Calvino. There are genres and works that eschew fantasy throughout this span, and in the nineteenth century fantasy was consciously pushed to the periphery by the upholders of the realistic novel, but fantasy has generally been a well-established part of mainstream narrative, and is now well re-established in contemporary fiction. To do justice to this all-but-universal phenomenon, we must abandon the assumption that mimesis, the *vraisemblance* to the world we know, is the only *real* part of literature; give up the notion that fantasy is peripheral and readily separable. We must start instead from the assumption that literature is the product of both mimesis and fantasy, and talk about mimetic and fantastic elements in any one work. Only then can we hope to approach literature without the distortion of perspective bequeathed to us by Plato and Aristotle.

My working definition is therefore of the simplest sort, and much like W.R. Irwin's. *Fantasy is any departure from consensus reality*, an impulse native to literature and manifested in innumerable variations, from monster to metaphor. It includes transgressions of what one generally takes to be physical facts such as human immortality, travel faster than light, telekinesis, and the like. Telepathy, although it may show up as a statistical effect in Rhine Institute studies of card-calling, does not work on the communication-as-if-by-telephone principle that some fiction displays, so that too is fantasy. I would include as a departure from consensus reality some technical or social innovations which have not yet taken place, even though they may well happen in the future: cloning of humans and utopian societies are both examples of this sort of fantasy. I would include alternate worlds and universes, for though other forms of life probably exist elsewhere in the cosmos, any current literary portrayal is the embodiment of our desires, a metaphor and a subcreation from matter we know in our own world, not an intuition of another world. We can also include as fantasy those stories whose marvel is considered "real", although not in the same fashion that a chair is real. Miracles and some monsters may have been thought to exist by their original audience and even their author, but were often acknowledged to be real only in a special fashion: they only enter the lives of the spiritually or heroically elect; they are *miracula* or things to be marvelled at, precisely because they are not everyday occurrences and cannot be controlled by just anybody who has a mind to try. We know we are dealing with a form of fantasy if the rhetoric of the text places the dragonfight somewhere else or once upon a time. Such distance and time markers commonly denote an awareness of fantasy.

Todorov and Brooke-Rose ban allegorical and poetic interpretation of the fantastic event or action. Although Jackson does not actually exclude the non-subversive, she relegates it to a position of insignificance in her treatment of fantasy. Suvin excludes from consideration as science fiction any story that does not include a "cognitive novum" or intellectual novelty (rigorously defined); hence both he and Jackson would pass over most popular "fantastic" escape literature. Many of these critics would deny utopias to be fantasy, preferring instead to call them speculative fiction, since they do not violate any laws of physics. I would embrace utopias along with allegories and science fiction as having fantastic elements, and therefore of concern in a study of fantasy. Utopias seem felicitously included by Jackson's "literature of desire, which seeks that which is experienced as absence and loss" (p. 3). The perfection of utopias may well be impossible in our world, and yet be desirable.

It may seem that I am trying to claim all literature as fantasy, or at least all but the realistic novel and occasional earlier picaresque and satiric tales. Not so. I am saying that most literature includes fantastic elements, even as it includes mimesis. I also grant that some forms are not best served by using the idea of fantasy as a means for analyzing them critically. One such form is any mythic narrative so undisplaced that teller and audience believe absolutely in the accessibility of the fantastic phenomenon to anybody. It is doubtful if we have any such tales in literary form, but some religious narratives may qualify. Another exception is escapist literature which is unrealistic but not a departure from what could physically happen in this world. Stories in women's magazines about ordinary girls marrying men who are brilliant, wealthy, fascinating, and besotted with them are sometimes called fantasy because of their raw daydream content, but they do not contravene the laws of physics or physiology. The third exception is simply what we normally call fiction. Plausible stories set in times past or present, which use invented characters in real or imagined situations, are not trying to depart from consensus reality, for all that they describe something which did not actually happen. If there had been a man like Horatio Hornblower during the Napoleonic wars, he might have enjoyed a career like that of C.S. Forester's hero; most of the upper ranked characters in that enjoyable series are historical and do what the history books say they did, but Hornblower himself is fictional. However, if historical characters are made to depart substantially from historical fact, as is Nixon in Coover's *The Public Burning*, then we are dealing with fantasy.

If we turn to the diagram of texts and contexts with an inclusive definition in mind, we can compare some of its concerns with those of the exclusive theories, and also chart the subsequent concerns of this book:

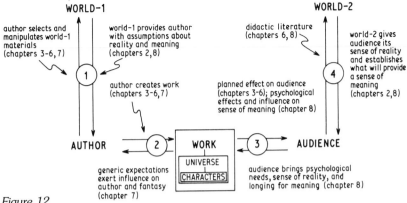

Figure 12

Since departure from consensus reality can only be registered from its appearance in the text, one might, at first, class this inclusive definition as work-oriented, but "consensus" immediately refers us both to the world of the author and that of the audience. Fantasy depends on what world-1 has conditioned the author to think of as real. Fantasy originates in the phenomena of world-1, as acted upon by authorial desire, fear, and logic. The author can incorporate the departures from reality out of the motives traced by Bloom, or out of those suggested by Freud and Jung; or may wish to "express" desire in both of Jackson's senses. All of these possibilities must be taken into account by the theory. Moreover, the nature of the fantasy may partly be dictated by the form of the work; if one is writing romance or satire or science fiction, one usually aims to meet formal expectations. The fantasy may also be influenced by the occasion for which a piece is produced, or by the preferences of market or publisher, or by the internal development of the plot. The departure from consensus reality appears within the fictive universe of the story, but is not always recognized as such a departure by the characters. In many a work of science fiction, the worlds portrayed are the only ones known to the characters, and so not alien or wondrous. Their adventures may or may not include brushes with what they deem magic. Rabkin's and Todorov's emphasis on a barrier between characters and the fictive universe seems too exclusive to me. So long as the departure is recognizable to the reader, we are talking about fantasy.

Some fantastic departures are peripheral: n-space travel is usually not magic to the characters within the work, and in any event is of less concern to readers than the plot it makes possible. Other departures, such as an escape from human mortality, can be central to the effect of the story. The nature of the mix of fantasy and mimesis has much to do with the complex effects of the narrative. The audience may respond intellectually, emotionally, and subconsciously, each response differing in content and strength. The audience will also react according to generic expectation, according to cultural background, and according to personal concept of reality. Some of these responses will be influenced by the audience's experience in and perception of its own world-2. Moreover, the fiction, if effective, may at least temporarily modify each audience member's relationship with his or her own world-2. If the work is extremely effective – as Jackson's subversive agency, as Tolkien's bringer of joy, or as C.S. Lewis' awakener of a sense of enchantment – it may permanently alter the reader's relationship with world-2.

An inclusive definition cannot confine itself to treating fantasy as a genre (Todorov) or even as a mode (Jackson). Tolkien moves beyond literature when he calls fantasizing a natural human activity, and that seems to me an important point when we try to locate fantasy within the system. The author fantasizes, creates inner fantasies using and altering materials he perceives in world-1, and turns them into a text which embodies fantastic departures from reality. The reader in turn absorbs the literary fantasy and turns it into virtual memory, and even into personal fantasies. We can see only the literary text, but without some consideration of the human desires motivating both supply and demand of that text, we cannot understand fantasy. A work-orientation to fantasy criticism is insufficient. We can deal with the textual manifestation because that is what we can see, but fantasy and the activities producing it go beyond that text. I have tried to gather and subsume these various facets of fantasy under the term "impulse", and I suggest that this impulse is not inferior in priority, scope, or significance to the mimetic impulse.

As the epigraph to this chapter suggests, fantasy has not generally been granted parity with mimesis in critical thinking. Even in this post-romantic era, Ransom could speak of mimesis as the best foundation for any aesthetic. One can indeed build elaborate intellectual edifices on an essentially mimetic foundation, as western critics have done, but the complexity and beauty of such structures should not blind us to the flaws inherent in this foundation. Moreover, the potential presence of fantasy and its effects in each of the relationships among the contexts and text suggests that fantasy is much more central to literature than a generic label. But I am not arguing that fantasy should replace mimesis. Robert Scholes is correct in theory when he states:

> what we can no longer accept is precisely this Joycean faith in the transcribability of things. It is because reality cannot be recorded that realism is dead. All writing, all composition, is construction. We do not imitate the world, we construct versions of it. There is no mimesis, only poiesis. No recording. Only constructing. [19]

In practice, however, we know it to be quite possible to recognize an imitative and realistic intention in narratives. Zola's *L'assommoir* and Updike's *Rabbit is Rich* may be fiction, and as stories they are certainly poiesis, but the plots use no fantastic elements and hew to consensus reality. No one would call them fantasy. Hence, I continue to use the traditional terms, mimesis and fantasy, and as *impulses* behind the creation of literature, the terms are accurate and usable as they may not be when used to describe the transformation of thing or action into words.

If we look beyond mimesis-oriented critical assumptions, we will see that fantasy is present in many literary forms throughout the ages. In some picaresque tales, pastorals, and novels, we find a systematic effort to avoid it. In the case of the novel, the exclusion of the non-real parallels and imitates the attempts of scientists to free their observations from the assumptions based on Christian myths, in order that they might establish facts. Fantasy, far from being a fringe phenomenon, is scarcely separable from literature as a whole. Fantasy and mimesis together are equally important impulses, and their interaction must be studied if we are to progress in our understanding of literature.

Assumptions about literature

As a coda to these definitions of fantasy, I would like to lay out the assumptions about literature made in this study. These can be important because assumptions about the function of literature strongly affect their proponents' attitudes towards fantasy.

Some of the standard assumptions about what literature is or does (aside from entertain) include the following. Literature has been seen primarily as *imitation* (the classical and neoclassical tradition). In a broad sense, this assumption extends to all the following approaches to literature. They all assume that literature refers to reality, whatever else it does. The role of literature has also been identified as *expression* (anthropological and psychological approaches, romantic lyricism); as *manipulation* of the audience through its affective power and rhetoric (Tolstoy, Sir Philip Sidney); as *communication* (Max Eastman, many didactic writers); as *creation* (Robert Scholes, Austin Warren); as expression of the author's mind which only becomes meaningful by *an act of mind by the audience* (Poulet); as *a dialogue between author and his predecessors* (Bloom); and as *an exercise of the teleological faculty by both author and audience* (Albert Levi). Obviously, some of these overlap and some contradict each other. The reader's teleological faculty may be exercised whether the opus is considered expression or imitation. Expression may mean lyric outcry, or may represent something like the author's attempt to manipulate unconscious anxieties. Communication may be the flatfooted exposition of a message, or may be something more subtle, such as Sartre's notion that literature has a thesis (though no extractable idea) whose point is to remind man of his freedom. For readers like R.G. Collingwood, who hold Kantian notions of the purely aesthetic, any attempt at explicit communication degrades a work from the status of art to that of propaganda. A work of literature deemed by one critic to derive its significance from the personal response of the reader may be seen by another critic as an embodiment of the spirit of its age.

All these approaches to literature seem possessed of some validity and usefulness, but each gives its proponent a characteristic ability to see or not to see fantasy in literature, to value it or not to value it. If one starts with the belief that literature consists of mimesis, one has an automatic bias against manifestations of fantasy. The presence of fantasy is taken to signal a kind of failure. Many classical and neoclassical writers used ghosts and gods in their high mimetic works, apparently feeling that these heightened the effects of pity and terror that they strove for, but Dryden, for instance, betrays defensive uneasiness over his use of such gimmicks; his protests on behalf of his practice imply uncomfortable belief that the titbits of fantasy were not the highest form of art, that they were, in fact, a bit regrettable, and entertaining though negligible. In no sense did they threaten the fundamental imitation from which his art drew its respectability.

Literature as expression is an approach taken by very different critical schools. Christopher Caudwell takes an anthropological and Marxist work-orientation, and discusses literature as emerging from expressions of community feeling such as work songs and celebrations of community events.[20] For Freud, the expression involves the author's conscious and unconscious anxieties, which are made palatable and even enjoyable to him and to his audience because they are artfully expressed.[21] For many romantics, literature was the author's lyric expression of feeling. Part of Wordsworth's celebrated definition of poetry calls it "the spontaneous overflow of powerful feelings". Theoretically, this approach to literature neither encourages nor discourages fantasy; in practice, it is sufficiently open to the fantastic and to images from the author's unconscious that it seems to foster fantasy, especially in the Romantic era, if only by contrast to the mimetic assumptions that had influenced previous ages. Gothic literature, with its sinister fantasies and subversive probes into bourgeois conscience, is often called dark romanticism. Jackson's Marxist and Freudian theory of fantasy rests on such assumptions about literature's expressive function.

If one considers literature as rhetoric, significant insofar as it has power to affect an audience, one should be able to admit and recognize fantasy. If swaying the audience is what matters, then any technique which succeeds validates itself, unless religious taboos limit the techniques allowed. The literature of sentimentality that flourished in the eighteenth century uses little fantasy because its rhetorical end is to persuade the audience to respond to the finer things of the extant world, but literature designed to frighten readers or entrance them often finds fantasy effective. Tolkien's emphasis on fairy tales bringing joy is an affective theory; C.S. Lewis' preference for enchantment is another. Theories that art should produce estrangement (*Verfremdung, ostraneniye*) make affective assumptions about the purpose of literature, and fantasy is a logical tool for inducing estrangement. Poetic metaphor and symbol are warranted by the aim of affecting the audience, no matter how surreal the metaphor or how fantastic the symbol.

Literature as communication is sometimes difficult to separate from literature defined by its affective power. The former, however, works more directly with ideas, the latter with emotions. Fantasy is possible within a communicative framework, but not necessary. Theorists who view literature as a medium for communication tend to be utilitarian, and hence consider the non-real insignificant. The more the communication of ideas is stressed, the less important the artistry and individuality of the text; as I suggested with figure 5, the text can be represented by empty parentheses in the line of flow between author and audience. However, fantasy can provide the *dulce* which makes the *utile* palatable, so it often surfaces in didactic literature.

Literature as creation is an approach that is open to the possibility of recognizing fantasy and making use of it. Robert Scholes, who stresses poiesis in his assumptions about literature, makes the following point:

> No man has succeeded in imagining a world free of connection to our experiential world, with characters and situations that cannot be seen as mere inversions or distortions of that all too recognizable cosmos. Thus, if we must acknowledge that reality inevitably eludes our human languages, we must admit as well that these languages can never conduct the human imagination to a point beyond this reality. If we cannot reach it, neither can we escape it. And for the same reason: because we are in it. (*Structural Fabulation*, p. 7)

This is a vital statement about the nature of literature; with commendable brevity, it suggests the basic grounds for my belief that fantasy is an impulse behind literary creation of no less importance than mimesis. Ultimately, we can escape neither one entirely. Both together are literature.

Poulet's characterization of literature is both expressive (for the author) and affective (in his concern for audience response).[22] Levi's description of literature seems to me to give a sharper focus and at the same time most resembles my own. Levi sees literature as the exercise of the teleological faculty by both author and audience.[23]

I accept all these assumptions about literature as useful and relevant, and by no means wish to exclude them when I state that my own primary assumption is that *literature is significant as a meaning-giving experience*. Both author and audience, in different fashions, receive corroboration for their standards of meaning, or find new frames of values. The myriad ways in which a sense of meaning is conferred will be discussed in chapters two, seven and eight. I grant that any sense of meaning is a myth of our

consciousness, but most of us seem to crave that myth. Literature, viewed
in this fashion, helps us find relationships between the I and the not-I,
between man and the cosmos, between consciousness and reality.
Although some limited and everyday affirmations of meaning can be made
using only reason and only mimetic techniques, and although fantasy has
other roles as well, I shall argue that it is the fantastic elements which allow
literature to convey most of its varied senses of meaning.

2

Historical perspectives on fantasy and realism

Throughout the span of western civilization, literature has served different functions in keeping with the shifting cultural patterns. Conceding the oversimplification, I would like to suggest that there have been three fundamentally different kinds of literature, each with its own typical function. Chronologically, they follow the sequence A-B-A-B-C. The first is the kind of literature fostered by traditional societies – societies with a unifying religion and morality – and we see this form in the Homeric epics (and much of the Old Testament) and in the literature of the Middle Ages (A, A). The second develops after the religious myths have been challenged (B, B). In late classical times, this development was cut short by the advent of Christianity and a new traditional society; in the later era, the long transitional stage found in the Renaissance eventually yielded a definitively new form of literature with a new implicit function: realism. The third stage (C), encompassing modernism and post-modernism, is arguably only another transition to we-know-not-what, but I believe that this literature has achieved a fairly clear new function, and feel that it can tentatively be recognized as a third distinct kind of literature.

Within these three stages, we find very different scope for the impulses of mimesis and fantasy. The characteristics of traditional societies have logical corollaries in their literature which help explain how that literature gives a sense of meaning, and help define the many varied functions of fantasy fostered during that stage. Skeptical philosophical and scientific stances likewise have corollaries in literature, and affect the ways of conveying meaning. I will discuss traditional literature in the first section, and then go on in the second to sketch the changes in cultural outlook that made realism possible. In the third section, I want to consider why realism has been so limited a phenomenon, historically speaking. What caused its synthesis of values to break down? How did it suggest a sense of meaning and why has this more or less ceased to work? Why was fantasy pushed to the periphery? In the final part of the chapter, I want to look at modern literature, at the kinds of effort being made to find new values. Fantasy has again entered the mainstream. What values is it asserting, especially given the continued tradition of skepticism and disbelief?

Several theorists of fantasy use so narrow a definition that they claim fantasy to be a post-Enlightenment phenomenon. Fantasy following the Enlightenment certainly is different from traditional fantasy in many respects, but, as this chapter should make plain, the impulse to depart from consensus reality is present for as long as we have had literature. It merely relies on a different logic and a different concept of reality.

These then are my main concerns in the following chapter: the implicit functions that distinguish these three stages of literature; the ways in which they give their sense of meaning to the audience; the ways in which they use fantasy; and the philosophical and scientific developments that brought about the changes from one stage to the next.

Traditional society and traditional literatures

A traditional society is one sustained in its values by a common mythology. The mythology tells man how he relates to the rest of the universe, or as Northrop Frye puts it, "A mythological universe is a vision of reality in terms of human concerns and hopes and anxieties. . . . All mythological universes are by definition centered on man, therefore the actual universe was also assumed to be centered on man."[1] The religious myths of a culture, privileged fantasies in that they are held to be true, are the spiritual axioms from which a society works out its priorities and values, be they to celebrate and exercise one's physical and mental powers, to mold oneself to the rules that define a chosen people, or to subordinate oneself to the disciplines and hierarchy that promise salvation.

The existence of these myths and the way society responds to them affect traditional literature in ways not generally recognized, although some of the social functions of the myths are well known. Mircea Eliade points out that reality in a traditional society is entirely different from reality in our own. We take the everyday, the nitty-gritty details, to be real. In a traditional society, only those essences within objects and actions that imitate the initial mythic truths are considered real. "If we observe the general behavior of archaic man, we are struck by the following fact: neither the objects of the external world nor human acts, properly speaking, have any autonomous intrinsic value." Eliade goes on, "The crude product of nature, the object fashioned by the industry of man, acquire their reality, their identity, only to the extent of their participation in a transcendent reality. The gesture acquires meaning, reality, solely to the extent to which it repeats a primordial act."[2] The mythic truth established *in illo tempore* (sacred time) is "real"; man living in profane time becomes real only to the degree that he imitates the sacred pattern and actualizes it within himself. In other words, imitation of the mythic pattern gives a sense of meaning. Man's highest aim in traditional society was to depart from what we would call consensus reality, the everyday dull detail, in order to imitate a state we would call privileged fantasy. The process involved in fantasy (departure from consensus reality), though called by different terms, is very much present in traditional society.

These assumptions about the need to imitate the mythic pattern affect traditional literature in several ways. To begin with, we find that much traditional literature describes mortals either living up to a set ideal, or failing to do so. This ideal may be the overall excellence of *aretê*, or a more limited virtue such as chastity or obedience. They do not decide between several legitimate choices; they must not count mere expedience. Their course is basically clear and we know by how much they fail or succeed. (The Greek *hamartia* literally means missing the mark.) Penelope's significance corresponds to the degree to which she has acted the faithful wife. We see Jesus conscientiously fulfilling a known pattern when he arranges for an ass to bear him (as proclaimed in Zechariah 9:9) and when he quotes from Psalm 22 while on the cross. Saints' lives show the heroic observance of proper pattern, no matter what the temptation or torment – witness the *Life of Saint Anthony*. Grettir, in his saga, forces himself to live the life of a legendary hero; his tragedy is being born too late, into a society that cannot cope with his kind of behavior. Patient Griselda in Chaucer's *Clerk's Tale* lives up to her ideal of submissiveness with inhuman success.

When the protagonist in traditional literature fails to live up to the accepted pattern, we usually see the dire consequences that follow such misbehavior. *In illo tempore*, Abraham set the pattern for obedient servants of God; when Saul refuses a sacrifice, he is judged by that example and found wanting. The misbehavior of Agamemnon and Achilles lies heavy over the *Iliad*. The ideal pattern in *Njal's Saga* is represented by the law; Gunnar Hamundarson is the nearly perfect hero, but when banished for his unavoidable part in a feud, he inexplicably refuses to accept the three-year sentence of exile and stays in Iceland, thereby ensuring not only his own death but those of all his friends as well. Roland's army is slaughtered because he lacked the *sagesse* such a leader must command. Malory's *Morte D'Arthur* is a magnificent study of men's failure to live up to their ideal patterns. One's obligations to God, to one's lord, and to one's lady should not clash in a well-regulated life. When Lancelot tries to combine devotion to the Grail and adultery with his king's wife, he violates all three obligations, and brings down the fragile network of allegiances that kept the chivalric society going. Given this traditional approach to basic mythic patterns, it is little wonder that much traditional literature strikes us as moral, even moralistic.

The concept of the individual, both in society and in literature, depends heavily on this imitative approach to the mythic ideal. To twentieth-century westerners, the sense of being unique seems naturally important, but this belief is exceptional. Anthropologists suggest that in many primitive societies, life is communal and members achieve their fulfillment not by individuating themselves but by identifying with the traditions of their culture. In large communities, identification may be with a subgroup, such as a totem, caste, profession, guild, or class. In the Middle Ages, this identification with the mythic ideal worked in religious as well as professional terms:

> Since the Renaissance we have tended to feel that a man has most completely fulfilled himself when he has been able most sharply to distinguish himself from other men in the development of what is peculiar to himself. The Christians of the Middle Ages felt, on the contrary, that a man most completely fulfilled his human potential as he shed what was peculiar to himself and let the image of God, in which he had been made, shine through.[3]

This concept of the individual affects portrayal of people in traditional literature. Villains can be more easily individualized than good persons. In *The Canterbury Tales*, we learn much more about the Wife of Bath than about the Knight or Plowman: her deeply personal thoughts and ordinary, unmythic actions are individual and hence for the most part sinful. We see Beowulf in half a dozen public situations, but never see him hung over or out of temper; we are not privy to his personal opinions of Hygelac's policies; nor do we have access to his misery when he was an unpromising youth. We are similarly in the dark about the individual thoughts of Griselda, Erec, Yvain, Roland, Sigurd, and any number of traditional protagonists.

We see this different theory of personality most obviously at work in biographical genres. Gombrich describes a version of it when he speaks of painting what you know rather than what you see.[4] When one's world outlook is oriented toward the ideal, one draws the ideal which one knows to be present and meaningful rather than the merely accidental. The ancient Egyptian practice of drawing eyes as seen from the front on profile heads, and the Greek idealization of bodies and faces to those of gods, are both examples of men drawing what they "knew" – knew to be meaningful and important – rather than the superficialities of visible reality. The same use of familiar models and the meaningful is seen in Einhard's *Life of Charlemagne*, which follows Suetonius' *Lives of the Caesars*. Historians have anathematized Einhard for following his model too closely rather than giving us Charlemagne as he really was, but Einhard saw himself as bringing out the *caesaritas*, and chose materials which would transmit this transcendent reality. Saints' lives likewise borrow miracles shamelessly from each other in a manner that strikes the modern mind as discrediting all claims to holiness for the saint thus beplumed with stolen feathers. If the miracles have to be imported from the Gospels or copied from earlier lives (as is the corpse miracle in the *Life of Ailred* from Sulpicius Severus' *Life of Saint Martin*) we hesitate to credit the later candidate for canonization with any proof of sanctity. Yet the author, from his own viewpoint, is affirming the *sanctitas* of his subject by providing this window onto the superior reality. In such a model-oriented aesthetic, we can be made very uncomfortable by the crudity of such borrowings. The final episode in *Grettir's Saga* changes the names, but arrogates unto itself the Tristan story. Modern scholars wince at this plagiarism, but it makes sense as a traditional literary means of creating an embodiment of the romance ideal, in order to contrast that ideal of heroic behavior with the other patterns explored in the saga.[5]

Meaning for the individual comes from imitating mythic patterns; meaning for the reader or listener comes from seeing these patterns imitated in the story, and from seeing attempts at imitation fail. If presenting the mythic ideal for imitation is the underlying function of traditional literature, what are the implications for fantasy? Departures from consensus reality abound in heroic Greek and medieval literature. Why?

To begin with, fantasy exists in the basic myths; they assert values that cannot be validated scientifically, and the stories they tell are most decidedly not verifiable – creation, activities of the gods, the deeds of semi-divine beings and culture heroes. Displaced from the mythic level, we find tales of men, many of whom still deal with marvelous adversaries since such enemies are necessary to define the heroes as heroes. The fantasy serves to let them copy the mythic pattern closely, and thus reinforces meaning. We find fantasy upholding morality, as happens when *deus ex machina* figures enter classical tragedies or when angels or the Virgin enter medieval tales. We find fantasy serving satiric ends; the dream elements in *Piers Plowman* and the animal fable of *Roman de Renard* uphold an ideal order while chastizing the abuses of the extant system. We find fantasy in allegory. What we do not find until the culture's myths have been seriously challenged is fantasy used to denigrate the ideal, satire without a high moral norm, black comedy, and the like. Those demand skeptical awareness as their first step, so let us turn to the effect of such skepticism on traditional values and literature.

Skepticism and the growth of realism

We see the challenge from skepticism fully formulated for Greek culture by the time that Socrates talks to Phaedrus about chimeras and gorgons. Not only does he know how to translate the phenomena naturalistically, he treats that process as a common game, one that any educated person could play. Socrates considers the process valueless. He not only apparently denies the myth primary truth, he denies it the truth of symbolizing man's mind and even the secondary truth one can salvage by admitting that the god Boreas is just a fanciful way of referring to the north wind. Socrates prefers to jettison all such myths as irrelevant in order to study himself.

The Enlightenment witnessed similar challenges to Christianity. The Faith had weathered many local threats in the form of heresies; it had suffered from *Sic et Non*-trained thinkers who could see incompatibilities between faith and reason; the sufficiency of the myth had also suffered under the attack of Protestantism, which insisted that some portions of the myth were merely symbolic. However, the basic mythic tenets remained unshaken until philosophy and, later, science raised the possibility of there being no God at all, or only a non-personal force. Atheism took well over a century to become commonplace, and has obviously not made great headway even yet, but the challenge to the primal myths of the God of Genesis, of a redeemer, of heaven and hell, was permanent.

Three developments in Enlightenment thought had crucial consequences for literature. One was Locke's concept of the individual as a *tabula rasa*. Each person is the sum of his or her unique experiences. These individual and accidental concatenations are what is real; there is no transcendent ideal. Unlike medieval nominalism, Locke's theory achieved widespread familiarity. According to its implications, we need to study as wide and varied a range of individuals as possible if we are to understand mankind, for we must now observe inductively rather than deductively. All humans and all situations are appropriate subjects for observation; social and moral elevation lose their preferential status as literary subjects. To understand a literary portrait, we will now need personal details; we will feel the portrait to be false to the extent that the author has let a literary type supply a pseudo-personality. Nor will we be satisfied with caricature or humours characters whose excesses are just givens; if every part of a personality develops from external stimulus, Lockean assumptions lead us to expect emotions to be logically explicable and logically coherent.

Once the mythic universe had crumbled, to be replaced with clockwork or the equations of physics, we find that the individual as object of literary study becomes more important than would ever before have seemed possible. If the physical world is composed of dead matter, intrinsically meaningless, then by contrast human responses seem more alive and meaningful. The concern to understand human emotions is very practical too, for that knowledge, properly applied, may help one ensure one's own happiness, as one must do if religion no longer dictates the basic terms of life. Even as later Greek drama and sculpture started portraying individuals, so too did European literature, and the individual's sensations and the logic of emotions gradually became the focus for the new form of literature which culminated in realism.

We can see the effect of Lockean assumptions if we compare the portraits of three women responding to their passions: Gottfried of Strassburg's Isolde, Flaubert's Emma Bovary, and Joyce's Molly Bloom. Very little that could be called individual emotion or raw feeling comes through in Gottfried's story. The emotions, indeed, are often replaced by objects, by props which can be used to pose set scenes, as if for panels in a tapestry. Thus, falling in love becomes drinking a potion; the one is invisible, but the other is easily visualized and described. The strength and generosity of Isolde's love is demonstrated by her throwing away Petitcreiu's magic collar and bell. Description of the love grotto appears where we might expect description of the lovers' unfettered passion. What a woman in Isolde's place would actually have thought while she slept with Mark, or would have said to herself when anticipating a meeting with Tristan, or what she would have daydreamed about, is not ours to know. The ideal is what matters, and its transcendent power is suggested by magic objects.

Isolde was an exceptionally well-realized heroine in traditional literature. Emma Bovary represents a Lockean extreme for the literature of her day. We know far more about her mind than we do about women in earlier literature. We watch her pass through romantic daydreams of herself as chatelaine of a castle awaiting her knight; she sings mawkish songs that express vague passions for angels and gondoliers. Her boredom and mental subterfuges are painstakingly exposed to our view. Flaubert too uses symbols, such as the curtained cab that wanders erratically, without destination, when Emma is capitulating to Leon, but the cab serves as an extension of the passion and as a reinforcement; it does not replace them in the text. Her emotions are the book's subject.

In Molly Bloom's soliloquy at the end of *Ulysses*, Joyce takes us further yet into the singularity of a mind. The degree of interiority is so far advanced beyond that achieved by Flaubert that we almost feel that no more detailed a Lockean study is possible. Stream of consciousness meets a natural limit imposed by the complexities of rendering into a linear sequence of words all the multiple levels on which a mind can operate, and all the quirks of individual associative leaps. We know Molly with a kind of intimacy new to literature then and rarely achieved since. This portrait would have been impossible without the change from the medieval Realism of traditional literary character to Locke's *tabula rasa*.

The second development in Enlightenment thought which affected literature was Descartes' finding his ultimate, irreducible point of validation in himself: *cogito ergo sum*. This had numerous implications. One may not be sure of a God, let alone of the truth of tradition and authority, but one can start with one's own thinking as the basis for further investigation and speculation. This reinforces the value placed on the individual by Lockean theory. In literature it implies to the author that he is the highest authority for what he writes; the play of his mind is ultimately more important than tradition or the rules made by others. We see practical consequences of this exaltation of the author in the steady introduction of more and more socially forbidden material as realistic literature developed. Authors wanted original subjects and seized them despite the long-standing rules of decorum. Likewise, we see the lingering influence of Cartesian assumptions in contemporary writers' indifference to the difficulties experienced by those trying to read their texts. Overall, Descartes' philosophical starting-point encourages a shift away from the concept of literature as communication and toward the romantic belief in literature as expression.

The third change in outlook had surfaced much earlier, in the Middle Ages, but it came into its own during the Enlightenment. This is the aesthetic distancing of knowledge. In a traditional society, knowledge concerns the society's traditions and the original mythic paradigms to be imitated. Naturally, that is sacred knowledge. With the rise of universities in the Middle Ages, information not directly related to salvation started to be accumulated and eventually disseminated, especially the natural history recovered from the Greeks via Arabic. Acquiring knowledge for its own sake, for the enjoyment of acquiring and deploying it, becomes more practicable as salvation fades from the central consciousness of western civilization. Art too becomes divorceable from its original matrix. Religious paintings and statues that had once served religious functions found themselves on display in the eighteenth century along with paintings of classical scenes and society portraits, all just labelled art. When collecting *orientalia* became fashionable in the nineteenth century, connoisseurs might mix objects from several cultures as well as from different centuries. In practice, aestheticization of knowledge and art means that one can admire performance for the perfection of its execution; one need not start to judge a work of literature by asking whether the subject is moral.

The cultivation of admiration for beauty, whether that beauty was to be found in literature, art, or landscape, is a skill that developed rapidly in the eighteenth century. Deriving pleasure from design for its own sake is an important preliminary to the realistic novel. *L'éducation sentimentale* and *Madame Bovary* are inconceivable without such aestheticism. Frédéric Moreau is of interest not as a super-hero, but only in ways that any person may be of interest: as a scrap of humanity, as an example of the interaction between environment and individual, and as an assurance to readers who feel insecure about their place in the universe that they are not alone in this feeling. Above all, his is not an attractive story unless one can admire the artistry that sets it forth. Emma Bovary is interesting, but also a bit disgusting. The pleasure we derive from learning about her is aesthetic: we see what makes her tick, watch the progress of her degradation, and enjoy our sense of understanding, even the unflattering recognition that we share some of her illusions. One cannot claim Emma as a negative moral example illustrating the evils of adultery – or at least not convincingly. Her behavior is unsatisfactory, but so too is that of everyone about her, and the bleak picture of provincial society suggests no way that such a life could be pleasant or even tolerable for someone with higher aspirations. Our interest in Emma is, broadly speaking, scientific. The realistic novel is successful as long as the knowledge it offers of human nature seems interesting to readers, and as long as the artistry compels our aesthetic admiration. When readers are no longer impressed by such knowledge and skill, the realistic novel ceases to be effective.

These three developments – the change in the concept of the individual, the focus on the individual's feelings, and the aestheticization of responses to art – make possible a literature with very different assumptions and functions from those found in traditional societies. The function of traditional literature – to display the ideals for imitation – gives way to a functional model analogous to scientific investigation and observation. Zola formulated this stance,[6] and may have seemed extreme when he put it forward, but in fact the novel had increasingly been functioning in a quasi-scientific mode – which is to say, it gave the impression of being a presentation of human nature which the audience would watch much as scientists would watch their subjects. Obviously the author is creating his data, but he offers it in a fashion that suggests it may be an unedited slice of life, from which we can draw conclusions. The scientific ambience is more pronounced once authors get past their early reliance on romance plots. What we find is characters being put into difficult situations, and we watch their responses.

This scientific model of literature rests on several scientific axioms. One is that observation can add to the sum of our knowledge. Another is that such data and such knowledge is desirable. Another urges the propriety of the author's being objective and withdrawn, and indeed most later authors eschew the chatty asides to the reader popular in the eighteenth century. In order to contribute to our understanding of mankind, this scientific author is free to look at any or all social classes, at vice as well as virtue, at individual responses. In its most crudely scientific formulation, the novel is a social experiment; the author sets up a situation and lets his characters develop logically, and we watch their responses. This scientific approach gave us studies of characters from previously unplumbed social depths (*L'assommoir*), studies of families through their quasi-evolutionary generations (*Buddenbrooks*), sophisticated analyses of social nuance (*Portrait of a Lady*), and explorations of crimes, passions, and obsessions (Maupassant, Maugham).

If scientific observation is to some degree the model for realistic literature, we might expect its ways of giving a sense of meaning to be related to those operative in science, and indeed they are. The most obvious quality of realistic fiction which validates what it offers is novelty. Any new situation, new kind of character, new social class or group portrayed, new extreme of personal interior detail, or new depth into low, unsavory, or repressed matter: these all, at least theoretically, affirm the worth of the fiction and offer the reader something that can be viewed as a personal gain. Readers learn something, thereby enriching their treasury of experience and knowledge. As long as we assume more knowledge to be a good thing, readers will naturally feel a sense of satisfaction, and the experience gained by assimilating the story will be meaningful if only because it is new, an augmentation of the state the reader enjoyed prior to reading. Much the same validation is offered in science by gathering data, no matter how obscure the information may be. Table filling is a recognized and worthy, if unexciting, scientific activity. Any new find is of interest, at least for the sake of the completeness of our understanding. The act of noticing something never before seen makes the observer feel that his own existence has been validated, and reinforces his sense of purpose.

Reading may also produce a reaction of triumph or satisfaction which makes the reader feel meaningful. This comes when pieces of a puzzle fall into place, when one suddenly understands what had been a mystery. Readers experience such moments in the later volumes of *Remembrance of Things Past*, when they finally understand relationships that were not clear to the protagonist in *Swann's Way*. *The Alexandria Quartet* offers similar revelatory shocks. The feeling can come from discerning pattern in what at first seemed chaotic (Schnitzler's *Reigen*). It can come from finding that one's predictions come true. Although some of these responses are possible in traditional literature too, we should remember that audiences heard fewer new stories, so surprise and the unknown were not a regular part of the traditional literary experience. In the novel, we rejoice when we finally understand the source of Pip's money (*Great Expectations*) or Esther's parentage (*Bleak House*), in part because we have been bedevilled by hints, and have been frustrated by our inability to solve the mystery. The subtler satisfaction of observing pattern, of discerning the proper action even if the character cannot do so, is a pleasure given to those who enjoy Trollope or Henry James. Seeing Freudian patterns of behavior emerge, as in D.H. Lawrence's novels, will please the reader familiar with Freud. One can feel satisfaction even at such commonplace patterns as seeing the new generation take its place in the adult society. These moments of discovery and satisfaction frequently involve the reader in a successful act of interpretation, of translating an unknown into a known. Our success makes us feel good about ourselves, and we feel that adding to our store of knowledge is a genuine gain. Hence, our sense of meaning.

Another value which may enhance a work's ability to convey meaning is its aesthetic perfection. Fine craftsmanship gives the discerning observer a sense of satisfaction. Insofar as the fiction attempts to solve a problem in narrative structure, we can applaud success. The intricacy of detail in Joyce or Proust is exciting. The delicacy and precision of implication in James can win admiration. This feeling has nothing to do with moral content. We can applaud a subtle portrayal of evil or ineptitude. We can congratulate the author, and then go on to congratulate ourselves as well for our perspicacity and aesthetic sensibilities. As a rule, therefore, enjoying a work aesthetically can give us a sense of meaningful intellectual activity.

All of these experiences of meaning are limited and personal. They help readers feel that they can relate to some local portion of the cosmos – to social patterns, to a love affair, to the interactions of Americans and Europeans. The experience given by reading fiction lets readers feel in control of anxiety-laden situations, some of which, in some guise, might arise within their own lives. As long as readers are satisfied with this limited kind of control, realistic literature is effective at conveying a sense of meaning. However, it quickly lost its effectiveness, as we shall see in the next section, and consequently ceased to dominate the mainstream of western literature in the twentieth century. The power of realistic literature in its heyday might have led one to expect a much longer life for the form.

The limits of realism

Why has realism enjoyed so relatively short a predominance in literature? Our culture still values science and reason, objectivity and observation, all of which once seemed to find in realism their true literary embodiment. The best-seller list still figures numerous realistic novels, but sophisticated readers find no substance in them, and few critics claim any lasting greatness for them. Realism no longer imparts an adequate sense of meaning to our experience with reality. Why not? And why is fantasy now regaining popularity at all levels of literature, although it once appeared to be permanently discredited, pushed to the edges by science and realistic literature?

Realistic fiction has eventually been faced with several kinds of limitations. One is an inherent set of literary problems, the issues being novelty and the degree of detail included. Another set is external to literature and involves the implications of advances in science and philosophy; if the objectivity of observation is called in question for science, this has ramifications for literature as well. Yet another type of limitation, one present from the outset though not inevitable, is simply the ability of nineteenth-century writers to impose a convincing sense of meaning on human experience, given their religious and social context. The convincingness of what they were achieving was under fire throughout the century in the peripheral literature of fantasy. I would like to look at these various limitations; among them, they have brought the values of realism into disarray, and have left thinkers in all disciplines facing the void, the implicit meaninglessness of the cosmos.

The internal limitations are logical corollaries to the aims and functions of realistic literature, one being the central significance of novelty and originality. If the function of literature is to repeat mythic patterns, readers neither expect nor want novelty; they want those unchanging patterns. If the novel is in some sense analogous to scientific observation, if its purpose is to explore and illuminate human behavior and manners, then there can be little virtue in repetition. Truly scientific knowledge is cumulative, and no one can usefully rediscover $E=mc^2$. Publication of rediscoveries is even harmful, since it wastes readers' time and distracts them from genuinely new work. Each narrative can be viewed as filling in the blank areas of a large map. As the map becomes detailed throughout, the difficulty of finding material that is both new and true increases drastically. What was once exploratory is now cliché. If the novelty of a recent story seems insufficient, we worry about the exhaustion of the form; if the truth or verisimilitude fails, we dismiss the work as an artistic mistake or acknowledge the departures from reality to be fantasy. Conditions of the world change so rapidly that new fictional possibilities continue to come into existence. A nuclear war or global famine might occasion dozens of effective realistic novels, and their realism would not be any shortcoming. Overall, however, the accessible novelties have worn thin.

The pressure to present original material made itself felt in many dimensions as the novel developed. As the normal concerns of upper-middle and middle-class protagonists were exhausted, writers moved lower down the social scale for subjects. The nineteenth century saw Zola's brilliant studies of washerwomen and actresses and peasants. The twentieth century has seen studies of criminals, junkies, and the insane. Not only taboo members of society but their illegal actions as well became legitimate objects for consideration. As the twentieth century wears on, however, the serious quest for novelty has forced writers to examine the grotesque, the acutely abnormal, and the unique, all of which contribute marginally at best to our understanding of human nature. Without originality, the novel loses some theoretical justification (although it may still entertain undemanding readers), but material too peripheral makes readers unwilling to give the story time or attention.

The other kind of internal, literary limitation can be explained by analogy as a limitation of scale. Look at a newspaper held at normal reading distance. You can take in words, sentences, and subheads at a glance; a minimal effort puts you in possession of the meaning. Hold the sheet so it touches your nose, and your field of vision narrows. You may be able to see a few words, but you must move the sheet or your head to take in a full sentence, let alone the whole news item. Put that sheet under a low-powered microscope. The single letter you see can no longer communicate meaning, although you may surmise it to be part of a message. A higher powered microscope reveals light and dark paper fibers, the ink giving no such crisp distinctions as it did at eighteen inches. An electron microscope would reveal an entirely different reality from the one initially being observed.

As this analogy suggests, closer and closer focus on human experience can cause meaning to evaporate. Stream of consciousness, for instance, as it is pushed toward greater fidelity, can lead to such fragmentation that all message disappears, and if multiplied detail does not produce incomprehensibility, then it may evoke boredom. Many of the sensations of everyday life are repetitive. An unedited presentation of breathing and heartbeats would provoke any sane reader to close the book.

Limitations external to realistic literature but influential upon it come from the advances and changes in philosophic and scientific thought, and from recognizing the limitations in these areas. For instance, where once the scientist was assumed to be impartial and non-interfering, we now know otherwise. In microscopy as well as art, humans see what they know or think they know. They are constrained by their language to force data into imperfect classifications – as does the observer whose language admits only of sacred and secular as modes of action when he tries to classify ceremonies in a culture with five or six modes of action. In fictional terms, we no longer consider the author objective in his presentation of social classes, for instance. Marxist critics like David Punter (in *The Literature of Terror*) and Rosemary Jackson make us aware of the many ways the author's own values are encoded in the stories and distort his presentation with strong unconscious biases.

Then too, we have learned to doubt the reality of what the author shows us – indeed, to doubt the interpretability of what we see or learn. Scientists have had to reconcile themselves to one kind of uncertainty; they cannot fix both position and momentum of an electron any more than they can pin a butterfly to cork and still expect to study its flight patterns. Science has also made it hard for us to ignore the illusory nature of our sense data: art may help us experience the stoniness of a stone – in Shklovsky's phrase[7] – but that experience may seem meaningless when we remember that the stoniness is an illusion. The stone consists of empty space, a tiny proportion of which is occupied by atoms, and they, in turn, prove to be only a form of energy, whatever that may be. Physicists are increasingly aware that our exploration into the nature of the universe via mathematics is really a mathematical projection onto whatever is out there.[8] Psychologists remind us of the degree to which what we see in other people is really a projection of ourselves rather than any objective reality.[9] Philosophers and linguisticians point to the tautological nature of language and remind us that all we think we know is really only a set of arbitrary linguistic structures. Barthes took such observations to their logical conclusion in *S/Z*, where he applies this logic to realistic literature and shows it to have little connection with reality. Its values refer rather to other linguistic and literary conventions. Upholding realism as a means of giving meaning to experience seems naive in the face of such deconstruction of its axioms.

A final shift in our scientific and social thinking has also changed our responses to the aims of realism. Where once we were sure of the importance of the individual and of mankind, where once we felt it natural to focus on the individual, we now live with a society and sciences in which the individual is a negligible statistic. Even whole populations are mere numbers on paper. In the Middle Ages, an individual, subordinated as he was to the traditional group, had very little personal freedom, and as a man had very little importance. But as a soul, that same individual was second only to the angels. As C.S. Lewis puts it, "There are no *ordinary* people. You have never talked to a mere mortal. Nations, cultures, arts, civilizations – these are mortal, and their life is to ours as the life of a gnat."[10] Science has freed man from one kind of insignificance, only to precipitate him into a far more complete state of aimlessness. The immensity of the macrocosm and the complexity of the subatomic microcosm alike make man aware of his own pitiful finitude. Yet we crave a sense of meaningful relationship with the universe, as our history of myth-making testifies, but the relationships that science can properly trace – physical, biological, and chemical – do not give people that sense of their own importance that they crave. For many, this lack of meaning spells depression and alienation, and makes literary focus on the individual pointless. Tragedy, being predicated on an individual's significance, becomes impossible. Romance heroism appears to be silly fairytale material. The affirmation of society proffered by comedy seems absurd. Only irony can flourish under these circumstances, and even irony must feel the weight of its own pointlessness.

When we turn to the limitations present all along in nineteenth-century realism, we find contemporary reactions to these inadequacies in the peripheral literature of the day. These limitations are not necessarily inherent, but reflect the blindness of the authors, their class outlooks, their moral assumptions, and other such individual and social characteristics. Realism as practiced was very far from being objective, but whereas mainstream authors repressed some of their darkest fears, writers in the gothic tradition and the literary descendants of such writers seized on these fears and magnified them. Fears of the dark races, of "letting go", of suppressed savagery, of sex, and of obsession: these all well up in de Sade's stories, in *Dracula*, in *Dr Jekyll and Mr Hyde*, *The Island of Dr Moreau*, in *Heart of Darkness* and *Moby Dick*. Fear and resentment of women emerges as early as *Clarissa*, and the anxieties are played upon to the point of parody in *She*. Fear of man's own intelligence and ingenuity give a sinister cast to *Frankenstein* and *The Invisible Man*. Numerous authors realized that the demythologized world, shorn of both divine and demonic, was not entirely true to human experience. Much of what we feel in life can easily enough be represented in realistic terms, but some of the experiences that move us most derive from more alien realms of experience, which we have represented in literature through the use of fantasy.

Certain inadequacies of realism were felt throughout its history. Others became apparent as the obvious veins of novelty were stripmined and exploited. Still others developed as sophisticated thinkers realized that realism was not and could not deliver what it implicitly promised: a valid interpretation of reality. And if realism were not succeeding in this aim, it could hardly give readers the sense of controlling experience and knowing reality which had sustained this literary form, even though the sense of meaning it gave was admittedly limited and local. In the first half of the twentieth century, writers and readers alike had to face the implicit void of meaninglessness. Literature and criticism, language, philosophy, and science were revealed to be tautological, imprisoned within the artificial unrealities of their own conventions. Or, as Scholes puts it:

> Once we knew that fiction was about life and criticism was about fiction – and everything was simple. Now we know that fiction is about other fiction, is criticism in fact, or metafiction. And we know that criticism is about the impossibility of anything being about life, really, or even about fiction, or, finally, about anything.[11]

Realism led step by step to this nothingness. At first, the great realistic novels evoked wonder, made readers feel that the fictive explanations of experience were correct. In such novels, one met people and problems that one half knew, and learned to see them whole. Realistic literature gave its readers a sense of power and insight, an outlet for feelings, and a reinforcement for social mores. This genuine richness and strength has proved ephemeral, largely because of its fundamental dependence on novelty and on validatable truth. Scientific gathering of evidence has a much vaster field of data to draw on so it has not suffered quite the enervation suffered by realistic literature. With all these problems, we can see why realistic literature would fail to give much sense of meaning to sophisticated readers. No one form has replaced it with a generally accepted way of asserting value. In the next section, however, we can look at at least four of the kinds of literature that are wrestling with the problem of meaning. Modern literature is in its way a literature of quest, a literature which first strikes the reader as being in search of its proper form rather than already possessed of that form. This questing gives it the appearance of being transitional, but unless some fairly major mental changes take place in western consciousness, this searching for answers may be as honest and effective a function as is possible for literature at present. The function of traditional literature was to present mythic patterns; that of realistic literature was observation; in this third stage, we find a quest for ways of giving a sense of meaning. Modern literature works from the acknowledgment that science does not allow us to assert mythic fantasies as "real", and from the knowledge that man is ill-equipped psychologically to live without a sense of meaning. Clearly there are no easy answers, but contemporary authors are striving, sometimes very impressively, to reconcile these apparently incompatible demands.

Beyond the void

According to contemporary theorists of modernism and post-modernism, realistic literature assumed that the world was rational and describable; that there was a correspondence between a description and reality; and that even if there were a mystery at first, you could unravel it.[12] Modernism has hacked and bashed at all such assumptions. Gabriel Josipovici illustrates the modernist technique with a single sentence from Kafka's *The Castle*: "Her hands were certainly small and delicate, but they could equally well have been called weak and characterless." Josipovici goes on to point out that in the realistic novel, we find a

> world where people will be either guilty or not guilty but never both, where hands will be either delicate or weak, but never both. No traditional novelist could permit himself Kafka's doubts about the precise way to describe Frieda's hands. And we rarely have such doubts in ordinary life. But what Kafka is suggesting is that our decisions that hands or events or people are one thing or another is really a convenience rather than a reality – it simply allows us to get on with things, with the business of living. But living to what purpose?[13]

Modernism, in many of its manifestations, has proved to be a literature of reaction. It has provided data for the theory that fiction is about other fiction. When Cortázar disrupts linear flow in *Hopscotch*, we are dealing with technique that is partly explored for its own sake, but also being exploited to upset and deny our expectations. Unity of plot and finally plot itself vanish: Brautigan's *The Tokyo-Montana Express* has no story. Character becomes more fluid until, in the works of Vonnegut, his science fiction writer, Kilgore Trout, has a different life history and personality in each novel. Readers are not allowed the security of separating daydream or drug vision from reality in Burroughs' *Naked Lunch*, and Fowles' *The Magus* leaves us far from assured that we have seen the many-layered mystery truthfully and fully unravelled.

Samuel Beckett's literature, especially his drama, presents confrontation with the void in an exceptionally pure form. Kafka's fiction not only shows us the void, but fills us with inchoate feelings and batters us into limp bewilderment. Both brilliantly catch nuances of man's quest for meaning, be it through tramps waiting by the road or through a burrowing creature's anxieties. But where can one go from such zero points? How does one get beyond the void?

Contemporary fiction seems to be going in four directions. (1) Writers ignore the void and its implications; they retreat from the edge and try to write in essentially conventional, realistic veins. Or they retreat even further to fantasy with strong traditional roots. Beautifully crafted fiction is still possible in the realistic vein; Saul Bellow and John Updike exemplify work being done of this conservative kind. Among writers of fantasy, we find Tolkien and his ilk, and the politically conservative writers of science fiction, in whose works the adventures serve to uphold the status quo of a benign technological elite. If the void does no one any good, they reason, we may as well stick to values that have worked in the past until something better comes along. Since these values are what we have, we should cherish them. (2) Writers continue to broadcast the breakdown of authority, the tautology of language, the self-referential nature of art and the other negative messages of modernism, all more or less forms of acknowledging the void. Calvino's *The Castle of Crossed Destinies* is such a work. (3) Writers recognize that they lack answers to our problems, but they go over and over the questions, checking out possibilities, looking at our fictional tools and techniques. Metafiction by Barth, Borges, Sorrentino, and Barthelme not only help us understand literature as criticism, it makes the argument that we can and should enjoy this state of affairs rather than long for a new naiveté. Borges, for instance, half-persuades us in "Pierre Menard" that the ironic twentieth-century text of the *Quixote* is richer and more profound than the original. (4) Some writers are trying to assert a new kind of meaning, a new sense of conviction and involvement; a new relationship to the cosmos; sometimes even a new mythology. In this group would go some works by writers called "post-modernist", although that slippery term is also applied simply to metafiction. John Barth, in an essay on post-modernism, suggests Gabriel Garcia Márquez' *One Hundred Years of Solitude* and Calvino's *Cosmicomics* as post-modernist fictions. I concur enthusiastically with *Cosmicomics*, and would suggest adding some of Doris Lessing's space fictions and Pynchon's *Gravity's Rainbow*.

Since all of the authors of these various kinds of contemporary fiction have somehow escaped the silence implied by the void, and since all find some meaning in the act of writing and even in the action of their characters, it is worth looking at their solutions. No obvious new genre or even single kind of answer has yet coalesced, except insofar as the quest itself is a kind of function. From the various schools of literary endeavor, however, we can see what kinds of meaning are being sought, and are being upheld as still valid. We can also see the efflorescence of various kinds of fantasy and note possible reasons for its re-entry into mainstream literature.

Writers who follow reactionary paths, whether realistic or fantastic, seem primarily concerned to find ways of asserting the importance of the individual despite the burden of negligibility assigned to him by science and by our mass societies. In a way, this is their basic myth: man is important, no matter what the scale of the universe. Since humanity seems to live rather poorly without some kind of belief in its importance, this is a defensible artistic stance. If we grant that their axiom need not be proven, we can only ask how persuasive they are in asserting their message of positive thinking, given that all the most coherent and systematic arguments supporting it crumbled in the latter half of the nineteenth century.

John Updike's Rabbit books are modern *Madame Bovarys*. *Rabbit, run* (1960), *Rabbit Redux* (1971), and *Rabbit is Rich* (1981) portray the ups and downs of an ineffectual but reasonably happy man. One can almost predict *Rabbit Retired* (1991?) to round out the saga and take us from the hero's gradually becoming reconciled to life into the later struggle in which he becomes reconciled to death. Rabbit is a Lockean *tabula rasa*. In the three books so far published, we see how Rabbit is gradually broken down until he accepts his life with all its rubs – imperfect and unreliable employment, a sour marriage, trouble with parents, the nagging recollections of glory as a highschool basketball star. Rabbit achieves his reconciliation very gradually – in the first book, indeed, he refuses to acquiesce and runs away instead. Such reconciliation as he does achieve is not won by his transcending the mundane or by his learning to shut it out through some esoteric mental discipline or interest, but through submerging himself in the flow of the minutiae of the everyday. He focuses on one thing at a time, be it the song on his car radio or the incidental beauties of a body emerging from the swimming pool. He is the sum of his impressions, and can never aspire to be larger than life; he is merely a mosaic of life. Readers not offended by his ordinariness come to cherish him for the completeness of Updike's picture, for the consistency which makes the rather disparate parts of his life seem a plausible whole – and for Updike's enchanting powers of observation. They not only make us see the stoniness of the stone, they make that stone magical. Nothing in Updike's technique is new. All that sets Rabbit off from ourselves or other fictional characters is the increasingly well-developed equation between Rabbit and the American middle class he exemplifies; this symbolism gives the portrait a national as well as an individual coherence. In a mental act halfway between surgical dissection and playful, lyrical dance, Updike invites us to enjoy the object of his study, to enjoy Rabbit for his own sake – an aesthetic stance – but also for our own sakes, for if we cannot enjoy this avatar of life-around-us, what can we enjoy in life?

Tolkien is an outstanding representative of those who have turned their backs squarely on the void. In his own life, he had Christian doctrinal reasons to do so, so in a sense he is a throwback to an earlier stage of mythic thinking; but he writes during and after the horrors of World War II, and is familiar with the idea of meaningless life preached by many of his contemporaries, so his assertion of medieval values is not a simple affirmation of a culture's unchallenged ideals. His stance is much closer to being "wouldn't it be nice if this were true", or "I would far rather find this true than what I see everyday". This is literature of desire. In it, Tolkien rehallows the idea of dedicating oneself to a larger cause. He diminishes personal professional obligations and emotional tangles in order to stress individual actions freely given to the aid of a cause. He upholds the possibility of heroic action; sacrifice of self for others is his highest good. In his zeal for such exalted ideals, Tolkien outdoes his medieval models in purity; the lust and violence tingeing Malory's vision are absent; the passion which can lead Gottfried's or Chrétien's heroes to misery and madness is excluded. Love is more dynastic than passionate, a *hieros gamos* rather than an individual experience. Tolkien is positively traditional in his preference for public issues and moral choices over individual emotions and private psychological quirks.

Since Tolkien loudly claims to dislike allegory, we are not encouraged to translate his *Ring* trilogy into other terms, and the attempts to read "the bomb" into "the ring" have not been persuasive. If we are not to allegorize, though, we are left to swallow the logical flaws in his creation. The Shire is not economically viable. It reflects a child's understanding of the world: food is delivered, put into the pantry, and eaten, but not paid for. The labor going into its production and the problems of isolated agricultural communities are ignored. The wealthy families have money but no source for it in tenant peasantry or stock-exchange investments. Another artistic flaw is the ineffectuality of the evil; the quasi-industrial damage done to the Shire is quickly rectified; the fellowship of the ring is too little damaged – Gandalf is even brought back to life. Heroism that exacts no price loses its meaning. If we are not to stumble over these logical flaws and thereby lose what Tolkien does have to offer, we are forced to concentrate on his exaltation of heroic action. He offers us a paradox as answer to the question of the value of the individual: the individual's private and personal life is insignificant, but he can achieve significance through commitment and dedication to a cause. As an answer to the problem of meaning in life, this has served well in the past. It is dangerous – causes vary in their worth and morality – but it has proven effective.

If we turn to modernist writers, what do we find them offering in place of answers? Characteristically, they force us to accept that we can never find certitude, that there are no fixed points from which to explore reality.

Some push us to this conclusion by stressing the negative, by saying there are no valid answers; others deny our either/or categories and insist on and/and, where the answers provided would, by normal logic, exclude each other. The typical protagonist is an interpreter of data. In Vladimir Nabokov's *Pale Fire*, the literary critic, Kinbote, embodies the argument that interpretation is the projection of self onto data. The interpreter in Italo Calvino's *The Castle of Crossed Destinies* tries to understand the stories his fellow travelers are attempting to tell by means of tarot cards. So polysemous are the symbols that when we look at the cards laid out as a story, we know that we would not have derived the same story as did the interpreter from that evidence. The interpreter as detective appears in Thomas Pynchon's *The Crying of Lot 49*. Oedipa Maas crisscrosses the California-culture world of San Narciso, seeking the principle of organization controlling the events in her life. She thinks she is about to arrive at some answers when lot 49 is cried at auction, but the book ends as the doors to the auction room are locked, and we never learn whether she finds answers or not. Pynchon challenges us to make what we can of his material. He and other modernists tear down our comfortable bourgeois fixities and set up situations in which there are no answers or a plethora of answers. Our need to create answers in this chaos can be a sign of our weakness (we want a security blanket) or strength (we reshape the world to our desire). Or, on the and/and principle, we may be left to conclude that the quest for answers is both weak and strong. Pynchon and Calvino, in these particular books, give us compelling reasons to consider pluralism a valid way to interpret reality.

One particular branch of modernism – I put it with modernism because it offers no solid answers – is metafiction, narrative concerned with the nature of fictive reality and with the problems of writing fiction. We see the conventions of fictive reality exposed by authors who put themselves and their characters on the same plane of reality, where the characters promptly become unruly and uncontrollable. Such challenges to our neat levels of reality are explored by Flann O'Brien in *At Swim-Two-Birds*, Raymond Queneau in *The Flight of Icarus*, and Gilbert Sorrentino in *Mulligan Stew*. The problems of writing fiction bedevil John Barth, who tries to work himself out of his *cul-de-sac* by discussing the problems. A many-sided piece of metafiction is his collection of three novellas entitled *Chimera*. In the first story, "Dunyazadiad", Barth explores the realist's problem in the person of Scheherazade's younger sister, Dunyazade, who is to be married to another virgin-a-night man. This man, Shahryar's brother, has heard all of Scheherazade's stories from his brother by letter, and knows all possible sexual practices as well. What can Dunyazade do to save her life? As Barth talks about the problem, he finds that "the key to the treasure is the treasure", that he has an effective story, and a solution of sorts to both Dunyazade's dilemma and his own.

The chimera is a tripartite beast, so Barth follows this tale with two others. The "Perseid" asks what a hero does after he has completed his monomyth pattern and settled down to humdrum marital and regal life. At the same time, Barth asks what a writer can do when the heroic story is played out. The hero tries to recapture his former sense of invincibility by retracing his steps, but at each site of former triumph he loses something or has it go bad on him until he realizes that he is only a man, one who no longer cares if kissing Medusa will petrify him or not. Thus, as he comes to terms with unheroic human limitations, he wins a place among the stars. Or, in authorial terms, you turn to the psychic patterns and images from the second half of life and worry about coming to terms with human limitations and death rather than assume that one should write fictions about airily transcending them. In the "Bellerophoniad", Barth starts with two lads eager to be heroes and supplies them with schematic knowledge of the hero monomyth (as worked out by Joseph Campbell and Lord Raglan). This knowledge allows Bellerophon to live a heroically patterned life, but that life feels inauthentic to him, a mere imitation. He is sure that his twin, who died, is the real hero. Bellerophon moreover achieves immortality not as a star but in narrative, petrified in the written word. Authorially, Barth comments on what happens to the writer who becomes self-conscious of patterns he had drawn on unconsciously; the knowledge makes subsequent writing seem inauthentic and imitative.

Such work with the hero-narrative forms clearly reflects the desire to be re-illusioned, the longing to find that the old stories work for us as one believes them once to have worked. Freud and Jung see the myths as tapping our psychic depths; we wish that we did feel thus moved by them, and long to find significance in narrative, in heroes, in pattern. That Barth should hope new meaning will emerge from myths but be unable to affirm it is not surprising. He settles for the intermediate state of deriving pleasure from the process of tackling his problems. Implicit in his procedure is the belief that in trying, not in silence, lies the only comfort. Talking about the problems, even if no answer is forthcoming, still seems to Barth worth the effort. Metaliterature is solipsistic, and probably a dead end, but *Chimera*, on its own terms, is extremely successful.

Finally we come to some of the writers who have been called post-modernists, or who might qualify for the name in that they go beyond modernism and metafiction and try out various possible answers and positive assertions of value. They work with full awareness of the void, and do not fall back on old answers or faith. In a series of stories quite unlike the pessimistic *Castle of Crossed Destinies*, Calvino enjoys an extraordinary success in creating a new, positive, mythic universe. For him, this does not mean rejecting science and its universe of "dead" matter. Rather, in *Cosmicomics* and *T Zero*, he juxtaposes absurd, homely, human behavior with the physics, chemistry, biology, and mathematics of the developing universe, and goes on from there to create a new sense of wonder, a new human scale for measuring and admiring the infinite. We learn all over again the miracle of vision, the indescribable length of eons, the nature of signs, and the wonder of a woman who longs "to make some noodles for you boys". Another writer who is managing to assert new values, albeit mystical ones, is Doris Lessing. In her *Canopus in Argos* series, she seems to be looking at her world from a supernatural perspective – mythology from the gods' point of view, as it were. She not only turns mythology inside out, she turns outer space into inner space, with the result that the god-like figures she studies become at least potentially some part of ourselves.

These and other post-modernists form no coherent group or school. They point in no obvious direction for contemporary literature. We may note, however, that the authors mentioned, modernist and post-modernist alike, sanctify the quest for meaning. Even the characters of Barth and Pynchon are seekers. Rabbit wants meaning and Updike is quite sympathetic to this desire. Calvino celebrates man's ability to adapt to the new scientific cosmos. Lessing makes the inner recesses of the mind our universe and works to help us relate to those inner realms.

Other ways of advancing beyond the void will be sought and found, and other ways of conveying a sense of meaning. Some will be variants on those already tried, others may be new. But among those being tried, we should note that most rely on some form of fantasy. In the cases of Calvino, Lessing, and Pynchon, the mythic elements are symbolic and metaphoric. In Barth, they are allegorical. If our mind craves a sense of meaning, writers are finding, we must speak to it in its own language, the language of symbol. Hence the recurrence of fantasy as a serious literary technique.

Given that we recognize meaning as internal to ourselves, not an eternal and external fixity, we can see why realism cannot be expected to supply that sense of meaning any more. Insofar as realism concentrates with quasi-scientific disinterest on what is there in the "real" world, it cannot validly express value judgments, they being human likes and dislikes. If writers are to work their way back out of this blind alley, they are essentially compelled to try fantasy – deliberate departures from consensus reality. So far, we have seen no absolute return to a new mythology, no assertion of a privileged fantasy as the new truth. But the modernist reliance on and/and rather than on either/or lets such writers refuse to label their fantasies as "merely" symbolic. We are far too ignorant of right hemisphere brain functions and of our own unconscious to be able to prove that there is only one kind of truth, the scientific. Writers of the future may find themselves engaged in a search for a kind of Grand Unified Theory – not to reconcile the various types of physics, but to integrate the various kinds of truth that give man and his universe their sense of meaning. For the literary critic of the 1980s, however, the challenges are obvious. We need to enquire into the uses and technical possibilities of fantasy.

Introduction

Part I concerns itself with definitions of fantasy, and with the historical forces which affected its popularity and caused its functions to change. Overall, Part II offers some answers to the question "How is fantasy used?" A literary work can offer readers four basic approaches to reality, namely, what I am calling illusion, vision, revision, and disillusion. Further, it can attempt to disturb the reader's own assumptions, or reaffirm those assumptions and comfort the reader. It can also invite emotional engagement or disengagement. These four approaches to reality and the variables in the artist's aim are the subjects of the next four chapters.

Literature of illusion, discussed in chapter three, is generally known as escape literature. Whether such a narrative is mimetic or fantastic, its author assumes our agreement that everyday reality is boring, unromantic – even depressing. Furthermore, the author believes nothing can be done to change that reality, so he offers to disengage us from its grey unpleasantness and to enfold us in comforting illusions. We wander through gardens of bright images, enjoying vivid sensations: wonder at the beauties of nature (pastoral); sexual excitement (pornography); delightful fear (tales of the uncanny); excitement (adventure stories); suspense (detective stories, the *fantastique*); and above all, the delicious pleasure of freedom from responsibility. In real life, we would have to pay something for these sensations. Suspense and horror are unpleasant if real, and leave an aftermath of exhaustion. Sex usually entails obligation to the partner. Search for the beauties of nature requires long hikes and high tolerance of mosquitoes and poison ivy. Escape literature thus offers us roses without thorns and pleasures without payment.

Literature of vision, the subject of chapter four, invites us to experience a new sense of reality, a new interpretation that often seems more varied and intense than our own. Instead of turning our backs on everyday reality, as we do when seeking illusion, we absorb a new vision. The author tries to present his interpretation as vividly and tellingly as possible, hoping we will respond with "I never realized that before!" or "So that's how it really is!". Either fantasy or mimetic techniques may be appropriate. This literature is expressive: the author often pours forth a passionate protest and invites us to join in his fervor. The visions of Vonnegut, Beckett, and Kafka take this approach. Literature of vision aims to disturb us by dislodging us from our settled sense of reality, and tries to engage our emotions on behalf of this new version of the real.

Whereas literature of vision offers us a new reality for consideration, *literature of revision* (chapter five) lays out plans for revising reality, for shaping futures. These two categories, vision and revision, relate to each other as the opposite ends of a continuum. At the one end, the author expects only reaction; at the other, he strives to push the reader from passive agreement to action. Because overt didacticism is not popular now, we find numerous works of revision clustering near the mid-point, their programs for action reduced to brief sketches, or left implicit. They differ from similar expressive works only in offering hints as to how mankind could improve the situation.

Whether as fiction or as sacred writ, this didactic literature concerns itself with two planes of reality, the personal and the cosmic. It proclaims the laws of behavior, or it makes pronouncements upon the nature of the universe, life after death, and man's place in the cosmos. Because didactic literature affirms absolutes, its claims are ultimately founded on a kind of fantasy, for not even the laws of nature, let alone those of everyday life, are traceable to ultimate fixities. Any work, sacred or fictional, that makes assertions about creation; or about life after death; or that claims to have universally applicable rules for human behavior – such a work goes beyond what we can know through reason. Didactic literature seldom advertises its dependence on the suprarational, and literature of revision need not use overt fantasy techniques, though it often does. As the vehicle for fable or satire, as a source of expressive metaphors, fantasy is a potent device for convincing an audience not just to agree but to act. Like literature of vision, such didactic literature strives to engage us, but unlike it, the aim is not so much to disturb us as to offer the eventual comfort of order, of a program, of decisions made and rules laid down. It offers us the emotional pleasures of absolutes.

Literature of disillusion insists that reality is unknowable. It strives to dismantle our comforting myths and offers us no replacements. Discomfort for the reader and disengagement are its aims. Such literature is the outcome of the author's dogmatic relativism or perspectivism, philosophies which assume all interpretations of reality to be worthless because they are unprovable. In works like *Naked Lunch* (Burroughs) and *The Universal*

Baseball Association, J. Henry Waugh, Prop. (Coover), the problem lies in our inability to stand outside the limits of our individual consciousness and its set perspective. The authors attempt to crack our mental barriers with material from dreams, drugs, and psychosis. Writers like Tolstoy (in "Kholstomer"), London (in *Call of the Wild*), and Barth (in "Night-Sea Journey") see our limitations as species-related; they challenge our blindness by using nonhuman narrators. Queneau and Calvino find inadequacy of language the obstacle to valid interpretation. Robbe-Grillet's *The House of Assignation* and Coover's "The Baby sitter" challenge our arbitrary interpretations by forcing contradictions upon us and refusing to resolve them. As critics who write about perspectivist literature often point out, the militant doubt it asserts is parallel to that forced upon modern science by Heisenberg's uncertainty principle, and by the principle of complementariety, the necessity of treating light as both wave and particle. We must abandon not only the fundamental assurance of mutual exclusivity but also the belief that we can observe and codify reality, for, as Heisenberg shows, some kinds of observations cannot be carried out without distorting the natural patterns of the thing observed. Despite the negativity and destructiveness of this disillusioning literature, readers can find ambivalent pleasure even in rejecting all interpretations of reality, as we shall see in chapter six.

The usual relationships among these four approaches to reality are easier to see if they are put in tabular form:

	illusion	vision	revision	disillusion
aim:	comfort	disturb	comfort	disturb
effect:	disengagement	engagement	engagement	disengagement

Of course, occasional works violate this pattern of associations, and we must remember that disturbing readers does not rule out pleasing them as well. While these four categories lack the memorable symmetry of Frye's seasonal *mythoi*, they do cover the possible approaches to reality available to authors who are concerned with the nature of reality. Escape literature, with its enchanting illusions, is an arbitrary starting-point, but it is what most people think of as fantasy. Literature of vision, instead of offering retreat, challenges us with the new, but still offers us this experience as a pleasure for our consideration, whereas literature of revision wants a stronger commitment from us. Literature of disillusion gives up on the positive approaches and rounds off the negative possibilities. Even if we personally started with a positive interpretation of reality, the literature of disillusion tries to persuade us that our happy beliefs are nonsense. When we accept its destructive proofs, we are free – whether to go on living without false props, or to bury ourselves in illusions, that we may not have to face the void.

Problems can arise if author and readers disagree too strongly on their basic assumptions about consensus reality. Where an early author is being read by a modern audience, the readers must make allowance for the differences if they are not to be cut off from the pleasures of a new perspective on reality. Throughout the next four chapters, I shall deal on an ad hoc basis with the shifts in assumptions about reality which have taken place during the past 2500 years. Homer and Vonnegut start with very different realities, yet when these are taken into account, their messages are complementary. Throughout, my main concern is the role played by fantasy in each of these four kinds of literature. How is fantasy used? I shall discuss both fantastic and mimetic works in order to show what contributions are peculiar to fantasy. Only when its basic uses and effects are clear can we go on to answer the question posed in Part III: "Why use fantasy?"

3

Literature of illusion: invitations to escape reality

Chapter two discussed the desacralization of the cosmos. Chapter three is about escape literature. Readers may feel as if they had been enjoying the view from a high window until pushed from behind – whereupon they find themselves fallen onto the dunghill beneath. This defenestration is deliberate. Cosmic vision and escapist daydream are both fantasy, yet the visionary is often forgotten, overshadowed by fantasy's role in popular literature. Most fantasy is dismissed by hostile critics as "escapist", and most escape literature is dismissed as "fantasy". We need to disentangle the two if we are to understand the variety of fantasy's functions. Escape literature has seldom fared well with commentators because it needs no explications and provides no opportunity for sophisticated analysis. However, the hostility engendered by simplicity should not be carried over to fantasy at large, and indeed is misplaced for much escape literature, as we shall see.

The forms discussed here are the pastoral, the tale of conquest and adventure, the comic novel, and such affective forms as the detective story, the thriller, and pornography. With the exception of classical pastoral, which has become an acquired and sophisticated literary taste, all of these forms are widely read. On television and in movies, they reach a still broader audience. The sex and violence which help create their appeal have often been found objectionable on the grounds that the audience feels encouraged to indulge in the behavior depicted. This objection seems odd; few great novels and very little didactic literature can be credited with this kind of power to influence their audience's behavior. Another, contradictory objection lies in this literature's very power to provide escape from social reality and thus *prevent* direct action. A believer in the work-ethic would call such an escape an evasion of obligation; Marxists denounce it for dissipating a frustration which might impel the reader to work for social reform. Yet another objection is that this literature does not push us to think. Since the first two faults are controversial and contradictory, and the third simply a characteristic of the form, I prefer to focus on what the various kinds of escape literature can be expected to do, and not just dwell on their weaknesses. Of the works discussed or alluded to in this chapter, some are full-blown fantasy; they break the laws of nature and permit occurrences we would label impossible. Others are only unrealistic and improbable. Studying these varieties together lets me pursue such matters as the differences which using fantasy can make to the kind of escape offered, and the nature of what fantasy can achieve that mimesis cannot.

The pastoral: retreat from society

The impulse toward pastoral simplicity has taken two main forms and emphasizes two concerns. The concerns are sensory experience and escape from responsibility. The two forms, each imposing its own kind of perspective on the reader, display Arcadia from within and from without. We see Arcadia from the viewpoint of an observant and sensitive inhabitant in Virgil's *First Eclogue* and Ray Bradbury's *Dandelion Wine*; we remain sophisticated outsiders on a vacation in Arcadia in *As You Like It* or Joseph Wechsberg's *Sweet and Sour*. Insider-pastoral, which usually stresses sensory experience, is rooted in the myths of paradise and the Golden Age, and offers readers the passive pleasures of bucolic perfection – intellectual retreat, ego deflation, and redefinition of life in radically simple terms. Although we naturally gain new insights, they crystalize into clear thoughts only after we have returned from the book to our own world. While reading, we enjoy the sensations without trying to analyze the contrast. Outsider-pastoral usually takes the romance form. The pastoral landscape is the special world where the hero tests himself and his ideas. He then returns to his own world, to take an active part in its affairs. In Arcadia, he – or she, in the case of Rosalind in *As You Like It* – remains an outsider on vacation, constantly aware of the gulf separating this paradise from the real world, so we likewise remain conscious of the contrast.

Insider-pastoral is clearly escapist, but its pleasures are so innocent that it has avoided the condemnation so often shown escape literature. Whether the Arcadia is literally the land of fleecy flocks, crystal streams, and fair-mannered herdsmen, or just some small town enriched by the author's childhood memories, the enchanting realm invites us to enjoy the singing of birds, the taste of sun-warmed fruit eaten in the noonday shade, the sight and smell of the summer landscape. Theocritus' *Seventh Idyll* and Virgil's *First Eclogue* celebrate such sensory feasts. In the latter, our awareness of the pleasures is poignantly sharpened by the realization that

Meliboeus has lost his land and is seeing the beautiful countryside for the last time. His loss makes us respond more deeply to Tityrus' savory offering of chestnuts, curds, and cream. When we stand back from the text, we know that country life is nothing like this. Tending sheep in sickness and health is dirty and unpleasant work not calculated to preserve white hands or please the imagination. The margin of existence is narrow. One's fellow shepherds are more likely to steal one's lambs than sing songs. We realize that Arcadia is not a world but an anti-world, set up in opposition to the cities inhabited by Theocritus and Virgil: "If we know the world to which a reader escapes, then we know the world from which he comes."[1] The strains of city life in classical times apparently shared some tensions with those of today: we see abundant evidence of pastoral longings in the utopian sorts of literature that celebrate organic living and homesteading in Alaska.

Arcadia and its equivalents give man independence. His responsibilities are limited. His flocks may need him, but few classical pastoral figures have wives or children or larger political obligations. Nature is benign. In this paradisal world, as in infancy, the principals are fed, clothed, and sheltered without exertion on their part. Economy, wars, ambition, and want are not much understood or worried about. Leisure is abundant. The chief gratifications are sensory: taste, smell, and sight predominate, and enjoyment of such pleasures takes one back to a childlike state. Readers are not exhorted to overthrow the city-world. Rather, they take a vacation, a sensorily rich rest.

In order to remain restful, the pastoral must eschew significant plot, for plots involve tension. Hence it is more often lyric than narrative. Few pastoral novels are true pastorals, though some come close: O. J. Sigurdsson's *Ljósir Dagar* (*Light Days*), Lord Dunsany's *The Curse of the Wise Woman*, and Richard Llewellyn's *How Green was my Valley* resemble classical poems in the simple life they describe, and in the relaxation they offer the reader. Ray Bradbury's *Dandelion Wine* is almost purely lyrical, a compelling patchwork of a summer's sensations experienced by twelve-year-old Douglas Spaulding in Green Town, Illinois. Here the small town replaces the open country, and the nostalgic veins tapped are not our personal memories of sheep and bees, for few readers have any, but rather recollections of the feel of new sneakers at the beginning of summer, the taste of midwestern cooking, the savor of ice cream on a hot day, the eerie darkness of the town's ravine. Readers are encouraged to relive, to reabsorb, any similar memories from their own childhoods which are brought to consciousness by the fleeting episodes of the book. One need not have known an old man just like Colonel Freeleigh; to have known any nostalgic old person is enough. We and Bradbury know that life in Green Town as it was in 1928, just before the stock-market crash, is not recapturable. Within the context of the story, however, no sophisticated distance intrudes. The events are seen through the eyes of an insider, not an outsider.

Insider-pastoral – classical or modern – encourages the reader to draw upon personal recollections. Readers with no appropriate childhood memories will probably find the form pointless, or will ask its thin character studies to bear a weight they were not designed for. The intellectual content is necessarily slight. For readers who do have suitable memories, however, such pastoral offers a Proustian experience. Whether the trigger be a taste, a sight, a sound, a smell, or a feel, the readers can meet their own memories, and after returning to the real world from a brief vacation in the golden past, may view their surroundings differently. The crust of *habitude* is cracked, and with eyes still filled with pastoral stars, readers cannot fail to find the real world overcomplex, frenetic, or even silly. Whether one then tries to change society, or merely shoulders the load again, one has gained a respite and experienced a sense of newness.

Fantasy pastoral is relatively rare, because the triggering of sensory memories is best done with verisimilitude. Fantasy does occur, however, when freedom from responsibility rather than sensory pleasure is the author's main interest. That freedom is enshrined in works like *Winnie the Pooh* and *The Wind in the Willows*. The songs and the abundant food from no visible economical source are typically pastoral. The adventures are more exciting than those usual in classical pastoral, but that is not saying much, for there are no genuine catastrophes, no villains, and no real suspense. Eeyore and Toad would be intolerable in real life, but as animals they are lovable eccentrics. Wol is a bit pretentious, but not as estranged from the rest of society as he probably would be in our world. Occasionally Milne and Grahame drop the mask for the adult audience and call attention to the artifice of the idyll, such as the time when Christopher Robin bids farewell to his world, or when the Great God Pan speaks to the little furry ones. For the most part, however, even adult readers are content to be amused by and immersed in the pastoral, and do not feel compelled to compare the story at every step to real life. This insulation from the everyday world and its responsibilities is what makes parodies like *The Pooh Perplex* and "Hell at Pooh Corner" so funny.[2] The former uncovers dark psychological passions and deep allegorical significations lurking beneath the surface of the idyll. The latter, a *Punch* interview with Winnie the Pooh (age 61, and suffering from terminal moth), tells us what the real Pooh wanted. He was scripted to sing inane hums when what he liked was jazz. 1926 was the era of short skirts, nightingales singing in Berkeley Square, two-seaters, and Le Touquet, Pooh moans, but he was forced to pass his evenings with Piglet and Eeyore. "'*The Great Gatsby* came out that year', said Pooh bitterly. 'The same year as Winnie-the-Pooh.'" "'Why didn't I get the breaks? Why wasn't I a great tragic hero, gazing at the green light on the end of Daisy's dock? Why didn't Fitzgerald write *Gatsby Meets a Heffalump* and Milne *The Great Pooh?*'" This kind of witty inversion is so startling because the fantasy of the original has kept us from standing aside from the idyll while inside it. We experience it uncritically and relax in never-never land.

Outsider-pastoral internalizes a sophisticated perspective. Characters from city, court, or any complex sector of society, enter the green and pleasant land, but self-consciously and temporarily. Free play based on personal memories is mostly eliminated. Because the logic of this mode is romance – excursion into a special world, proving one's ability to survive in it, and return – the experiences readers undergo tend more to affirm capability than exercise sensory awareness. If insider-pastoral embodies something like childhood, outsider-pastoral echoes adolescence and initiation. Many authors who use outsider-pastoral to revisit their age of innocence remain fully aware of the adult knowledge that makes the idyllic world unobtainable to them now.

Robinson Crusoe, *Walden*, Faulkner's "The Bear", Hemingway's "Great Two-Hearted River", Godden's *Greengage Summer*, and Wechsberg's *Sweet and Sour* are variations on this form of pastoral. *Walden* is unique in that Henry David Thoreau really did retreat to nature. His Arcadia was as real as the beans he tended. Nonetheless, he remains aware of the contrast between his cabin life and that of Concord, and he eventually returns to life outside. In *Sweet and Sour*, and *Looking for a Bluebird*, Wechsberg tells about Europe between the turn of the century and the end of World War II. His kind of pastoral is a mental journey through the realm one lived in before one's innocence was lost. Again, there is a dual perspective. The boy he used to be often does not understand what is going on, but the man who describes the events is putting them down in the aftermath of World War II. Many of the incidents he describes, especially those prior to World War I, are as pastoral as those in *Dandelion Wine*, but the sweet is tinged with sour, and the teeth set on edge by the sophisticated outsider-awareness which hovers on the fringes of the child's perspective. The child did not understand antisemitism; the Czech Jew whose friends and relatives disappeared into concentration camps does. Memory and history cast their shadow over the story of Uncle Absalon who, in 1913, enthusiastically arranges with the village authorities for an antisemitic riot against himself lest the village lose face with its neighbors. The mayor tells the firemen, footballers, and young men's clubs that there will be rioting on Sunday at 11 a.m. The doctor selects the stones to keep them small. Uncle Absalon's wife bakes apple strudel for the hungry organizers of the riot to eat afterwards. When one member of this mob (a resident of only eight years' standing) actually throws stones in earnest and breaks the large plate glass window, the angered villagers rough him up. As Uncle Absalon happily sums it up: "The Mayor said they'll pay for a new one, from the lamp account. I guess the folks in the park district will have to stumble around in darkness for a couple of months."[3] Wechsberg lovingly renders the sights, smells, sounds, and tastes of this lost world. As a musician and former member of the Vienna Opera claque, he is competent to guide us in the realm of sound, and as a lover of good food – he wrote for *Gourmet Magazine* – he is expert at describing flavors, whether of delicatessen specialities or holiday feasts. In between the sinister events are patches of sunlight, funny experiences, naive and amusing episodes that have idyllic qualities, even though their landscape is not the actual countryside.

Both insider- and outsider-pastoral invite the reader to escape from complex contemporary life. What effect does a successful escape have? None of the pastorals I have chanced upon make a serious pitch for abandoning civilization permanently, let alone overthrowing it. Many admit implicitly that the idyll is unobtainable. In fact, those that argue its obtainability, because they build complex arguments, become didactic utopian fiction. If all literature is to be directed to social action and moral improvement, the pastoral will not rank high, but those are parochial standards to apply to art. Better to be grateful if a pastoral can sharpen our sensory awareness and remind us of ways in which our lives lack simplicity. The appreciation of beauty and the basically positive mind-set encouraged by the form seem beneficial, and the static nature of its illusion would keep most readers from wanting to lose themselves permanently in its solace.

Adventure: refuge in daydreams

Deflation of the ego, simplicity of life, passive openness, awareness of sensory data: these provide an escape for one kind of personality. For another, the desiderata are nearly the opposite: ego inflation, excitement, the illusion of strenuous activity, violence, and intense emotions. The only shared feature is the protagonist's freedom from unpleasant responsibilities. Tending a flock of sheep and ruling a kingdom are similarly glamorized. Marriages are passionate for ever after. Of such stuff are daydreams made; or conversely, from daydreams are such stories spun.

Classical literature supplies no true equivalent to this form of popular literature. Daydreams are private, and often anti-social, in the sense that the protagonist imagines himself or herself scaling the barriers erected by society, and gaining power that belongs to others. Traditional societies are founded upon the rightness of the status quo, so naturally such aggrandizement, by violence or marriage or cunning, is seen as sinful and threatening.

Mimetic examples of daydream stories are *Pamela* and *The Three Musketeers*; fantastic examples are *The Wizard of Oz*, Andre Norton's *The Year of the Unicorn*, and Heinlein's *Time Enough for Love*. What qualities of life not found in the real world do these works supply? And why should the qualities seem so attractive in reverie when they would be found frightening and upsetting if they were to become real?

Pamela and *The Three Musketeers* adhere to female and male stereotypes respectively, but the rewards they offer to the protagonists are similar. The female success story figures the heroine's defense of her virtue, her perturbations, and her marriage to a man of much higher status than herself. D'Artagnan of *The Three Musketeers* is the son of a poor gentleman – that much rank is necessary if he is to be permitted a sword – but he starts with only his bravery and weapon-skill, and rises to become a lieutenant in the musketeers and the trusted henchman of Cardinal Richelieu. In the course of winning higher status, both challenge and defy social norms, she by refusing to take her virtue lightly and then by marrying above her station, he by his thoroughly illegal duels. Both create their new selves by going against society's rules and then forcing society to acquiesce.

When authors defy the limits of the physically possible, a new dimension is added to the daydream material, one which enriches and enhances its significance if properly used. *The Wizard of Oz* describes in colorful fantasy terms a child's need to feel equal to the adult world. Dorothy starts her adventures by inadvertently killing a witch who has tyrannized a nation of child-sized people. Her companions' quests are her own since they seek brains, a heart, and courage. Brains represent not so much IQ as the accumulated knowledge that separates adult from child; a heart, besides its association with the adult emotion of love, offers emotional knowledge in general. When the child learns the heart's reasons, she will be adult. Courage is necessary if she is not to be daunted by the adventures and pressures of growing up. In the course of the journey, Dorothy kills the other witch by an act of defiance, and demands treatment as an equal from the wizard. But Dorothy has also to realize that she is not yet ready for independence. She must go back to her aunt and uncle in Kansas and accept the normal pace of growth. Dorothy would have been quite unable to articulate her problems, except by complaining that life was dull, and that she wanted to be grown up. Few children would find an analytic account of her needs interesting or comprehensible. Symbolically, however, at subliminal levels, they can learn what qualities are necessary. They are also urged to be patient and accept their own Kansas. Fantasy is effective here in a way that realism could never be.

Andre Norton's *The Year of the Unicorn* uses magic to give a body and name to problems faced by women at the age of marriage. Gillan has powers unknown even to herself, and this psychic reality is translated into the fantasy of her having witch powers. Ordinary problems are again translated into fantasy terms when her husband in a socially arranged marriage, a were-beast sorcerer, appears to her to have his were-animal nature only imperfectly under control. Through her adventures, which include schizoid journeys in the mind, she comes to terms with the sorcerer. To reduce the magic to psychology – the problems of self-definition and sexuality, and the difficulties of combining career with marriage – would impoverish the book. It attempts to communicate on the emotional, not the intellectual level.

Heinlein's *Time Enough for Love* supplies a cynicism lacking in *The Three Musketeers* or in a sword and sorcery fantasy like *Conan the Conqueror*, and tones down their crude zest, but does not subtract from the hero's powers. Lazarus Long is not only credited with limitless fighting skill and tremendous mental agility, he is over 2000 years old when the story starts, and is apparently immortal, capable of unlimited medical rejuvenation and of regenerating amputated parts. With more than two thousand years in which to lead every kind of life, the hero is in a better position than most to determine what makes life worth living. His experiences all point to love: not sex (although the tale is frequently adorned with sexual encounters), but family togetherness. Like Don Juan, Long goes from one woman to another (though he is often married for fifty years at a time), but reaches a sense of rounding off and completeness only after he has time-travelled back to his childhood (during World War I) and slept with his mother. Otto Rank's analysis of the Don's seeking the one unobtainable woman is thus played out to the full conclusion – a fantasy of enthusiastic, happy incest.

It is no coincidence that fairy tales, many romances, many heroic legends and myths, and most adventure stories share the same narrative pattern, yet the values inculcated are not identical. Today, there is no generally accepted mythology or religion, so our adventure literature offers a completely secularized, ego-centered equivalent to stories that once had transcendent elements. Without the mythic signification for the exaggerations and monsters, the form seems cheaper. Its lack of concern for ultimate questions – questions irrelevant to a totally materialistic world – similarly lowers the spiritual level. Since adventure stories proliferate rather than being told over and over, they remain individualized and further displaced from archetypal patterns, and become more displaced as later authors strive for originality. One might call them crippled myths, forced to operate in a material universe which has no heaven and no gods.

Their most enthusiastic readers would like to think of themselves as crippled heroes, forced to operate in a materialistic universe which has lost its myths and its monsters. Trekkies and Tolkien fans clearly find bourgeois life deeply unsatisfying. Its democratic ideals, and its petty-minded betrayal of even those ideals, give no sense of personal significance. Readers of *Lord of the Rings* or Julian May's *The Saga of the Exiles* or Ann McCaffrey's *Dragonworld* series identify with the aristocratic Aragorn, or with the inner circle of humans who have developed metapsychic talents, or with the dragonriders, not with the untalented masses. Readers can glory vicariously in competence and the accompanying self-confidence, qualities that come to the stories' heroes with little unpleasant effort and may even be inherited. Part of the pleasure lies in joining an inner circle of likeminded, powerful people. Such comradeship, the sense of being part of an elite fellowship, is hard to resist if one otherwise feels alienated and disenfranchised and finds one's daily actions meaningless. Being part of a system, psychologically, can give readers a sense of meaning.

Myth, too, gains meaning from being part of a system, and in this characteristic it has advantages over many modern adventures. Monsters like the gorgons in the Perseus story have an ancestry that links them to a total network of divine and demonic powers. In dragon stories, a dragon may not have a genealogy, yet western dragons share family resemblances which give them predictable powers (such as breathing fire) and predictable weaknesses (soft underbellies). Evil or unpleasant such monsters may be for a hero, but at least the hero knows himself to be in touch with something more than an ad hoc obstacle; the monsters have significance beyond the fight itself, as Odysseus found after he harmed Poseidon's son. Such transpersonal significance for fantastic monsters is often lacking in contemporary popular literature.[4] Thus two fantastic monsters, one known and the other unfamiliar, may serve the same function within the story yet have differing effects on the imagination. The Morlocks of *The Time Machine* disturb us as we learn that they are our descendants and also represent a facet of our present society. The Ur-viles of Donaldson's *Lord Foul's Bane* remain meaningless, although they too are frightening underground creatures.

These and other shifts in world picture may account for some of the shortcomings of modern adventure stories. Daydream material not subordinated to a mythic universe is crude stuff in its egocentricity. If the reader responds to it as if the story were myth or fairy tale – that is, symbolically – then it may well have some of the same potential for socializing and for integrating the self that they appear to have, according to Bettelheim and others.[5] If adventure stories help create a positive mind-set, or encourage bravery, or reinforce development of the unconscious along its hero-myth path, then this form of escape may offer benefits to some of its readers. Even the self-transcending act of reading can be beneficial, especially if the reader forms images and imagines emotions in later daydreaming. Total passivity, if habitual, is not healthy, and neither is the occasional unbalanced response, but there is no way to guard against the eccentric case.

Escape literature is the dismissive term for such tales of success and conquest. But we cannot even assume that the desire to escape is weak or unworthy. Tolkien argues that escape from the modern world is beneficial:

> Why should a man be scorned if, finding himself in prison, he tries to get out and go home? Or if, when he cannot do so, he thinks and talks about other

topics than jailers and prison-walls? The world outside has not become less real
because the prisoner cannot see it. In using Escape in this way the critics have
chosen the wrong word, and, what is more, they are confusing, not always by
sincere error, the Escape of the Prisoner with the Flight of the Deserter. . . . They
would seem to prefer the acquiescence of the 'quisling' to the resistance of the
patriot.[6]

Both Tolkien and C.S. Lewis argue that escape into an admittedly illusory
world can make the responsive reader aware of mythic powers beyond the
material world – the religious world of Christianity. Even without their
religious concern, though, one can feel that the illusions of escape
literature offer possible benefits. Trashy though many adventures are, they
encourage belief in the possibility of meaningful action. They deny that the
individual is worthless, a negligible statistic. Even at lowest valuation, this
reassurance has psychological value, for people who cannot believe in
themselves have trouble engaging themselves with life in any fashion.

Indulgence in the amusing and the farcical

Success-and-conquest literature is often disparaged for pandering to very
crude egoism. Amusing and farcical literature is not disapproved of,
although most theories of humor explain humor as making us feel
superior, and some forms of humor invite us to enjoy the injury of others.
Moreover, the comic world is rarely criticized for its escapist nature, yet any
extended comic narrative is an escape from reality. What so differentiates
this form of escape from others? What lets it successfully avoid the distrust
and disapproval of judicious minds?

D.H. Monro classifies comic theories according to whether they are
based on superiority, incongruity, release from restraint, or ambivalence.
The following comments owe much to his discussion.[7] Each of these four
theories is useful for explaining some forms of humor, but none covers all
types of the amusing, and within a comic narrative one may find all at
work. There is considerable overlap among them.

Hobbes, Bergson, and Aristotle are exemplars of the superiority
theories. Aristotle defines comedy as portraying those lower than
ourselves. In *Leviathan* (Part I, chapter 6), Hobbes declares that laughter is
the "sudden glory" arising from the sudden perception of some superiority
in ourselves by comparison with the infirmity of others. A continuous state
of arrogance gives its possessor no amusement, but sudden boosts lift us
from our normal state, and we naturally feel pleased at being better than
before, or better than others. Hobbes' definition helps explain our
response to viewing comedy on stage, to reading satire or to watching a
person slip and fall, and it can be stretched to cover our amusement at
children's errors, and the laugh or smile that occurs when one reaches the
summit of a mountain. Clearly, a sensation of superiority is a welcome
escape from the everyday.

Bergson modifies the concept of superiority with that of incongruity. According to his famous exposition, life and man are informed by a vital force which is essentially vigorous, flexible, and alive. Any stiffening or rigidity, mental or physical, is discerned as contrary to this natural force and hence deathly, and is corrected by ridicule. The rigidity may be that of a man unable to adjust his stride to a banana peel, or the improper use of one set of rules in an unsuitable situation – social rules in a criminal situation, or ecclesiastical behavior in the bedroom. To the degree that man appears to be a machine by being mechanical, repetitive, or unable to adjust, he becomes funny. Many of Bergson's examples are illuminating, but ultimately something more is needed, as Koestler points out:

> If automatic repetitiveness in human behaviour were a necessary and sufficient condition of the comic there would be no more amusing spectacle than an epileptic fit; and if we wanted a good laugh we would merely have to feel a person's pulse or listen to his heart-beat, with its monotonous tick-tack. If "we laugh each time a person gives us the impression of being a thing" there would be nothing more funny than a corpse.[8]

Kant is the font for the incongruity theories, which stress the "sudden" rather than the "glory". Laughter is "an affectation arising from the sudden transformation of a strained expectation into nothing".[9] One line of thought collapses by a lesser replacing it. The relief of strained expectation is a semi-physical sensation, one to be enjoyed by the reader. Kant stresses the downward fall, but incongruity can work in other directions. Monty Python farce routines often involve random incongruity, the refusal to move from important to trivial, and the refusal to stick to related concepts; they build on the *non sequitur.*

Release from restraint and discharge of tension are Freud's means of explaining most humor. This release is physical as well as psychic, a pleasant sensation for the reader. Civilization rests on repression. Humor touches strain points and triggers laughter, a temporary flash of the energy that has previously been used to enforce the repression. According to Freud, the most common repressed bases for humor are sex and aggression. By his focus on the mechanics of repression, Freud helps suggest why superiority should call forth a laugh, why we are insecure enough to welcome the sudden glory, why the aggressive component of humor is so noticeable. Koestler takes study of the physical dimensions one step further by suggesting the causes of laughter to be in the biochemistry of the fight-flight mechanism, and in the necessity of releasing the tension that it generates.

J.Y.T. Greig introduces another possible basis for humor – ambivalence.[10] Genuine hatred and strong hostility do not provide much amusement. For the funny side to be felt, one must both love and hate the butt; one must feel both joy and fear in a situation. Sexual jokes work because our attitudes are divided: part of the mind assents to the repression, after all, with at least as much firmness as the other part resents it.

With these various theories of humor in mind, let us look at some comic narratives. The stories of P.G. Wodehouse come to mind as perfect examples of comic escape. No one would claim that they ever offered any deep meaning or social message. His *comédie humaine* (approximately ninety novels and over 200 short stories) stresses the *comédie* rather than the full scope and variety of the *humaine*, but the sheer number of interconnected stories and characters makes his world more than a mere setting. Wodehouse can be called the man with just two plots: boy and girl get each other; or boy gets into a scrape and manages to evade the consequences. His stories hold no genuine suspense. The proper troths will be plighted, the necessary escapes engineered. Because the reader knows what the outcome will be, what one enjoys, variation by variation, is the virtuosity of the comic complications and the comic style. These adorn a landscape that embraces British country houses, London clubs, New York nightclubs, and Hollywood studios. Never was there a cloud-cuckoo-land this side of Cockaigne more removed from the unpleasant facts of life. Wodehouse's world is innocent and unthinking, both socially and sexually. The only flies in the ointment are domineering aunts, henpecking wives, and temporary "sticky situations".

Some of Wodehouse's humor is susceptible to standard analytic approaches. Such a passage, brilliant but not puzzling in its effect, is found in *Leave it to Psmith*, when Lord Emsworth's much-hated secretary, the efficient Baxter, hears a noise the night after a burglary, and investigates:

> With stealthy steps he crept to the head of the stairs and descended.
> One uses the verb "descend" advisedly, for what is required is some word suggesting instantaneous activity. About Baxter's progress from the second floor to the first there was nothing halting or hesitating. He, so to speak, did it now. Planting his foot firmly on a golf-ball which the Hon. Freddie Threepwood, who had been practicing putting in the corridor before retiring to bed, had left in his casual fashion just where the steps began, he took the entire staircase in one majestic, volplaning sweep. There were eleven stairs in all separating his landing from the landing below, and the only ones he hit were the third and the tenth. He came to rest with a squattering thud on the lower landing, and for a moment or two, the fever of the chase left him.[11]

The failure to adjust, the non-human nature of his swoop, the anesthesia of the heart we indubitably feel for his sufferings (ensured by his very unsympathetic behavior prior to this scene) are all pure Bergsonian humor. Wodehouse adds delay after delay to his exposition, building tensions to be released. Baxter's fall, unusually violent for Wodehouse, is well calculated to relieve a lot of the dislike we feel for the man. Because this comeuppance seems "justified", we relish this fall. At last we can feel superior to Baxter, and we are glad to do so because he rouses subliminal guilt in us. He is always morally in the right, and we know we should praise him rather than blame him, but all along we are identifying with Psmith, who is helping steal a diamond necklace and carrying out an impersonation.

Pinning down the comic effect of other Wodehouse humor is rather more difficult. The introduction of "Catsmeat" Potter-Pirbright in *The Mating Season* is characteristically Wodehousean:

> Today he is the fellow managers pick first when they have a society comedy to present and want someone for "Freddie," the lighthearted friend of the hero, carrying the second love interest. If at such a show you see a willowy figure come bounding on with a tennis racket, shouting "hullo, girls," shortly after the kickoff, don't bother to look at the program. That'll be Catsmeat.

Catsmeat is usually so sprightly that

> he is more like Groucho Marx than anything human. . . . Yet now. . . he was low spirited. It stuck out a mile. His brow was sicklied o'er with the pale cast of thought and his air that of a man who, if he had said "hullo, girls," would have said it like someone in a Russian drama announcing that Grandpapa had hanged himself in the barn.[12]

We laugh at seeing social comedy thus reduced to so simple a formula, and perhaps there is a Bergsonian element to Catsmeat's dramatic type being so narrowly (i.e. mechanically) definable. We enjoy the lowbrow smirk at this incongruous lowering of Shakespeare and Chekhov, and we enjoy the self-inflation we feel at looking down on the great writers. Groucho Marx is undercut by the implication that he is not human, but that works out to be a compliment, not a Bergsonian reification. What we come away with is not a release of aggression, but a sense that we see the theatre world afresh. Bit players, social comedy, Groucho Marx, Shakespeare, and Russian dramatists have all been viewed incongruously askew in each other's presence, in a fashion that lightens and enlightens.

Wodehouse's comedy remains mimetic. When we add fantasy to light farce, new effects are possible. To take a dramatic example of comic escape, consider *Ruddigore*. Few Gilbert and Sullivan operettas can be accused of making sense or of mounting serious satiric attacks, but *Ruddigore* qualifies for a prize in lack of significance. A former baronet of Ruddigore enjoyed burning witches. One witch laid upon him a curse that he and his successors must commit one crime a day or die in agony. The true heir, to escape the curse, lives disguised as the farmer Robin Oakapple, while his younger brother bears the burden as Sir Despard. When the true heir's identity is revealed, his fiancée breaks off the match. By a legerdemain even more outrageous than the one at the end of *Major Barbara*, Robin breaks the power of the curse: disobeying is tantamount to suicide, but suicide itself is a crime. Hence, none of his ancestors who died for refusing are rightly dead, so they all come back to life by stepping down out of their portraits.

Ruddigore's world offers no commentary on our own. We feel far less engagement with the fates of the couples than in most Wodehouse plots. We stay for the music, the humor, and the unexpected incongruities that startle us into laughter, such as the behavior of Rose Maybud and Mad Meg. Theorists of humor can isolate elements that gratify aggressive or ambivalent feelings, for it would be difficult not to feel superior to this crew. Many a time one train of thought collides with another, derailing both and earning a laugh from the audience. Overall, however, what strikes us as most immediately attractive is the preposterous irrelevance and irresponsibility of it all. By entering this fantastic world, the audience declares a mock war on seriousness, mock because no one expects to come out of such a show and apply anything seen there to real life. If pastoral offers life without responsibilities, and success-and-conquest adventures give the reader power without responsibilities, farce makes fun of the responsibilities themselves.

In a more serious vein, Gogol's "The Nose" charts some of the possibilities of mixing fantasy into farce. The early stretches of the story might be read for horror, although the barber's domestic comedy makes serious sympathy with his fears difficult. Once a man is identified by the police as the missing and mischievous nose, we pass beyond horror to a kind of feverish gaiety. The possessor of the nose is, we realize, not in truth possessor (nor are we of ours), but beneficiary of his nose's co-operation, and when deprived of it, he feels like a leper. He can face nobody; he feels he ought to hide. The grotesquerie mounts as an apparent human shows no surprise at being accosted as a nose, but merely denies a close relationship with the accoster. Later, when the policeman returns it, he says:

> Your nose was caught as he was getting on the stagecoach for Riga. He had a passport made out in the name of a government official and the strange thing is that, at first, I myself took him for a gentleman. But luckily I had my glasses with me, so I put them on and recognized immediately that he was a nose.[13]

With the return of the prodigal nose, Kovalev is a different man – confident, cheerful, a great pursuer of women. He makes no spiritual improvement upon recognizing his blessing, but at least he now counts his nose as a blessing, rather than taking it for granted. One can talk about the story as satire on human nature: the loss of an eye, though substantively more serious, would not have upset Kovalev nearly as much. Overall, though, the peculiarities overshadow any such specific satire. The humor is not incidental or stylistic. One joke does not lead necessarily to the next. Rather, the situation is novel, and we are led on because each step is unexpected. We "identify" with Kovalev, and then have to readjust our rules about reality. The fantasy allows us to see many common social concerns anew. The use of fantasy is not necessarily a farcical technique, but it can provide the material for humor: incongruity, the unexpected, the disguised obscene, the butt with whom we identify and at the same time feel superior to. The fantasy can be manipulated to provide a comic atmosphere. Remove that humorous element, and "The Nose" would have the nightmare qualities of Kafka's *Metamorphosis*.

When we ask why the escapism and sadism of humor usually avoid reprobation, we see that the comic benefits from excellent protective coloration. The cream-puff form of comic narrative is not directed at a single butt, so its audience cannot be criticized either for arrogance toward another person or for satiric subversiveness. One almost laughs at one-knows-not-what. The precise triggers of laughter are extremely difficult to pin down, and look relatively innocuous (morally speaking) or insignificant. Yes, one feels flashes of superiority, but the ego-inflation that humor gives us *cannot grow*. Success-and-conquest stories get woven into daydreams, and the inflation they foster may linger in our private thoughts for days as we relive and reshape the stories with ourselves as hero. Humor cannot be thus re-used. The "sudden glory" arises only when our mind makes an unforeseen connection. We cannot preserve this quality of surprise, nor can most of us manufacture a steady stream of humorous situations for ourselves. Humorous narrative is an ephemeral gift to the audience from an author. It cannot be re-experienced until forgetfulness has blotted out some of the original experience.

Detailing all the modes of farce and the comic would be difficult. At one extreme, Monty Python skits make war on sense and logic; at another, the animal fable shades into success-and-conquest (trickster-style) wish fulfillment. Rabelaisian humor of size and body modulates into satire, and out of the escapist realm. The kinds of experience offered the reader differ. The pleasure of being surprised can be fairly passive, but many forms of humor, by their understatement and economy of means, leave the reader to supply the missing link, and thereby demand active participation. Most humorous narratives build a world noticeably better than ours because funnier, but these worlds are not offered as if they might be real, and we do not expect any carry-over to real life. The world of humor remains delightful but illusory. It exercises the mind and relaxes some repressed emotions. We all enjoy feeling superior, and to those readers who actually laugh aloud, the escape obviously offers a direct and pleasurable physical stimulation.

Puzzlement and pleasing jeopardy:
the reader at a stimulating disadvantage

So far, we have examined kinds of escape literature that encourage passive relaxation, that stir active thoughts of aggression, that arouse and discharge minor tensions, and that feed one's sense of superiority. If we turn to affective literature, we find forms of escape that in one way or another raise and maintain tension, usually causing a sense of inferiority. Surprisingly, this inferiority is perceived as pleasing. Mental and emotional involvement with characters and situation are demanded because the primary point of such stories is the degree to which they stir the reader's emotions: one does not read ghost stories if one can feel no thrill. Affective literature is written to produce a specific effect on the audience. The appeal is primarily emotional, not moral or intellectual, and usually is the arousal of a single emotion – puzzlement, or sexual desire, or fear, or terror. In mimetic fiction, puzzlement is the intended aim of the detective story; in non-mimetic, it is produced by the uncanny and the *fantastique*. Pornography, ghost tales, and horror stories exemplify the other forms.

Tension in the reader is not produced solely by affective literature. All literature rouses expectations which cause a tension until they are satisfied, but the expectations can be of anything. Excitement too is a kind of tension, but it is non-specific, and in an adventure story the nature of the excitement shifts, as the hero hunts or is hunted, disports himself in bedroom or battlefield. The tensions of affective literature are narrower and more totally sustained. The reader's tensions may be released at the end of the story, as in a detective story, or the reader may not achieve release until returning from the horror story to the everyday world. Or the tensions may need a physical outlet, as in masturbation. Throughout such stories, readers are at a disadvantage: they don't know "who done it", yet have the clues which will solve the mystery. They feel helpless before ill-disposed superior forces, the unknown, the diabolical. They feel sexually roused, but cannot take the centerfold playmate to bed. Tension without the prospect of relief is not pleasing, and few would seek it deliberately. In real life, there is no joy in learning that one of your four best friends must have committed a murder. Going over the clues in one's mind would make one exhausted and irritable, not pleasurably stimulated, and the relief afforded by knowledge would be mixed with pain.

In fiction, the sensation attendant on all these is pleasurable, particularly when we know that an answer will be provided. In other words, this kind of fiction offers pleasure without payment. In real life, sexual arousal with no possibility of satisfying it is a nuisance: ask someone in a body-cast whose arms are in traction. Most pornography, however, offers vicarious gratification, and those interested in physical release can seek it, their imaginations stimulated by the story's actions. In real life, no one would welcome terror. Yet we accept the fictive nature of these tensions as a kind of protection, and we anticipate the satisfactions internal to the story, and those we will feel upon leaving the story for real life. Again, the kinds of escape offered by affective literature are diverse, and again the introduction of fantasy can alter the ways in which the story grips us.

Rex Stout's detective stories offer the would-be escapee a mimetic haven that has much to recommend it. Nero Wolfe's enchanted brownstone supplies gourmet meals, a good library, and orchids always in bloom. Wolfe is an extremely demanding chief, but he is so hedged in by his own rules – he will do this, he will never under any circumstances do the other – that Archie Goodwin (and the reader) can maneuver to avoid serious conflicts, and can enjoy the sense of manipulating so overbearing an authority figure. With Archie, readers can enjoy the company of good-looking women and the casual handling of large sums of money. When confronted with a corpse, those readers who lack war experience would be likely to have hysterics, vomit, faint, or at least feel terrible, but Archie handles bodies effortlessly. Since death is a subject most readers are touchy about, *savoir-faire* in the face of death in a tenuous way assuages our fear of dealing with it. The corpse rouses latent anxieties; the detective's behavior quiets them. Goodwin's calmness is not exclusive to him. Most detectives are cool, but some make no issue of it, and others concentrate on the disfigurements of the body. Stout rarely does more than allude to the corpse; he focuses on the emotion and on cool, collected action. Readers batten on this emotional reassurance.

Styles of control and competence vary. Raymond Chandler's talk-tough-out-of-the-side-of-his-mouth Marlowe is not the suave socialite and superficially frivolous Lord Peter Wimsey of Dorothy Sayers, but both always just happen to have the information needed, or the lead which will produce it. Although mere mortals need not be too bothered at failing to out-guess such masters, the similar failure of the police is comforting. Indeed, the more intelligent the police or helpers, the more enjoyable their failure is to readers – a fact not properly recognized by Conan Doyle and Agatha Christie, who use irritatingly stupid helpers. In most stories, the detective's need to hand the criminal over to the police and the need for the police to go through all the messy technicalities of wrapping the case up serves to pull readers back to approving of the police again, and thus leads them back to socially acceptable stances.

Like the detective story, pornography rouses one major tension – here sexual interest rather than puzzlement – while at the same time offering a number of subliminal assurances which the reader craves. At the primary level, pornography puts the reader at a stimulating disadvantage in at least two ways: (1) by arousing sexual desire without completely satisfying that desire, and (2) by making the reader's own sexual experience seem unimaginative and pallid compared to the orgasmic virtuosity and lurid details described. The latter characteristic is particularly true of stories in magazines like *Playboy* and *Penthouse*, where finding material for twelve issues a year drives the producers to seek unusual combinations and actions to provide their readers with new daydream material. Pornography of an earlier era, when explicit reference to sexual experience was in itself exciting, was not as drawn to exaggeration and the bizarre.

Fanny Hill, a sunny, early example of the form, demonstrates the kinds

of subliminal assurances offered by this form of escape literature. The story
purports to be told by the woman involved, a device unequalled for
offering the male reader assurances he is glad to receive. According to
Fanny and her friends, women really want sexual contact, enjoy it, climax
easily, and are game to try any erotic practice. True, there are men like the
egregious Mr Norbert, who do not win her approval, but he is portrayed as
sexually inadequate, and is in no way a figure the reader would identify
with. One need be only tolerably endowed by nature and behave
considerately and one will be welcomed by Fanny and her associates. She
does not even try to wangle marriage from her clients, and she accepts
marriage to her first and only love with an odd show of reluctance; she
agrees to wedlock in part because she is superior to him in fortune, and she
wishes to bestow her financial security upon him. She offers the men in her
life great pleasure and satisfaction, and her whore's price is left discreetly
vague. In short, though female, her set of values is almost identical to those
of a man who can afford to seek casual gratification. Cleland sets up as
possible the whore's lack of emotional engagement, but eliminates the
whore's usual underlying hatred of men and desire to debase them, the
whore's boredom and lack of personal pleasure, and her fears of
impregnation and disease. All the charms of dealing with a pretty and
sympathetic woman are invoked and none of the responsibilities or
obligations that a real-life relationship normally entails. Sexual revolution
may change average social values to the point that such casual
relationships will be common, but to date they would have to be
considered moderately rare.

Besides eagerness and undemandingness, another quality offered in
such sexual escape literature is female subordination and passivity. In
Fanny Hill's time, it could be assumed. In the works of an author like
Heinlein, who has used sex imaginatively in his recent science fiction, the
passivity is still there despite the changes in the facade. In the futuristic
Time Enough for Love, women are technicians, world leaders, and
spaceship captains. They are sexually independent, yet willing and even
eager to bear children for all the men they like. Nevertheless, their normal
tactic for getting their own way in an argument is to cry, and the first
contingency plan proposed by a pair of twin girls (should they be stranded
without any money on a strange planet) is to become hookers, despite the
assurances we have received that they can do space-travel mathematics in
their heads. One might add that most pornography, besides flattering the
masculine ego, sings siren songs of a world in which all women are
effortlessly beautiful. The protagonist never has to make do with a plain or
dowdy woman, nor with one too old, nor with one whose hair is in curlers
and whose face is covered with gooey creams. Pornography for women
offers an equivalent range of assurances – promises that the reader can
reach spectacular orgasms, insistences that she is beautiful enough to

attract any man she pleases, and soothing statements that she will be respected.

Such jejune assurances for the insecure are not an essential element in pornography, as a text like Georges Bataille's *Story of the Eye* demonstrates. Operating on the knowledge that most people have "gelded eyes" and will look away from lewd and horrifying events, Bataille pursues such actions with zestful obsession. His private associations of eyes, testicles, and eggs supply a nightmarish coherence to the episodes that climax with sexual abuse of the sacraments, erotic strangulation, and the sight of a blue *eye*, surrounded by pubic fur, staring out of a vagina. Pornography of this sort does little to comfort readers – unlike most literature of illusion, it rather seeks to disturb us – but the creation of a single-minded emotional tension is otherwise typical of this affective form of literature, as is the escape from quotidian reality.

Pornography and detective stories stay within the realm of the empirically possible, however unrealistic the action may be. Their effectiveness depends on their events being possible: were mystery-writers allowed to reveal that the murderer had physically been in two places at once, thanks to his time-travel machine, we would feel cheated. For our puzzlement to be meaningful, we must believe in the possibility of a rational solution. Ghost stories, however, and some other affective forms, derive their power from contravening normal reality. We want to dismiss the ghosts in Brian Moore's *Fergus* as figments of Fergus' imagination, but to insist on diminishing them thus would greatly limit our pleasure in the story. They are so much more solid and real than, say, the golem in Cynthia Ozick's "Puttermesser and Xanthippe"; there the golem never achieves an existence much beyond that of metaphor. Henry James' *The Turn of the Screw* would be greatly impoverished if we could not allow ourselves to entertain the possibility that ghosts may exist. Part of the story's effectiveness lies in its refusal to resolve the ambiguities: in one sense the tension is not released within the story, and our sense of release comes when we transfer back to our own armchair and world. That form of organization leaves some tensions unresolved. We remain puzzled over what the story means. The novel is popular because we ponder it even after the experience of reading it has ended. Is it about real ghosts, or a governess' hallucinations? Is it about the dual nature of man? The corruption of goodness? Or is it about all of these? The possibility that ghosts exist is usually perceived as a pleasant alteration in our concept of reality, for their existence, even if they are malign, presupposes life after death. This implication helps explain why ghost stories are escapist and are enjoyed, even when the ghosts are troublesome.

Horror literature, at first glance, should not be escapist at all, yet appears to be so. One reads Ambrose Bierce or H.P. Lovecraft for entertainment, even as huge crowds have edged their way into theatres to thrill to

Hitchcock films. Lovecraft attempts, by means of heavy mystery and witnesses too overcome to comment intelligibly, to build an atmosphere conducive to fear. He uses such fantastic effects as monsters (*The Dunwich Horror*), witches, and demonic possession. He speaks of "remainders" from puritan witch-hunting times, powers which escaped the hunters and remain in hiding in Boston and in isolated rural communities in Massachusetts.

A variant form of affective literature is what Todorov calls the *fantastique*. Such stories build a world which we continually try to pin down and label: are the events uncanny but susceptible to rational explanation, or are they genuinely supernatural, and ought we to revise our notions of reality? *The Turn of the Screw* is such a tale. So is Jan Potocki's *The Saragossa Manuscript*, one of Todorov's chief examples. Potocki inclines toward rational explanations, but in many stories the mystery is apparently inexplicable. His fragmentary decameron of interwoven tales features underground caverns, awakening under gibbets, dead men alive, secrets leading to treasure, a family with Christian, Jewish, and Moslem branches, gypsies, and the Wandering Jew. One is always guessing. Is the story meant to be taken at face value? Is it a dream? A drug vision? A lie?

The effect of fantasy in horror stories, ghost stories, and the *fantastique* depends heavily on the reader's outlook. To the mind that is childishly self-centered and unmoved by the suffering of others, a Lovecraft offspring of the devil is probably more effective at churning up appropriate sensations than the protagonist of a mimetic story. To the mind of a religious believer, moreover, contact with the supernatural has the potential for more meaningful excitement than a strictly human situation. To a humanist, however, human suffering is the ultimate horror, and hence mimetic fiction is likely to be more stirring. Ambrose Bierce's Civil War stories create "intolerable" human situations for our delectation. Captain Coulter of the Northern army carries out a suicidal gun attack and survives to learn that the bombardment has killed his child and secessionist wife. A Union son kills his Confederate father to prevent the father from betraying the approach of the son's troops. Many of these stories work on two levels. The primary one tells of horror, and we read for the frisson. But these plots mask fundamental conflicts with political issues. The man who shoots his father with the most honorable of patriotic intentions enacts an Oedipal drama. Men who kill their wives or brothers touch similar psychic stress points.

Horror literature offers a wide variety of experiences, be they thrills, tragedy, or semi-serious religious terrors. (Serious religious experiences take one beyond the realm of escape.) Any tingles of horror, disgust, vicarious hatred, or nausea are desirable from the author's point of view, but they must be carefully controlled, for the reader who puts the book down unfinished is evidence of failure. People submit to being upset, perhaps because feeling strongly is one proof that one is alive, just as feeling a pinch is held to prove that one is awake. But few would seek out strong negative feelings in real life. Waiting in court to hear whether the jury has acquitted one of a murder charge or has condemned one to death is doubtless a situation of great emotional intensity, but few would willingly enter it in order to feel alive. Books and movies provide that pleasure without the drawbacks of deep, grinding fear, and the aftermath of exhaustion. For someone willing to enter into the horror story, a good deal of adrenalin is stirred up, providing what Huxley calls Violent Passion Surrogate, a physiological experience that his *Brave New World* rulers deem necessary to health. The reader not only gets the benefits of having darker emotions whipped to a froth, but can also enjoy the relief that comes when the experience stops. The relaxation following one's return to the safe world of everyday can transform one's ordinary surroundings from their usual dullness to a kind of blessedness.

The pleasures of literary escape

At the outset of this chapter, I stated that most fantasy is dismissed by hostile critics as "escapist" and most escape literature is dismissed as "fantasy". The one-to-one equation is patently preposterous. No one escapes to Kafka, and, as I have tried to demonstrate, escapist literature need not be fantastic, even though it is unrealistic. The interrelationship is rather the familiar one of overlapping sets, two partially overlapping circles. Fantasy is a larger and more varied realm than the literature of escape. The realms overlap, but each maintains a separate domain as well. Within the set comprising escapist works, two characteristics unite the fantastic and the mimetic: the first is their overwhelming emphasis on appeal to physical sensations and emotions rather than to the intellect; the second is their portrayal of man freed from responsibilities and limitations. The sensations evoked, the responsibilities and limitations expunged, however, differ with the relationship of the narrative to empirical reality. Fantasy is an effective tool for tapping some veins of emotion in the reader, but useless for others. Two kinds of escape are thus possible, neither one necessarily better, just different.

Materialistic assumptions about the universe underlie much modern thinking and provide the basis for most mimetic escape. Sensory impressions alone among the escapes described are viable in both traditional and historical societies. A pastoral like Lord Dunsany's *The Curse of the Wise Woman* keeps us aware that the joys of the senses should not outweigh our responsibilities in the long run, but both we and the narrator are refreshed by exposure to the pleasures of the Irish countryside. In any complex culture, religious or scientific, man loses some contact with nature and may benefit from being reintroduced to its beauties. The other mimetic escapes, although possibly known, are not written down in traditional societies. To write extended pornography, for instance, (as opposed to enjoying a dirty joke), demands serious rebellion against the traditional interpretation of sexuality in moral terms and presupposes control over the printing or copying process. When classical or medieval authors use sex, it is usually as a satiric tool, a means of debunking man's misbehavior, and consequently its use can be justified as a reinforcement of the moral code. Only since the Enlightenment do we find many examples of extended sexual detail without satiric intent. A similar focus on the human without a distancing or detached perspective produces horror literature. In a world where man has been able to find no measure but himself, death and the suffering an individual can undergo are the ultimate horrors; hence it is these mimetic subjects that Bierce invokes to stimulate maximum emotional arousal.

Mimetic escape accepts the world we live in, but suggests we can succeed within it. It accepts our prejudices – such as the high value we place on good looks, or our cultural sex-role stereotypes – but insinuates that the reader can beat the system, whether through talent or through such loopholes as luck or socially advantageous marriage. The pattern set by *Pamela* is still alive in women's literature like Mary Stewart's *Nine Coaches Waiting*. Mimetic escape may let us substitute for both our fear of nothingness and our desire for metaphysical answers the lesser question of "who done it?" and then invite us to enjoy the relief of discovering the lesser answer.

Fantastic escape is different in its possible effects. One cannot simply add a dollop of fantasy to sensory pastoral or pornography or the detective story and come up with "the same, only more so". The first two forms depend on verisimilitude for their effect, and the assumption that a rational answer exists is central to the third. Fantastic escape is not bound by materialistic assumptions: it considers standards of measurement other than man, planets other than our own, worlds other than that of dead matter. It does not necessarily accept man's limits or the status quo. The departures from reality can be put to stimulating uses or to dull ones: the limitations of human physique are dissolved by Robert E. Howard to give his hero Conan superhuman strength, but to what end? The gift is only used to kill opponents more numerous and varied than swashbuckling heroes can usually manage. However, Tolkien goes beyond physical limits with a ring of invisibility, which starts as a mere plot convenience in *The Hobbit*, but develops intriguing moral dimensions in *The Lord of the Rings*. Monsters bear witness to the quasi-sacred power of the heroic individual who overcomes them, and provide the opportunity to uphold the possibility of heroism. They can also focus yet more complex feelings, as shown by the affectionate amusement many cinemagoers feel at the sight of King Kong manhandling a skyscraper. Man can thus enjoy fantasy and, as a secondary benefit, enjoy consciousness of its artifice. Overall, mimetic escape is bound to our materialistic assumptions. Fantastic escape allows authors to draw on a wider range of value systems.

The chief drawback of escape literature is not its fantastic elements nor its lack of realism but rather the fact that it rarely challenges us to think. It is sensational, literally producing physical sensations and unfocused feelings. In this respect, fantastic escape has a slight edge over the merely possible. It need not appeal more directly to the intellect, but it can more readily let new ideas, values, and social systems form part of its tapestry. If the feelings they arouse are pleasurable, we may think more seriously on the underlying subject later. Fundamentally, however, escape literature offers blind, passive enjoyment, and demands no obligation toward the source of the pleasurable stimulation. We disengage from the real world in order to engage with these comforting illusions.

The desires evident at the literal level of many escapist stories may seem silly – success-and-conquest kingship, elite fellowship, or communication with ghosts – but those to whom they seem silly should ponder the reasons for the popularity of such fantasies. They point to the lack of fulfilling and satisfying values in everyday life. The democratic and bourgeois ideal leaves many desires unfulfilled, and, as Rosemary Jackson has argued, fantasy is, among other things, a form of subversion and protest. Even if the fantasy only offers escape, that desire to turn away is not necessarily contemptible. Readers who feel no lacks in their everyday lives are quick to scorn the means by which others gain satisfactions, but the scorn may be misdirected. The readers for whom this literature does nothing are well supplied with alternative forms of literary experience.

4

Literature of vision: introducing new realities

Most fictions present an individual concept of reality and, in that narrow sense, a new reality. Some fictive worlds, however, do not seriously call attention to the differences separating them from the reader's own world. When we submerge ourselves in an exotic adventure story, we know its illusory world is not ours, but we do not bother to analyze the differences with a mind to improving our own. Nor do we feel drawn to compare the world of a popular novel set in our own day with our own, not because it is different, but because its world is too similar in values to our own to offer any challenge.

The works I wish to examine next invite conscious comparison of our own vision of reality with that which we confront in the stories. They seem designed to call attention to the differences. They make us feel the limitations of our notions of reality, often by presenting one that seems more rich, more intense, more coherent (or incoherent), or somehow more significant. Not only do these visions invite comparison, they encourage strong emotional response. Creating a separate reality and calling attention to it is one characteristic of great, as opposed to merely competent, fiction.

They may express an outrage we are expected to share. Vonnegut fosters bitterness at human stupidity in *Cat's Cradle*; Beckett cries out in *Waiting for Godot* at the cosmic joke being played on man, and insofar as we can accept his symbolic depiction of the human plight, we share his feeling. Some kinds of narrative persuade us that reality is finer than we had supposed. Epic and heroic pieces like *Beowulf*, *The Song of Roland*, and saints' lives exclude all that is trivial, and present black-and-white worlds that preach an intense, narrow commitment to one kind of life.

Some present a richer, more varied vision of reality, such as we find in Calvino's *Invisible Cities*. Barthelme expresses despair in *Snow White* at reality's aimless fragmentation. Calvino produces such a fizzy cosmic joy in *Cosmicomics* that it is difficult not to rejoice with the narrator. Such expressive visions are a mean between escapism and didacticism. The sensations of the former make no demands upon us, the latter asks total commitment. Expressive literature appeals to both emotion and intellect. An expressive vision may imply that some action is appropriate, but encourages emotional response and reflection rather than action, and provides no blueprint for a future program. As a rule, the fictive world is at least as important as the plot to the work's overall effect, for a complex story would distract the audience from the comparison of visions of reality.

The techniques which help a fictive world comment on reality are additive, subtractive, and contrastive. An author may use all three in a single work, but most works rely heavily on one approach to reality. If the world presented is notably fuller, richer, and more varied and vivid than our everyday reality, or if it reminds us that our own has much that we pass over unconsciously, then we can speak of an additive or augmented world. Whether the addition is merely realistic detail, or a fantastic gimmick like a magic carpet, the technique involved is still additive. Subtractive worlds are either very narrow definitions of reality which leave out large portions of human experience, or they are worlds in which the author has deliberately erased expected material, especially the logical connections between actions. Heroic worlds and metaphoric worlds like Borges' library are the former, absurdist literature the latter. Contrastive worlds are a special subset of the subtractive, in that they refine the complexity of reality down to two centers of interest; the tension between these two constitutes a comment on the nature of reality. The two poles about which experience is ranged can be two sets of values, such as Emma Bovary's silly romanticism and her village's bourgeois dreariness. They can be people: Gregor Samsa as bug versus his family. Frequently, one of these foci is fantastic, an additive feature in an otherwise subtractive approach to reality. Contrastive works differ from the subtractive dualism seen in heroic black-and-white, in that readers have a foot in both camps. We are emotionally committed, or at least intrigued, by both sides in contrastive works.

An author can stimulate our awareness of reality by manipulating our literary expectations, giving us a different presentation of reality than we expect from the form or story (as Gardner does in *Grendel*). Or the author may force us to notice the differences between our own mixed and banal worlds and the burnished simplicity of the heroic ideal. Or he may revivify day-to-day material that we normally banish to our subconscious. Most of the basic additive, subtractive, and contrastive effects are available to authors writing in both the mimetic and fantastic veins. Although I shall cite mimetic examples in passing, my chief concern is to explore the paradox of using fantasy to comment on the nature of reality.

The creation of augmented worlds

We are only dully aware of everyday life. We can get up and dress in a semiconscious state, and many repetitive professional tasks require little more engagement or concentration. We indulge in mannerisms like chronic coughs and cracking knuckles, totally unaware of the habits which so irritate others. The same sort of low-grade consciousness characterizes many of our responses to the world. To some people, a good dinner is just something to be eaten before the Monday night football game. To the gourmet, the food will evoke consciousness of the steps needed to prepare it, speculation on recipes, and reminiscence of previous encounters with the dish. To a food-industry specialist, the awareness might extend beyond cooking to the raising of the animal or crop, to processing conditions, and to marketing problems. Our consciousness automatically narrows our awareness, and we get out of an experience far less than is available. Professional training affects our response as well. Ingmar Bergman's film of Mozart's *Magic Flute* intrigued me with the strongly symbolic hero monomyth pattern. A theatre historian's attention would be riveted by the Drottningholm theatre's eighteenth-century stage machinery; a musician would focus on the performance and conducting; a singer on the effectiveness of the vocal performances; a film specialist would register camera work and integration of the frame with the opera.

When a fiction offers us a world whose values basically agree with our own, we feel no pressure to review our assumptions about reality. When values coincide, the reader and author agree on what parts of life are admirable, and which are too trivial to be mentioned, or must not be brought up on the grounds of decency or good taste. Most popular literature thus lulls and flatters readers rather than challenging and contradicting them. If an author persuades us not to reject his selection because of its strangeness, but succeeds in enticing us to explore and enjoy those differences, then we can compare a new reality with our own.

An augmented world, one created by additive methods, presents a reality fuller than our own. Mimetic literature accomplishes this augmentation by reintroducing to our notice material which our consciousness normally filters out; by introducing us to outlooks we would not otherwise take because of our class, race, sex, or other limiting factor; or by giving us several different views of the same scene or event.

Aldous Huxley argues that human consciousness is a reducing valve whose function is to screen out inessential stimuli so that we need not process them. Were it not for this filter, we should go mad from the bombardment of stimuli needing to be classified and responded to.

Without a limiting mechanism, we should never be able to ignore the sound of raindrops or traffic. Braces on the teeth would remain vividly uncomfortable forever. Every sound would put us on fight-flight readiness until we had consciously analyzed it and reassured ourselves. To function efficiently, we exclude from our consciousness a great deal of daily life.[1] To be reminded of the sensations we automatically exclude can be a pleasant gift of the unexpected, even if the sensation is a trivial one. *Ulysses* is famous for offering us such suppressed material as something new. Bloom's fleeting pleasure in passing a bowel movement of just the right consistency is a sensation known to all, but one that we rarely bring to the conscious level.

Vonnegut extends our consciousness in the realistic portions of *Breakfast of Champions* by taking us along his mind's associative rambles through normally repressed material. His drawing of an ass-hole (six irregular intersecting lines) is extremely funny when one remembers all the taboos surrounding that anatomical feature. His picture of a "wide-open beaver" similarly undercuts the moral and emotional charge associated with crotch pictures:

> When Dwayne was a boy, when Kilgore Trout was a boy, when I was a boy, and even when we became middle-aged men and older, it was the duty of the police and the courts to keep representations of such ordinary apertures from being examined and discussed by persons not engaged in the practice of medicine. It was somehow decided that wide-open beavers, which were ten thousand times as common as real beavers, should be the most massively defended secret under law.[2]

The reality Vonnegut exposes us to is made up of vignettes concerning blacks and whites; rich and poor; the commercial world of car dealers, fast-food chains, motels, trucks, and a polluting factory; an American midwestern town with its correctional institution, its much-advertised cave, and its highways. Vonnegut avows his determination to free us from our normal rules of selecting realities. He says, of a conventional author, that she made "people believe that life had leading characters, minor characters, significant details, insignificant details, that it had lessons to be learned, tests to be passed, and a beginning, a middle, and an end" (p. 209). Having decided that life imitated art, and governments treated citizens like bit-part characters, Vonnegut says, "I resolved to shun storytelling. I would write about life. Every person would be exactly as important as any other. All facts would also be given equal weightiness. Nothing would be left out. Let others bring order to chaos. I would bring chaos to order" (p. 210). Naturally, he does no such thing, and as an artist he quite consciously orchestrates his material, but the effect on the reader is that of introducing chaos, because the trivial and repressed materials are all mixed into the story. The result is a new, more inclusive reality.

V. S. Naipaul enjoys some of his popularity because he introduces white

middle-class Britons and Americans to "third world" perspectives. The
Muslim Indian from the east coast of Africa who narrates *A Bend in the
River* gives us a new view on slavery, and introduces us to everyday details
of living through an African revolution. In *Guerrillas*, Naipaul enriches our
sense of reality by exploring economic, racial, and political tensions in a
Caribbean island, making readers see how white attitudes look to others.
Zola created similar effects when he revealed that a washerwoman had as
complex a personality and as serious a set of problems as any society lady
(*L'assommoir*). Patrick White expands readers' horizons by describing life
from a transsexual's point of view in *The Twyborn Affair*. Richard Fariña's
Been Down So Long It Looks Like Up to Me shows squares what a cool,
hip outlook is like.

Juxtaposing several views when they represent a cross-section of society
is especially effective for forcing us to realize that our view of reality is not
privileged. Norman Mailer tells white, middle-class, Protestant Americans
about war through the eyes of a Mexican, a Pole, a Jew, a black, and
various classes of white. He also tells America things it didn't want to know
about war and about what happens to American boys when they put on
khaki. We watch the mental zigzags of the innocent who forgot to keep a
tight ass-hole, and watch him, in his determination to get cleaned off, go to
a beshitten death. The sort of clean, tormented heroism popular in World
War I literature had not prepared folks at home for Mailer's picture of the
reality of war: the stresses created by old school ties and fiancées at home
knitting socks found in R.C. Sherriff's *Journey's End*, for instance, belong
to another world from the one where the sergeant tells one of his men:
"Suppose you just set down and beat your meat if you're gettin' anxious.
I'll do the goddam masterminding."[3] Nor did standard literary decencies
prepare an audience for the flashbacks dissecting unsatisfactory marriages
and sleazy premarital experience. Mailer does not let his readers shrug off
this taboo material by saying that only niggers or yids or polacks or
greasers have those troubles, for so do the WASPs, up to and including
General Cummings.

Adding suppressed or repressed material, and contrasting views, are the
chief techniques available to mimetic literature of vision. Fantasy
contributes two further techniques: one is the magic device; the other, the
addition of a mythological or metaphoric dimension to the mimetic level of
the plot.

The device may be purely a gimmick, something which imparts an
exotic flavor. Although its particular function may be irreplaceable – as is
Bilbo's ring of invisibility – the general plot of *The Hobbit* would need only
cosmetic changes to do without the gimmick. Cloning of humans is a
superficial device of this sort in Arthur C. Clarke's *Imperial Earth*. Adoption
of a child would have produced almost the same effect, for the story is
really about quarrel and reconciliation. Ursula Le Guin's "Nine Lives",

however, is genuinely concerned with the implications of human cloning. What would a member of a clone-group feel when the other members were accidentally killed? What would ordinary "singletons" feel when they had to work with such a group? A new planet is often a gimmick, equivalent to "Darkest Africa" as a suitable backdrop for derring-do. In Wells' *The Time Machine*, however, the setting is its own justification. Encounter with the new is the meaning and focus of this tale. An author's taking the trouble to develop his gimmick does not guarantee that the literary results will be good, but it usually does ensure a more potent new reality for our delectation.

The other technique open to fantasy is the addition of a mythic dimension. This may introduce a divine or at least superior world, a demonic one, or even one that is superimposed upon our own, coextensive with it but invisible, as are some versions of Faerie. In any of these numinous worlds, beings with supernatural or superhuman powers penetrate the fabric of everyday existence. The hero achieves some of his status because he is able to deal with the numinous or demonic more effectively and familiarly than can lesser mortals. Achilles benefits from his divine connections when Athene keeps him from striking Agamemnon. Circe sardonically encourages the beast within man, and Odysseus seems more heroic for receiving the divine aid needed to arm himself against her enchantments. Saints and the Virgin protect those in medieval tales who have learned to invoke them properly. If we allow ourselves to enter this kind of augmented world, we are made uncomfortably aware of the thinness and insignificance of our own material reality. Mary Renault forces us to this awareness in *The King Must Die* and *The Bull from the Sea*, in which Theseus receives signs from Poseidon at key points in his life. He is free to refuse, and when he misuses this power, he loses it. When he cultivates the right receptiveness, however, he can open his consciousness and wait for conviction to seize him, and he develops his abilities to match the vein of wisdom he taps, whether you wish to call it a god or his inner self. Similarly, Odysseus is enviable for his relationship to Athene. Gawain is blessed in his devotion to Mary, whether in trifles like finding lodging or in a crisis like the third temptation.

Gawain also has to face mythic forces allied to the demonic: Morgan le Fay appears in fairly malevolent guise. Beowulf too occupies a world augmented by demonic beings. Whether these antagonists were considered real or allegorical by the original audience, they challenge the assertion of order made by the heroic hall of Hrothgar, and possibly the order of the audience's own mundane world as well.

These mythic figures, divine and demonic, are often a culturally shared fantasy: Grendel may not exist outside of *Beowulf*, but man-eating ogres are folktale commonplaces. When Mary Renault takes the Greek gods seriously, she is calling up powers we have heard about already: Poseidon,

Artemis, and Apollo all have characteristics and histories known to her audience. Such mythic additions to reality carry a resonance beyond that possible for mere fantasy creations. The more exposure we have to a fantasy tradition, the more easily it can work upon us. Those nontraditional fantasies which command some of the power of traditional myth usually imitate or echo known patterns: Tolkien's Gandalf owes much to Merlin. Márquez' miracles in *One Hundred Years of Solitude* – bodily assumption into heaven, flying carpet, prophetic knowledge of the future – have roots in Biblical myth, Eastern tales, and in vatic writings like Geoffrey of Monmouth's "Prophecies of Merlin", and Márquez' Melquíades also owes something to Merlin. Mythic worlds not rooted in known traditions have trouble communicating their reality to the reader. David Lindsay's *A Voyage to Arcturus* suffers some degree of audience rejection because its mythic components are too alien.

The *Odyssey* relies on a mythic layer which seems added to the mimetic. Athene is its prime representative. She emphasizes for us Homer's world view: the vertical set of values, especially to past and future, to father and son, to the gods and the dead. Yet Athene does very little in the plot that would not have happened in any case. She rouses a spark of rebellion in Telemachus, terrorizes the suitors, and gives Odysseus and Penelope beauty. One could call her the religious equivalent to a gimmick, were it not that her doing these things makes us focus on them, and approve them gravely as proper, desirable, and just.

A more involved mythic or metaphoric addition is found in Vonnegut's *Breakfast of Champions*. Vonnegut presents himself as a persona within the story, and travels to an Arts Festival in order to meet the characters he has created, including his oft-used science fiction writer, Kilgore Trout. Although Vonnegut approaches only Trout directly, all the characters in the Holiday Inn dining-room are walking and talking with their God. Trout, as Vonnegut admits, has many features of Vonnegut's own father, yet as creator, Vonnegut is a kind of father to Trout. Vonnegut mentions Maxwell Perkins' advice to Thomas Wolfe that a writer should have a good, solid theme like "a hero's search for a father". There are passing references to Trout's inadequacy as a father, and implied too, a sense of the inadequacies of the father-child relationships in Vonnegut's own life, and of those between humans and their heavenly father. All the characters are very weak in this realm of family alignment where Odysseus is strongest: the vertical relationships of the generations. In *Breakfast of Champions*, characters cling insecurely to their coevals because no sense of tradition helps them stand on their own. When Vonnegut gives Trout his freedom, all Trout can plead is "*Make me young, make me young, make me young!*" (p. 295). In Vonnegut's world, people cannot make the decision Odysseus made when refusing Calypso's offer. They cannot accept the human limitations of age and death. They have no mythic frame to give life and death meaning for them.[4]

When Vonnegut departs from a relatively mimetic narrative presentation, whether his own stream of consciousness or his Arts Festival material, he adds this pseudomythic or metaphoric dimension involving the creator and his creations. Mythically, the creator is analogous to God, and his relationship to his world is a comment on God's to us. If interpreted metaphorically, the author is analogous to the imagination, the creative, law-inventing force of life. Coover, Barth, and Borges all use such mythic/metaphoric additions in their search for meaning, Coover with his Uncle Sam in *The Public Burning*, Barth with himself and various deities in "Bellerophoniad", and Borges with the creator of the dream-son in "The Circular Ruins".

The mimetic techniques for augmenting reality can be mixed with fantastic. Brunner's *Stand on Zanzibar* combines social cross section with an imaginary future world. Gardner's *Grendel* combines the fantasy of a monster and the reintroduction of repressed materials. Grendel sees and comments on the brutal side of life that is left out of the heroic presentation of the world in *Beowulf*. *Grendel* augments our *Beowulf*-conditioned expectations by extending reality to include material not considered decorous in presentation of the heroic:

> The enemies' horses would thunder up into the clearing, leaping the pig-fences, sending the cows and pigs away mooing and squealing, and the two bands of men would charge. Twenty feet apart they would slide to a stop and stand screaming at each other with raised swords. The leaders on both sides held their javelins high in both hands and shook them, howling their lungs out. Terrible threats, from the few words I could catch. Things about their fathers and their fathers' fathers, things about justice and honor and lawful revenge – their throats swollen, their eyes rolling like a newborn colt's, sweat running down their shoulders. Then they would fight. Spears flying, swords whonking, arrows raining from the windows and doors of the meadhall and the edge of the woods. Horses reared and fell over screaming, ravens flew, crazy as bats in a fire, men staggered, gesturing wildly, making speeches, dying or sometimes pretending to be dying, sneaking off. Sometimes the attackers would be driven back, sometimes they'd win and burn the meadhall down, sometimes they'd capture the king of the meadhall and make his people give weapons and gold rings and cows.[5]

I have called *Grendel* additive because someone familiar with *Beowulf* is struck most by this anti-heroic criticism and finds it a shocking but useful addition to the heroic interpretation of facts long accepted as near-ideal by romantic critics. Gardner reminds us of what the "Christian" critics have insisted upon: that the so-called heroic life is nasty, brutish, and short. He supplies something which we know must logically have been there all the time, but has been ignored as contrary to heroic decorum. Of course the book's appearing in 1971 during the Vietnam war has a good deal to do with this desire to debunk the heroism of war.

We welcome almost any enrichment of our sense of reality. Nonetheless, it seems odd that fantasy should be seen as a valid or useful enrichment. What does the gimmick do, or the metaphor, that is worth having? How is the avowedly non-real useful in explaining the real?

Many fantastic additions really belong to escape literature. They contribute nothing to our greater understanding of reality. Interstellar travel simply takes one to new scenes. But a gimmick which could be rationalized can nonetheless have some literary usefulness. Vonnegut's ice-nine in *Cat's Cradle*, for example, refers at least in part to the atomic bomb. The narrator of the story was writing a book about the day the bomb fell on Hiroshima, which he planned to call *The Day the World Ended*. One of the "fathers" of the bomb is the creator of ice-nine. As the story works out, ice-nine does destroy the world and the narrator is writing the account of how it happened. Vonnegut could have written a book with a similar warning, using the bomb itself, but bombs operate on national and international levels, and his concern is with the motives of individuals. Humans are infinitely stupid, clumsy, greedy for happiness, lonely, and selfish. What operates on the individual level guides the national, but we see and respond more directly to a demonstration of the importance of the individual's weaknesses. Ice-nine can be carried around in a thermos by anyone who owns a sliver. A bomb would not be so casually available, nor would people operating on a personal level be able to bring about global nuclear holocaust easily, though that scenario has been shown in Kubrick's film, *Dr Strangelove*. Ice-nine is easily manipulated by an everyman. In his presentation of what he feels to be the significant level of reality, Vonnegut emphasizes the personal. Fantasy lets him focus on his preferred subject in a fashion that a more mimetic treatment of a similar theme would not.

Gimmicks, myths, and metaphors are more important for what they contribute to the author's presentation of values than for their literal function in the story. A strictly mimetic piece is well adapted to the presentation of material values, or even humanitarian ones, but cannot readily get beyond these. Fantasy lets an author assert the importance of things which cannot be measured, seen, or numbered. Odysseus' affirmation of the human condition would be nothing more than whistling in the dark, or mindless repetition of a traditional piety, were he not being offered immortality by a goddess. To say that life as a poor peasant is better than lordship in Hades is meaningful only if spoken by someone who has tried the latter. From the shade of Achilles, the statement is spectacularly affecting. By bringing himself and Kilgore Trout together, Vonnegut makes implicit assertions about the powers of the imagination – its ability to create worlds and people in truly divine fashion. In a strictly mimetic work, someone would have had to talk about this subject. By meeting with Trout, Vonnegut can suggest this and much more that cannot be easily put in analytic terms – about seeking one's father or one's mother, about seeking the ever-absent God, and about human rebellion against the limitations imposed by mortality.

The creation of new worlds by subtraction and erasure

Subtraction, the exclusion of what the author deems inessential, is inherent in any artistic creation based on representation. Nonetheless, some subtractions are extreme enough to call attention to the differences between the reality which is being constructed and those we function by personally. The high mimesis of Greek tragedy is an example of slight subtraction. More extreme subtractions challenge our reality more sharply. Heroic literature, whether secular or hagiographic, offers many examples of such subtractive worlds. When the exclusions are not just the trivia of day-to-day experience but so radical as to call the meaning of the action into doubt, then one can speak of erasure. Erasure is the deliberate destruction of the logical connections we expect: cause and effect no longer function normally; motives disappear; actions seem random. Farce often relies on such erasure. Absurdist literature characteristically uses the technique. Subtraction and erasure also work in conjunction with fantasy additions. Some of Borges' stories combine extreme subtraction with a fantastic metaphor, a skewed image of human endeavor or life. Because subtractive techniques simplify reality so starkly, they naturally tend to crystallize out in an image, and thus are forcefully expressive of some new reality which challenges our own.

Heroic literature is the best known form of subtraction. The usual setting for a heroic tale and its related code of behavior have remained amazingly constant throughout the last two millenia, and they are subtractive. The principle behind the saying that no man is a hero to his valet (or his wife) expresses the need for this selectivity. We lose belief in the heroic if the hero is seen displaying daily habits, petty weaknesses, sillinesses, vanities, and moments of inferiority to those around him. We find it easier to credit heroes who are different from us than heroes who are just like us.

In *Beowulf*, we see the great hall adorned with woven hangings and filled with joyous and well-behaved celebrants. We would not thank the author for reminding us that there would have been fleas and flies, and dog droppings on the floor. Clothing and bodies would have stunk. Nor would we feel uplifted had the author reminded us that those who got drunk at the feast might not have made it outside to puke, and that drunken warriors were likely to be quarrelsome. The infinite dignity of Hrothgar's hall would have been marred by the sight of these fighters hurling bones at servitors. Beowulf's life is likewise presented very selectively, so much so that we do not even know if he was married. He fights three monsters, and interacts with half a dozen people. We never see him trying to crawl out of bed with a hangover. Life is refined to the heroic simplicities, those pertaining to a gold-adorned life of courage and to the dark patterns of dynastic treachery. Even the treacherous, though, are heroic, and villains in many northern tales die as valiantly as good men. Life consists of fights, gifts, feasts, behavior according to a clear code, and, if one is lucky, the chance to deliver a lengthy speech summing up one's life as one is dying.

In *The Song of Roland*, the same kinds of material are deemed trivial or indecorous, and are suppressed. Men are defined by their deeds against the infidel. In Roland's case, opposition is described in religious terms, but in both this epic and *Beowulf*, the heroes are allied with the powers of order and light against those of darkness. Marriage is almost as thoroughly excluded, and, in general, women are unimportant in secular heroic literature. The simplifications assert a male-oriented idealized reality, one the readers can strive to achieve not by eliminating trivia from their lives (impossible), but by recognizing its insignificance and ignoring the non-heroic details. Such a fictive world invites a narrowing and intensifying of consciousness, and promises a sense of meaningfulness to those who achieve the intensity of commitment. That promise is made by many religious works. Saints' lives urge commitment to a narrow set of rules and guarantee a sense of meaning to those who hold fast to their commitment. The aim may be to fight for Christ, give all one's goods to the poor, protect one's chastity, or avow one's faith, even unto death. If the heroism is secular, the invitation may be to proffer one's physical prowess to those in distress, or even just to fight for the sake of fame. The heroic world portrayed may be untroubled by doubts of its righteousness, or the author may show awareness of internal contradictions in the heroic code, as does the author of *Beowulf*. But in all these variations, the heroic world exists in opposition to the unsatisfactory, trivia-clogged lives we lead. It raises the problem of finding meaning, and offers a solution.

Erasure, destruction of normal order through removal of some element which gives logical coherence, produces a profound challenge to our sense of reality. The element giving connectedness may be emotions: Camus' *The Stranger* is a mimetic example of such erasure, where connections are missing in the narrator's mind. An author may erase motives or past experiences that would make sense of the present antagonisms: Pinter erases such material in his play *Old Times*. The whole of a past life may be erased, and all justification for a bizarre present lost, as in *Waiting for Godot*. Once we reach Beckett's degree of abstraction, interrelationships between people no longer make any sense. Neither do actions. One day a man and his slave bustle through, very much alive and kicking. The next, they are inexplicably blind and dumb respectively. We can force an allegorical interpretation: perhaps they are the capitalist exploiter and his underling, and on the second day, their physical state corresponds to their spiritual existence – but this is a feeble attempt to fill the gap caused by erasures, feeble because not verifiable. The element removed by erasure may be the logic of interaction that governs normal communicative dialogue: Ionesco throws all such basic logic out the window in *The Bald Prima Donna*; Claude Simon removes most such connective tissue in *The Flanders Road*.

Barthelme erases most of the usual linking elements in *Snow White*, and those remaining are mostly ironic. A gruesomely distorted version of the fairy tale mocks us with its insufficiencies as a giver of meaning. Snow White is waiting for her prince to come. She hangs her long black hair out the window (like Rapunzel), and finally realizes that life will not provide her with the proper happy ending. She has been living in group marriage with the seven "dwarves" (window washers and makers of Chinese baby food). The man she thought might be her longed-for prince turned out to be "pure frog", and he is poisoned before she can marry him anyway. We realize that she is crippled by a "failure of imagination", but find no satisfaction in the non-solution offered by the author. Our desire for the pieces to click together into the fairy-tale end is thus made to echo Snow White's own longing. When we acknowledge the impossibility of what she wants, we implicitly cede our own unreason in demanding such an order, in narrative or in our own lives.

Subtraction and erasure are available to mimetic fiction, although the more the author removes, the less realistic his story will appear. They can also be combined with fantasy additions. Thus intertwined, subtraction and fantasy together have produced some ensorcelling fictive worlds. Borges' "The Lottery in Babylon" and "The Library of Babel" illustrate the power of this mixture. In "The Lottery in Babylon", Borges starts by reducing life to a game of chance. A formal lottery is the basis for social class, profession, even for life and death. As the historical development of the lottery system is described, we realize that the all-powerful company, so silent in its functioning and so insignificant in daily life, becomes comparable to God. The multiplications of chance between stimulus and ultimate event lead us only to the world as we know it:

> Under the beneficent influence of the Company, our customs are saturated with chance. The buyer of a dozen amphoras of Damascene wine will not be surprised if one of them contains a talisman or a snake. The scribe who writes a contract almost never fails to introduce some erroneous information. I myself, in this hasty declaration, have falsified some splendor, some atrocity. Perhaps, also, some mysterious monotony. . . . No book is published without some discrepancy in each one of the copies. Scribes take a secret oath to omit, to interpolate, to change. The indirect lie is also cultivated.[6]

Borges starts by narrowing the world to a very limited image, that of the lottery, in order to describe human experience. Then, by a curious involution, he unfolds the intensely narrow world to show that all of human experience really is encompassed. All possible activities are governed by chance and hence are implicit in the lottery image. In its rigid, institutionalized form, this image seems extremely selective, but as all the stages of administering the chance decisions soften to indeterminable vagueness, the lottery process comes into focus as a much fuller world. In the hands of someone as inventive as Borges, subtractive methods clearly need not be simplistic.

The more acute the subtraction and erasure, the more inclined the reader is to see the world represented as an image with possible symbolic interpretations. We know that the image refers in some fashion back to the world we know, and it invites revaluation of reality. Although there is no necessity to add the fantastic, many authors feel its attractions. Erasure of such ordinary narrative features as logic and motive so lowers our assurance of what is real and what is fantasy that the distinction is almost meaningless; a strongly subtractive or erased world, by insisting strenuously on its truth, becomes fantastic. On us as readers, the effect of subtractive works is often very compelling. We do not feel that its commentary on our own world is as optional as the commentary from a purely additive fantasy. Subtraction overcomes our natural tendency to reject a comment based on fantastic material because fantasy may seem irrelevant to our reality. It succeeds because the reduced, skeletal worlds of such fiction are so effective in forming pictures in our minds. We are used to assimilating metaphors without insisting on their literal meaning. The images conjured up in such subtractive metaphors short-circuit rational objections based on words. They stir emotional response, and affect us more directly and personally than would a more explicit invitation for us to ask ourselves "what if?". "What if the world were seen as a library?" is soggy. Borges' assertion of the idea is luminous, and we derive emotional satisfaction from the image he conjures up. We enjoy savoring his depiction of reality because it simplifies the dizzy complexity we are used to dealing with. Simplification is emotionally gratifying. Putting a label on the inchoate and incoherent, pigeonholing something which has defied classification – these processes give us a sense of power and competence. A sharp, vivid image expressing an attitude toward experience that we have entertained gives us this sense of power. The attitude expressed may be one we only feel now and then. It may be very negative, even anguished. We can enjoy such expressive works, nonetheless, because we enjoy the sense of sophistication we feel when we can give a name to the unnameable.

Contrastive interpretations of reality

Additive and subtractive examples of expressive literature present single visions of reality for us to measure our own by. Contrastive literature forces us to try to make sense out of two clashing views of reality, as well as to contrast these with our own. Contrastive literature is in some ways a special form of subtractive: reality is greatly simplified, but it is pared down into two images instead of one. As a rule, these two poles are such that the reader feels some agreement with both. They must evoke approximately the same degree of response, usually on very different grounds. Another characteristic of this form is that one pole is often fantastic, and hence additive as well.

The aim of a contrastive work may be to invite us to affirm one of the views. *Something Wicked This Way Comes*, Bradbury's fantasy companion piece to *Dandelion Wine*, pits the pastoral world against a midnight world of an infernal carnival. The carnival traps souls by preying on human desires and fears, especially the fear of death. The carousel, when run backwards, can spin one's body back to youth. This is the attraction of the otherwise demonic party. The small town's library janitor, a fading little man who is perfectly open about his fear of death, is nonetheless able to make Odysseus' choice. He combats the infernal crew with laughter and wins. This crude description does no justice to the vivid portrayal of the two worlds that briefly coexist at each other's edge, the one of day, the other of night, one of plain folks, the other of carny freaks, one humdrum, the other exciting. The two boys being fought for by these good and bad forces echo the contrasts between the two worlds. One is blond, naturally good, a follower, and unwary when it comes to human evil. The other is dark, a leader, not bad but rather restless with unfulfilled longings, and unsurprised when evil appears. Both almost succumb. In this fantasy, the proper choice is never in doubt, but most of us can feel the temptation of the gifts offered by the carnival, even as we can feel the pull of the pastoral town. Indeed, the latter's purity is as unobtainable a gift as is rejuvenation. Laughter and love, the twin bulwarks against fear of death, have to be found within our own lives, but by naming these the weapons, Bradbury does make them detachable from the immediate pastoral context. The message is not affected by the pastoral setting nor by the fantastic aspect of the evil. No carousel can give youth, but that is immaterial. We can throw away our other pleasures in search of unrealizable desires. The criticism of our own ways of organizing reality and assigning meaning is valid even when one of the contrastive worlds is as fantastic as this piece of Halloween magic.

An ironic contrastive story that affirms both polar possibilities is Borges' "Pierre Menard, Author of the *Quixote*". Its two poles are Cervantes and Pierre Menard, a classic author and a modern. Borges' quixotic creation is a twentieth-century writer who comes to write *Don Quixote* word for word, as an expression of his own view of experience. He is not copying it; not pretending to be a seventeenth-century Spaniard. He writes as a modern man. What Cervantes could write as "mere rhetorical praise of history", when written in this century is bizarre. "History, the *mother* of truth: the idea is astounding. Menard, a contemporary of William James, does not define history as an inquiry into reality but as its origin. Historical truth, for him, is not what has happened; it is what we judge to have happened" (*Labyrinths*, p. 43). But Borges adds: "Cervantes' text and Menard's are verbally identical, but the second is almost infinitely richer. (More ambiguous, his detractors will say, but ambiguity is richness.)" (p. 42). The barrenness of twentieth-century experience, and the recycling of the old in desperate search for meaning, stand against the relatively settled world of Cervantes in open, if brief, contrastive opposition. We find engaging the labyrinthine complexities of Menard's ironic mind, and we recognize that Borges' mind is of necessity yet one step more complex for having invented Menard. Against the worried circlings and bewildering ingenuity of these twentieth-century figures, we see the comparatively assured Cervantes. He too felt that the literary forms were outworn, but he found a vital way of recycling them. He weathered a cultural failure of the imagination. The others are trying, perhaps not quite as successfully. We can look at the solution of Cervantes, compare it with Borges' own, and try to savor and judge the differences between them. Both attract us, the former for its vigorous irony at the expense of romance, the latter because its double ironies flatter our desire to feel sophisticated.

Contrastive literature can also encourage protest at both realities without suggesting a remedy. Such a work is Kafka's *Metamorphosis*. All the pent-up feelings of Gregor toward his society and family, of theirs toward him, and of ours toward what we sense of his tedious, sterile professional life are given an emotional correlative when he becomes a gigantic bug, a loathsome pest, unclean and disgusting. Opposing this concentrated image stand his family, depicted in pitiless detail. We cannot reject either, or side exclusively with either. We are both. Gregor is a victim, and we sympathize with his plight. We loathe his father's hectoring manner and insidious parasitism. We sympathize with Gregor's having to do uncongenial work to salvage the family after his father's failure. Once Gregor has become a bug, we feel for his terrors and deplore the torments, both physical and mental, which his family inflicts. We recognize his positive aspirations for his sister, even while noting their selfish, Freudian side. However, we also recognize the validity of his family's revulsion. Neither the primitive fear of the healthy toward the maimed nor the selfish concerns which detach the well members from the sufferer are admirable, but honest readers will admit their inclination toward these responses, and hence will empathize. As we struggle to find a balance between these polar interpretations of the situation, and the outlooks behind them – tarnished bourgeois complacence and bugdom – we reinterpret many of the characters' stances and find our understanding and loyalties shifting. We want to be able to pass judgment, to be able to state that the reality of the situation is thus-and-such. Kafka denies us this release. His ending is as twofold as all the rest: the family may be reborn into a hopeful new life and future, or the parents may be viewing their blossoming daughter as the means of securing a new breadwinner from whom they can suck sustenance as they did from Gregor. Yet throughout this exercise in frustration, we enjoy our fleeting feelings of agreement. The overall bleak portrayal of human nature works like a subtractive image. Insofar as we can agree, even temporarily, it is pleasant to call humanity vermin. One does not need all the evidence marshalled by Swift's King of Brobdingnag to reach that interpretation.

Another contrastive work embodying a lyric protest at both its inhering interpretations is Tom Stoppard's *Rosencrantz and Guildenstern are Dead*. Like "Pierre Menard, Author of the *Quixote*", this belongs to the special class of works which exist parasitically off prior artistic artifacts. The audience must know the original for the secondary piece to function properly. In *Rosencrantz and Guildenstern are Dead*, the absurd world of *Waiting for Godot* lies behind one of its interpretations of reality, for the main characters are close literary kin to Vladimir and Estragon. Also present, fighting to impose its system of order, is Shakespeare's *Hamlet*. As inhabitants of the twentieth century, we respond to the protagonists' lack of direction, their desire for guidance and roles. As students and viewers of *Hamlet*, we know the Elizabethan world picture, and we expect its values to dominate a play in which Hamlet appears and speaks none but the lines Shakespeare gave him.

Hamlet's world was an orderly universe. Values were fixed. Ideals were possible. Man could break the rules, but the rules existed. Hamlet is so exceedingly upset by his mother's behavior precisely because he had believed in the verities of marriage, love, kingship, and honor. Rosencrantz and Guildenstern do not start from Hamlet's firm base. They have no fixities. They recollect no past, they have no notion of what they are supposed to do. Their world is so erased that they are not sure which of them is which. Their only fixed point is the confused recollection of the messenger's summoning them at dawn. Whereas Hamlet's problems and failures produce tragedy, theirs result in failed romance. They want to be romance or fairy-tale heroes. They dimly recognize the message as their Call to Adventure. Guildenstern expects the conventional signposts that guide the hero of a fairy tale. He rejects the comedians for their vulgarity: "It could have been – it didn't have to be *obscene*. . . . It could have been – a bird out of season, dropping bright-feathered on my shoulder. . . . It could have been a tongueless dwarf standing by the road to point the way. . . . I was *prepared*."[7] Instead of finding their identity, proving themselves, winning their place in society – all of which they desperately want to do – they drift, looking for somebody to assign them their roles. They want logic, consistency, a pattern. Anything they attempt fails. Their probing Hamlet on his distemper is a disaster as a question-game, Hamlet beating them 27 to 3. When Rosencrantz and Guildenstern read the letter ordering Hamlet's death, they have a clear-cut chance to act. All they would have needed to do was raise their voices slightly and say "Look at this, Hamlet". That simplest of actions could have changed all their lives. The moment passes, however, and they rationalize their inaction. When they next read the letter and find their own names instead of Hamlet's, they ruefully find that they have at last acquired roles in which they are not expected to make any further decisions. Others will act for and upon them. They accept these roles and go to their death. The tension between the

Elizabethan and the modern world is especially acute because it is enshrined in the language. The short, colloquial bursts in a modern vein clash with all the portions taken verbatim from *Hamlet*. Neither their absurdist view nor Hamlet's traditional Christian universe comes off looking like an especially attractive interpretation of reality.

Besides encouraging affirmation of one interpretation, or the search for a new one, or rejection of both, contrastive literature can encourage reconciliation of the two polar views. Nowhere have I seen a more felicitous example of this form of contrastive literature than Calvino's *Cosmicomics* and *T Zero*. They are as radically divided in their centers of attention as *Metamorphosis*, but to very different ends. One reality is the phenomenal world of scientific theory and fact, especially physics and biology. The other is the human perspective, represented by the eternal narrator, Qwfwq. Calvino reintroduces us to the material universe, its unspeakable immensity in space and time, its imperviousness to our small beings. And beside this universe are ranged Qwfwq's family and acquaintances, each embodying particularly trivial human concerns, loves and longings, hopes and fears, failures to communicate, differences of taste. How humanity can interact with a non-divine universe and with the scientific outlook is the great question of our time, and Calvino poses it through his contrasts. How does the puny and imperfect human con-sciousness keep from being overwhelmed by its own insignificance? Calvino sets the problem out over and over in different forms, and manages to suggest the solution in the very process of battering these two realities against each other.

In "The Distance of the Moon", for instance, we are first struck by the tangle of petty human emotions. Qwfwq suffers a hopeless adolescent passion for Mrs Vhd Vhd, and she an unrequited longing for Qwfwq's deaf cousin, while Captain Vhd Vhd suppresses smouldering resentment and sensual desires of his own. These longings keep the main characters occupied with tiffs and schemes, and keep them from being overcome by the cataclysmic events taking place in the universe. Their very humanity can be a bulwark against too much awareness of the infinite.

The deaf cousin represents another way of interacting with the universe. His love is given to one part of the phenomenal world, namely the moon, and he is supremely successful at finding the moon-milk they all seek. Literally, he milks the moon of its secrets. His response to the lunar landscape is at once sportive and sensual. To others, his actions appear random, but his success in gathering the moon's riches confirms his possession of some sort of logic or higher apprehension. When the moon withdraws from earth, he accepts the change. His love is for the moon as it is, not clouded by selfish considerations. His virtuosity has no purpose, just simple fascination.

Out of this fantasy concerning the moon's separation from earth,

Calvino depicts three solutions to the contrast between man and the phenomenal cosmos. The first is immersion in the network of human attractions and repulsions. These relations delightfully echo the playful actions based on the attractions and repulsions of gravity between earth and her satellite. Gravity and love are both forms of "attraction". These forces make the world go round, and keep men from coming unstuck, physically and emotionally. For those whose longings are not satisfied by mere human intrigue, there is the course of mythologizing and of poetry. Qwfwq, as narrator, becomes poet-priest of the moon and its new myth, for Mrs Vhd Vhd stays on the moon, and for him therefore the moon becomes the ever-unattainable feminine. She "makes the Moon the Moon and, whenever she is full, sets the dogs to howling all night long, and me with them".[8] The third response to the universe is scientific: the cousin's sportive and inquisitive love suggests scientific quest.

"All at One Point" allows, for one brief moment, an apotheosis of the human perspective over the material. All the trivialities of man as social animal are present: racial and class snobbery, prejudice toward immigrants and clichés about lazy cleaning women, the gossip about who is sleeping with whom. All the rivalries of a small, crowded tenement are aired as Qwfwq describes the moment when the universe was contracted to a single point prior to the Big Bang. All the presences jostle and rub one another in predictable ways. Most of the inhabitants feel no great love for any of the rest, but all agree that Mrs $Ph(i)Nk_o$ is something special. Her frustrated desire to nurture her admirers with fresh-made noodles causes her to exclaim "Oh, if I only had some room, how I'd like to make some noodles for you boys!" These words bring about the Big Bang, and room is created. As this takes place, Qwfwq recounts, she is

> dissolved into I don't know what kind of energy-light-heat, she, Mrs. $Ph(i)Nk_o$, she who in the midst of our closed, petty world had been capable of a generous impulse, "Boys, the noodles I would make for you!" a true outburst of general love, initiating at the same moment the concept of space and, properly speaking, space itself, and time, and universal gravitation, and the gravitating universe, making possible billions and billions of suns, and of planets and fields of wheat, and Mrs. $Ph(i)Nk_os$, scattered through the continents of the planets, kneading with floury, oil-shiny, generous arms, and she lost at that very moment, and we, mourning her loss. (p. 47)

Hers, the motherly, is the love that moves the sun and all the stars, and brings them into being.

Calvino does something unique in these stories. He starts with the scientific world, and never allows us to lose sight of it. This phenomenal reality which we often view as lifeless, he shapes into a world vibrantly and staggeringly alive. The dry facts are reglorified. New wonder is found in their purely factual dimension. In a complex process, Calvino at once revivifies the material and teaches us to cherish the purely human as well.

As the human jostles the factual, the two fuse. The universe adds meaning to itself because we are here to enjoy its patterns. And, incidentally, by pitting the human against the material world as he does, Calvino creates at one level a new mythology, a human interpretation of the universe that is positive. Calvino gives us a mythic universe that does not deny science, but accepts and glories in scientific reality – an astonishing accomplishment.

As I suggested earlier, expressive literature, with its new vision of reality, lies between escape to illusion and revisionary didacticism in its effects. On the one hand, it does not explicitly urge us to change our ways or follow a specific course of action. We can agree temporarily with an interpretation of reality yet not be committed to making it our religion. One need have felt only occasionally that man is the victim of cosmic joking to respond to Beckett's or Stoppard's picture of human existence. On the other hand, the form does invite thought in a way that escapist sensation does not. It does make us revalue the assumptions which permit us to turn the facts around us into workaday reality, and this it does by presenting a new vision of reality for our delectation.

Delectation may seem an odd word. Many such visions of reality are anguished. Yet there are pleasures to be derived from many kinds of emotional responses. Vonnegut's interpretation of human nature is bleak, and we are condemned along with the rest of mankind in his history of human stupidity. Nonetheless, those who enjoy his books like the feelings induced by joining him in his low-keyed indignation. By adopting his stance, we can congratulate ourselves on our moral superiority and perspicacious consciences. Because we pity the people he pities, we feel superior. Beckett and Borges do not make it as easy for us to console ourselves, but they still provide us with the satisfaction of applying a vivid image as label to inchoate experience. As it snaps into place, we enjoy a sense of power and release. Literature with a traditional mythology holds out promise (if one is a believer) or a pleasant chance to experience life "as if", and try out the answers such a mythology offers. The heroic life tantalizes one with its shining simplicities and promise of intense commitment. Contrastive literature offers us two interpretations, but this by no means precludes its giving us an image for reality: Calvino's two poles are reconciled into one image; Kafka's are both so negative as to form a single indictment; Bradbury's finally resolve into only one tenable stance. Whatever the nature of the contrast between the visions these offer and our own, our feelings almost always have a pleasurable element because the reality is new and different. The everyday is so dull, if only because our consciousness screens out so many of the stimuli present. Literature which calls attention to the nature of its own reality helps free us from our automatic filtering and makes us freshly aware of our vision of reality.

Many of these expressive pieces work their spell through the power of an image or set of images: a man turned into a bug; two tramps in a roadside ditch; the universe as library or lottery; life as opposition between the circle of light in the hall and the outer darkness inhabited by man-eating monsters. If our emotions can be spoken of as uncommitted, suspended as if in a supersaturated chemical solution, such an image acts like a seed crystal. It attracts the emotions and gives them a form to attach themselves to. Their crystallizing out of suspension produces a sudden gust of agreement. This process works so efficiently because it relies on pictures. They enter our consciousness not as verbal argument to be accepted or rejected on logical grounds, but as a vision. Our defenses, especially of rational matters, are so often verbal that the non-verbal attack can breach them with relative ease. And such images, as often as not, are fantastic. They are so effective because new, because we have not seen them before and have not developed the automatic processing that would screen and classify them, making them dull again.

5

Literature of revision: programs for improving reality

In chapter four, I analyzed expressive literature in terms of technique, partly so that I could refer to additive and subtractive elements in subsequent discussions, but also because the literature of vision did not seem to have significant natural subdivisions to build from. Now that the techniques are familiar, nothing is gained by organizing a new group of works around them, so chapter five will use different analytic divisions, namely focus on man or on the universe. These two concerns do inherently divide didactic literature, so this is a logical choice. For these reasons, chapters four and five are dissimilarly organized, even though their subject matters are contiguous on the spectrum of responses to reality, and are indeed so similar that only the presence of a program of action sets apart literature of revision from the expressive works discussed as literature of vision.

One need not agree wholeheartedly with the outlook in a work of expressive literature in order to enjoy it. Partial agreement or temporary consideration of its views will make its pleasures accessible. Its very novelty and strangeness can be enjoyable. Didactic literature, however, is not so accommodating. If you accept its premises, you are given comfort, assurance, and guidance. If you do not accept the premises, you may just want to put the book down, and only very imaginative writing will carry you along. Didactic authors start by assuming that they know the Truth, or that they know what is good for the reader. Today we are reluctant to accept such authority.

Didactic literature concerns itself with two subjects: the nature of man and the nature of the universe. More specifically, didactic literature focuses on man and the morality of everyday life and lays down rules of proper conduct. Such rules may be presented in many forms: messianic romances, utopias, dystopias, satires and exposés, and works concerned with determining the essence of human nature. Or didactic literature may take the form of sacred and mythic narrative about creation, apocalypse, the cosmos, and man's place in that cosmos. The close relationship between the moral and the cosmological for religious writers can be seen in the work of fantasists like C.S. Lewis and David Lindsay. They wish to see personal morality revised in order to bring it into accord with their visions of cosmic truth.

Because didactic literature works with assertions and absolutes, it gives us what purports to be a sufficient system for classifying experience. We are given the grounds for saying that one action is good while another is bad – or effective and ineffective, or proper and improper. One can assimilate an experience readily if one can classify it and relate it to other experiences. A didactic system gives us that framework, and with it, prescriptions for our own responses and actions. This guidance helps lessen the indigestibility of chaotic experience. That a correct response exists is assumed by didactic literature, so much so that most such literature demands full affirmation of its vision of reality and by implication asks for revisions in the reader's life. Expressive literature encourages us to think as well as feel, whereas didactic literature, although it may present logical arguments, often aims to annihilate critical thought.

Fantasy is useful to many forms of didactic literature, for it can hold our attention and interest even when we disagree with the author's premises. One need not accept C.S. Lewis' Christianity to read *Perelandra* with enjoyment, thanks to his lush invention. Moreover, in cosmological didacticism, the fantasy *is* the message, for we have no verifiable knowledge of the ultimate source or beginning of the universe, and obviously can have no knowledge of its end. Nor is there any generally accepted theory about a creator, and very little agreement on some of the alternative scientific hypotheses either. Although cosmological didacticism is a natural place for fantasy, we find fantasy surprisingly common in moral didacticism as well. Social criticism does not logically need it: if readers believe the crimes being described are likely to affect them personally, they will pay attention without the inducement of fantasy. Upton Sinclair achieves this rapport with *The Jungle*. Some literary sermons would lose much of their point if they introduced the unreal. Almost all other forms of didacticism, however, draw on fantasy, whether to exalt humans or disparage them. The departures from reality may be emotional enticements, or images for bypassing verbal defenses. Given the premises from which didactic authors work, however, fantasy is important because the vision of reality is almost necessarily idealized or demonic. To put across the intensity and significance of either, the author departs from the dullness of the everyday, and that can be done most economically with fantasy.

Moral didacticism

When focusing on human behavior, didactic literature takes many forms. The broadest categories are the works which exalt human beings for our edification, those which disparage man and teach by negative example, and those which attempt to analyze him without bias. This last group is small, and shades off into non-literary forms like psychoanalytic description. What makes good didactic literature so difficult to produce is the problem of persuasion. Readers are rarely as dogmatic about moral behavior as they are about their concept of cosmic structure: an agnostic scientist will resent a religious explanation of the universe more fiercely than a religious code of conduct; the former contradicts what he considers fact, whereas the latter merely challenges social convention. Problems of behavior obviously could be discussed in strictly mimetic settings, and, given the immediacy of practical application, one might expect realism to be the most logical weapon for the author to use. In fact, fantasy is quite common, chiefly because of the problem of persuasion. A book's audience is voluntary. The reader's freedom to lay the book down after a few pages probably has more effect on didactic literature than on any other, for didactic literature, especially moral didacticism, aims to attack the audience. The need to keep people reading fosters fantasy.

One can teach by positive example or by negative. Both have drawbacks. Negative exemplars may be too unattractive to win our concern or too attractive to draw our censure. Positive examples may seem so virtuous that we feel indifferent, cowed, or resentful, rather than inspired. What an audience will accept and will identify with is bound to change with other cultural shifts. The anti-hero we accept today would have met with disgust and a total lack of understanding not long ago. Many ways of handling these problems of persuasion have evolved, and I can only mention a selection in the rest of this chapter.

There are three common types of positive didacticism: stories which center on a hero; stories which use a superhuman saint or messiah; and stories which present an ideal society. Many hero-centered tales are not didactic – tales of success-and-conquest often teach us nothing at all – but a hero can be created who sets us an example, whose overall conduct we are supposed to admire and imitate within our own context. Christian in *The Pilgrim's Progress*, Parzival, or the priest in Bernanos' *Diary of a Country Priest* are such protagonists. Saints are common, messiahs less so because they are in some sense divine and thus harder to sell to a secular audience. We do not aspire to be divine, but we can learn from messiahs and perhaps imitate their non-divine followers. Nevil Shute's *Round the Bend*, Heinlein's *Stranger in a Strange Land*, Lawrence's *The Man who Died* all present messiahs. Utopias offer us not just rules for personal conduct but a blueprint for improving society in general.

Exemplary heroes can teach us by preaching: in *Man and Superman*,

John Tanner broadcasts his principles in his own person, but also as Don Juan in the "Don Juan in Hell" interlude, and in "The Revolutionist's Handbook" appended to the play. Or the hero can teach by doing and suffering. If he does not suffer, we are apt to think him too far above us for us to feel we could imitate his actions. Parzival conspicuously fails when it comes to asking the right questions at the crucial time, and he fails to treat his mother correctly, so he suffers the consequences. Christian makes error after error in his struggle to attain salvation. An imitation of Christ might be beyond the audience, but imitating a stumbler like Christian shows us how to be a Christian hero. Bernanos' priest endures poverty, the indifference and hostility of his parishioners, and even their attempts to disgrace him. The deeper the humiliation and frustration, the more like an ordinary mortal such a hero seems, and the more able to demonstrate that even we can follow him up the narrow path. The priest affirmed his religious belief throughout his lonely and unpleasant period of service as an act of faith. Nothing reinforced him or helped him. Even God seemed silent, and fellow priests were able to contribute little to help him. On his deathbed, however, he was rewarded with a vision of grace. If we are to reach his reward, we must commit ourselves without any more positive reassurance than he received. He suffered. So can we, and we are meant to recognize this shared characteristic as our only assurance.

Messianic figures are rare, since they must bring new interpretations of the cosmos, assign new meanings to life, and find new ways of coping with death. Some authors interested in the messianic phenomenon have created messiah figures without creating didactic literature: Herbert's *Dune* tetralogy, Gore Vidal's *Messiah*, Barth's *Giles Goat-Boy* all give us too little doctrine for these figures to offer us a new way of life, so they are best seen as escapist or expressive. Heinlein's *Stranger in a Strange Land*, despite the thinness of the ideas and the dishonesty of giving all true believers telekinetic powers, does offer enough of a program for new life that cults and rites sprang up in the wake of that book. D.H. Lawrence's retreaded Christ in *The Man who Died* is a messiah with a strong implicit message. He did not die on the cross, but revives in the tomb, escapes, and, while recuperating, commits himself to a totally different way of life, one whose sacred, meaningful act is sexual coupling. Another true messianic figure, one less dogged by incongruity than Lawrence's, is Nevil Shute's Connie Shaklin in *Round the Bend*. His message is openly preached and aimed at a technological society, his own and that of the readers. What he taught to his fellow workmen was how to be an airplane mechanic and how to bring God – whatever god or gods one believed in – into one's every professional action. The narrator is an ordinary, nonmystic, British aviator trying to run a freight airline in the Persian Gulf. His reluctant and incomplete capitulation to the notion that Connie might be more than man proves to be Shute's tool for bringing us to the same affirmation. Shaklin's teachings are eminently practical. In brief, he teaches us to free our minds from petty concerns and open them to an absolute. After tightening every nut and soldering every connection, he asks whether he has done the job to the best of his ability and waits for the inner answer. His followers are good workmen, responsible, well integrated into their societies, and well balanced spiritually. We can apply his principles if we feel drawn to do so.

Utopias preach at us from many directions. We see people who exemplify the virtues of the system. We see children being educated to fit and fulfill the ideals of the society. We usually follow the adventures of an outsider, surrogate for ourselves, who ultimately wishes to convert to this new way of life. Reason and conditioning are key themes in utopian fiction. Plato, Huxley (in *Island*), and Bellamy (in *Looking Backward*) stress training; Skinner (*Walden Two*), Callenbach (*Ecotopia*), More, and Morris (*News from Nowhere*) stress man's natural capacity to adapt and see reason.

The preachiness and the static plot structure of utopias are flaws well enough known to need no further description. Anyone who has read a typical utopia will recognize these characteristics at once. Ursula Le Guin's *The Dispossessed* is an intriguing attempt to get around the problems. She changes the ground rules, and by doing so makes character development and plot possible. Her utopia is a small anarchy situated on Annares, the moon of a much larger planet, Urras. All work and co-operation on Annares are voluntary, but social consciences are highly developed and children are conditioned to do their part in this sharing mode of life. Unlike many utopias, however, this one is spartan. Standards of living are adequate, but any kind of excess is treated as exceedingly bad taste or is impossible. So long as crops and weather are good, the community can survive, and its members enjoy a materially minimal but a spiritually rich life.

Another departure from the stereotype is the degree of perfection attributed to the society. Le Guin does not make all humans sweetly reasonable or helpful. The hero, Shevek, is shown in a childhood scene being humiliated by a stupid and unpleasant teacher, for instance, and his adult life is complicated by the nastiness of a jealous senior colleague. Nonetheless, we sense that he is receiving a well-rounded education, one that makes him competent not just in crafts and practical work, but in theoretical physics too.

When a four-year drought causes widespread famine on Annares, the flexibility of the society's voluntary co-operation hardens into a demanding system, a denial of individual needs, and a requirement of service. Ultimately, Shevek's goal will be to try to save his society by shaking it up, reintroducing the anarchy of ongoing revolution. Le Guin makes no promises that he will succeed. Indeed, martyrdom and helplessness look possible, for the society has shifted far enough from its original freedom that perhaps only violence great enough to destroy the society could budge it. Nonetheless, Shevek has made it clear for us that the society is very much worth trying to save. It appears to be as close to equitable as any human society could be, granting the imperfections of human nature.

The third alteration in the utopian formula is the plot movement. Shevek is an insider in his own society, but he goes to Urras, the mother planet, and plays the outsider there. Urras is recognizably our own earth in the sense that it has thinly disguised equivalents to the USA, the USSR, the UN, and other such institutions. Its natural resources and landscapes seem incredibly beautiful to one from the parched moon, even as its cultures seem vulgar, its wastefulness repulsive, and its exploitation and repression frightening when seen through the eyes of the outsider rather than through our own dirty windows of acceptance and indifference. To keep Urras from usurping the center of our attention, Le Guin interweaves episodes of Shevek's early life (from childhood to departure for Urras) with his Urrasti experiences, letting the two counterpoint each other, and letting us understand the depth of the contrast between the two cultures. The camaraderie of Annares looks attractive compared to the paranoia, conspiracies, and riots of Urras, but the hardships of Annares are not slighted, nor are its hardening political arteries ignored.

The amount of preaching didactic authors can indulge in without losing their audience varies with the subject, the engaging power of the fantasy, and the standards of the readers. In the latter part of the twentieth century, resistance to overt didacticism is so fierce that one persuades students to read utopian fiction only with difficulty. *The Dispossessed*, Huxley's *Island*, Skinner's *Walden Two*, and Callenbach's *Ecotopia* are by their nature so dependent on description and on explicit comparisons that preachiness is unavoidable. Authors who try to engage with ideas directly suffer for this commitment. Mann's *Magic Mountain* is more talked of than read. If some former ages have been unduly harsh in rejecting entertainment, we have gone to the other extreme in demanding entertainment almost exclusively. Hence, most modern authors wishing to communicate explicit ideas are driven to make their didacticism palatable with fantasy. The technique has proved itself over the centuries. Saints' lives feature miracles; moral allegory gives wide scope to fantasy; *Parzival* uses the mystery of the Fisher-King; satire relies on the fantasy of caricature; *Man and Superman* makes its major points directly in the fantastic "Don Juan in Hell" interlude. Preachy that little act is, but the play is often done, and "Don Juan in Hell" is even performed separately. The Devil, Don Juan, Doña Ana, and the Statue are too intriguing for us to resent the talk as much as we would had it come from Mendoza, John Tanner, Ann Whitfield, and Ramsden Roebuck. Likewise, *Doctor Faustus* succeeds where *Magic Mountain* does not. It captures the imagination. The ideas are not hidden, but they become far more assimilable in the intriguing context of a pact with the devil.

Didactic authors who work with negative examples are better off in some respects than those with saintly heroes. Most readers listen with more amusement and interest to a Juvenalian satire than to an encomium or panegyric. Moreover, insofar as the proscribed actions represent deeds we feel some repressed longing to commit, they have a covert attractiveness. The attraction of evil is a weakness of the form. The sadistic sexual fantasies embedded in many tales of female martyrs undercut the spiritual elevation of the material. Villain-heroes like Faust and Don Juan are too attractive in some renditions for us to learn virtue from watching them being punished by divine justice. The sins of overreaching and sexual adventure are not calculated to disgust a modern outlook and even at earlier periods they enjoyed some glamor. The salvation of Faust by Goethe and the glorification of Don Juan by Heinlein in *Time Enough for Love* actually present these figures as heroes. A truly villainous character will not arouse such admiration, but very few stories focus exclusively on a villain. Usually some representative of good, a conventional hero, will serve as foil to the villain and hence acts as a positive example. There are few purely negative equivalents to the positive didactic use of a hero.

Other forms of negative didacticism are less open to audience misprision. We know where we stand with excoriations, dystopias, and other disparaging visions of man within society. Excoriations are a broad group ranging from the ranting and railing of the prophetic books in the Bible through outraged exposés of social wrongs like Sinclair's *The Jungle* and Steinbeck's *The Grapes of Wrath* on to social satire and black humor of the sort seen in *Slaughter-House Five*. Such satiric works frequently haunt the borderlands between expressive and didactic literature. In some instances, identifying a narrative as one or the other will come down to whether the reader is willing to consider a single idea enough of a program for action to qualify the work as didactic or not. However, putting works in convenient pigeonholes is not the point of reading, and the presence of borderline cases need not invalidate the basic classifications as long as we recognize that those represent tendencies toward opposite ends of a continuum, not absolute distinctions.

Many excoriations are mimetic. *The Jungle* is a good example. Sinclair can hold his audience so easily because he is lambasting not its members, but a third party – the slaughterhouses and packing firms. Moreover, he entrances readers with the revelations of their own victimization.

> There was never the least attention paid to what was cut up for sausage; there would come all the way back from Europe old sausage that had been rejected, and that was moldy and white – it would be dosed with borax and glycerine, and dumped into the hoppers, and made over again for home consumption. There would be meat that had tumbled out on the floor, in the dirt and sawdust, where the workers had tramped and spit uncounted billions of consumption germs. There would be meat stored in great piles in rooms; and the water from

leaky roofs would drip over it, and thousands of rats would race about on it. It
was too dark in these storage places to see well, but a man could run his hand
over these piles of meat and sweep off handfuls of the dried dung of rats. These
rats were nuisances, and the packers would put poisoned bread out for them,
they would die, and then rats, bread, and meat would go into the hoppers
together.[1]

This is pure hell-fire preaching, but we do not lightly put the book down.
These sausages were regular breakfast fare for the original readers. Even
now, when conditions are presumably better, self-interest keeps alive a
sickened fascination. Sinclair's concern, actually, is not so much our
breakfasts as the plight of the workers in such plants. Their misery is
documented in pitiless detail. After he has harrowed our feelings, both for
the workers and for ourselves, he introduces his solution – socialist
organization of labor. This gives our feelings an outlet, a channel to run
through once they have become so powerful that they seem ready to burst
the dam. Our relief is immense. Didactically, the book is very cleverly
conceived to play on audience emotions and produce affirmation of the
socialist program.

Excoriations of society that attack the reader rather than a third party are
more difficult technically. *The Grapes of Wrath* and Wright's *Native Son*
attack middle-class white America for economic and racial injustice. *Native
Son* is on the borderline of expressive literature: the message is that we
mistreat people on the basis of skin color. Wright offers no clearer program
for our reform than the obvious "Thou shalt not", but the corollaries to
that prohibition are so straightforward that I would tentatively call this
didactic. Other readers might demur. *The Grapes of Wrath* does offer a
sample program: at one brief point in their weary odyssey, the Joads stay
at a government-established camping ground. Its running water and flush
toilets, not necessities but glorious luxuries, suggest how little it takes to
give people great pleasure and pride in their camp. More important is the
humanity shown toward newcomers. They get a bit of credit at the store,
and their neighbors help them get settled. The community makes decisions
together and polices itself. Everyone shows pride and a sense of
responsibility, growing out of having decent living quarters, decent
treatment, and a chance to work. When intolerable labor conditions
deprive the Joads of these basics, violence seems only reasonable.
Steinbeck leaves us with an eerie minatory image: the stillborn blue baby
put in a crate and floated off on the floodwater, demonic parody of the
child in the rudderless boat – Moses, Perseus, St Gregory – who would
have grown up to be the savior of his people. Middle-class readers, smug
in their jobs, homes, and self-righteous snobbery, are Steinbeck's target,
but also his audience. Engaging their sympathies takes skill.

Steinbeck, Wright, and others who have cried out at social injustice
necessarily assume an audience willing to receive their message, one

willing to take on a burden of guilt, for little softens their accusations. Realism in excoriation demands complicity from the audience, or at least acquiescence. Satire lets an author reach a broader audience, for it makes good the deficiencies of realism with humor, exaggeration, and fantasy. An audience not willing to be lambasted in a realistic vein may enjoy the humor of satire.

> One recognizes true satire by this quality of 'abstraction'; wit and other technical devices . . . are the means by which the painful issues of real life are transmuted. But even more important is the element of fantasy which seems to be present in all true satire. The satirist does not paint an objective picture of the evils he describes, since pure realism would be too oppressive. Instead he usually offers us a travesty of the situation, which at once directs our attention to actuality and permits an escape from it.[2]

As inducements to continue reading, humor offers the pleasures of feeling superior and clever. Exaggeration, a form of fantasy, lets us comfort ourselves by arguing that the description *is* exaggerated, and more explicit fantasy intrigues us with the hunt for meaning, since most satiric fantasy is loosely allegorical. But satire as didactic literature encounters problems. If mild, it shades into comedy and has little if any effect on the audience's foibles. If serious, it may alienate its audience and may, in its wrath, fail to provide a clear plan for future improvement. Coover's *The Public Burning* is so total a condemnation of America that his wit and humor, his wildly funny fantasy featuring Uncle Sam, and even his curiously attractive and appalling portrait of Nixon have trouble holding the audience. Tertullian and Juvenal ran into the same problems. Both, for instance, rail against society women, and one deduces that if women want to improve, they must stop commiting the sins they are accused of. But this negative list is a poor plan for improvement. Coover's telling Americans that they have been wicked and stupid, blindly greedy for mythic reassurance of meaning, does not give them much help toward improving. William Burroughs' "Ah Pook is Here" tells us a lot about our lust for control, but not how to curb it. Satire spouts forth out of the author's boundless conviction of his own righteousness, and it certainly tries to wring affirmation from its audience, but in respect of reform, many satires are better treated as expressive literature than didactic. Their vision is too negative to lead easily to revision.

Dystopias labor under this same problem, one endemic to negative teaching, but their format allows them many chances to hint at positive patterns of reform. Like utopias, they must introduce us to a total society, and hence many indulge in a fair amount of description or preaching. Because the main character longs to change the system, his thoughts give us some positive standards. Although dystopias can grow out of any evil – pollution and overpopulation, for instance, provide the basis for Brunner's *The Sheep Look Up* and *Stand on Zanzibar* respectively – many grow out of the related problems of life, liberty, and the pursuit of happiness. Orwell's *1984*, Zamiatin's *We*, Huxley's *Brave New World*, Levin's *This Perfect Day*, and Vonnegut's *Player Piano* are all dystopias, and all seek solutions to the problems of teaching us something positive through a negative example.

All these dystopias struggle with a paradox: individuality is messy, inefficient, harmful to others, and often just as harmful and distressing to its possessor. Freedom is necessary for individuality. Making man into a happy machine, however, robs life of its sense of meaning. Freedom blights happiness for many people, but ensured happiness for the greatest number can only be achieved by abolishing freedom. These authors differ in the degree of happiness they see their societies as encouraging, but all postulate an advanced state of technology, and rub our noses in the fact that technological invention diminishes man's necessary functions, and thus force us to look closely at the meaning we wish to claim for human life.

Perhaps because the basic didactic stances are simple and similar, the plot patterns work with very similar units. D503 of *We*, a mathematician and engineer, is acutely aware of the square root of minus one, the irrational, which cannot be made to fit with ordinary reason, engineering, or his mechanical society. Smith of *1984*, an official rewriter of history, also hits on mathematics to symbolize the basic clash: "if you can allow $2+2$ to equal 4, all else, all other freedoms, are possible". Both start diaries, and these help bring unconscious, repressed discontents to the conscious level. Bernard Marx in *Brave New World* is alienated by his physical inferiority. (The hairy hands of D503 and different colored eyes of Chip in *This Perfect Day* are similar gimmicks.) In *We* and *1984* and *This Perfect Day*, woman is the temptress: she is already a rebel, and sharpens the hero's nascent awareness of his own nonconformist desires. In *We*, D503 continually remarks on the x-shaped lines of I330's face; to him, she is the mathematical "unknown", something he wants to find a value for. In *Player Piano* and *Brave New World*, by contrast, women exemplify their society's values. Lenina and Anita can bring personal pressure on the hero to conform. Because these heroes have not really embraced their rebellion as a deliberate intellectual development, but have drifted into alienation, others must articulate the intellectual problems. Finnerty (*Player Piano*) and Helmholz Watson (*Brave New World*) are rebels for intellectual reasons; Lasher and John the Savage, for religious and moral reasons. In *This Perfect Day*, an artist performs both functions.

All these books make similar pleas. Orwell's prayer that two plus two be unalterably equal to four is the simplest formulation of the problem, but the others ask for truth, for allowing man to have a soul or imagination, for letting man chose his own path to happiness, and for condemning compulsory chemical salvation. These are their basic programs for revision. Dystopian visions without such minimal programs are expressive rather than didactic. Whereas *Cat's Cradle* is an expressive outcry, *Player Piano* offers a description of human nature that we must accept if we are to recreate the possibility of meaningful life. György Dalos' *1985*, a satiric sequel to *1984*, seems expressive compared to its forerunner because it establishes no bedrock equivalent to Orwell's demand that two plus two must be allowed to equal four. *1985* satirizes the rebels and their ten-point program rather than affirming them, thus leaving the reader with no irreducible credo.

The heroes of the revisionary dystopias meet different ends, and these ends characterize their authors. Levin's Chip overthrows the ruthless benign dictatorship – unbelievably, and hence to the story's detriment. Huxley's Bernard Marx is sent to an island colony, where he will be allowed to live, politically impotent but unharmed. Paul, in *Player Piano*, will be executed. Winston Smith and D503 are forcibly converted. The horror of *We* is that the hero can be made totally obedient and happy by surgical means, yet apparently remain useful to the state professionally. The state has no cause therefore to hold back. In *1984*, we may hate to admit that a mind can be broken to the point that it really believes two plus two to be any amount Big Brother says, but Smith's obvious uselessness thereafter makes that torture process one not to be employed lightly.

Player Piano illustrates ways in which positive standards can be introduced through a negative framework. One method is through imagery and example. Many satires derive much of their power from some central image of violence:[3] Winston Smith and the rats, the glass bell in *We*. Vonnegut's image is particularly effective: a cat gets caught up by the sweeping machine, sucked through its works to the outside dump, survives and leaps hysterically up the nearest wall, only to be electrocuted by the guard wires at the top. Man caught in the machine is the tragic leitmotif of this dystopia.

Another way of introducing the positive through the negative is through personal manifesto. Paul has to justify himself in court while hooked up to a kind of lie detector. He has been accused of rebelling against society (which his father helped found) because he wishes to rebel against his famous father. "I suspect that all people are motivated by something pretty sordid", he admits, "and I guess the clinical data bears me out on that. Sordid things, for the most part, are what make human beings, my father included, move. That's what it is to be human, I'm afraid." He denies, however, that the sordid motives negate the value and beauty of the actions they inspire. Or, as he puts it, "The most beautiful peonies I ever saw . . . were grown in almost pure cat excrement."[4] Vonnegut fights the machine-dominated society and the efficiency ethic without glorifying man.

Indeed, he is clever at forcing us to make the affirmation of man he wants without letting it seem an easy, romantic assertion, based on nothing but wishful thinking. In Miller's *Canticle for Leibowitz*, the abbot sees in one and the same man a moronic peasant and the image of God. Vonnegut likewise sees in a rebel both a contemptible idiot and a man who deserves freedom and dignity. The luddite revolutionaries show their stupidity by attacking all machines, including the sewage plant and the bakery. As Paul and Finnerty survey the remains of the abortive rebellion, Finnerty muses: "If only it weren't for the people, the goddamned people . . . always getting tangled up in the machinery. If it weren't for them, earth would be an engineer's paradise" (*Player Piano*, p. 313). The paradox is inescapable. Man does so many mindbogglingly stupid things that those who can think feel compelled to try to straighten the mess out and see to it that such messes will not occur in the future. But, as Vonnegut insists, man controlled, man in a situation which prevents messes, is not worth having or being. Vonnegut affirms, however tenuously, the creature worthy of freedom over the idiot, though he, like Miller, sees both in us all.

Cosmic didacticism need be neither positive nor negative: it can just teach us what is, as a science text claims to do. Personal morality is irrelevant to its message. Didacticism that works on the personal level is usually moral, and hence positive or negative, but it need not be. One can view human nature almost as one views planets or atoms, as an impersonal phenomenon or as a puzzle to be solved. Few authors remain totally neutral, since humans, unlike planets or atoms, do govern their own actions, and those actions affect others. The more morally opinionated, the more an author in this last group belongs with those who exalt or disparage humans. Those who stay relatively neutral repay brief notice, however, because of their use of fantastic images.

Whether man be imagined as a creature of complexes and repressions or as the product of The Fall and Original Sin, we find the paradise image, to take one example, used to suggest a preconscious state. Erich Neumann uses paradise and the ouroboros to make assimilable his ideas of man's prenatal and early infancy stages. Indeed, according to Neumann, these are more than just images. They are archetypes in the mind, which actually help shape man's development. Freud's Id, Ego, and Superego, or Jung's Anima or Animus and Shadow are similar to the physicist's neutrino: a convenient name to cover a variety of observed phenomena. One talks of these psychological terms as entities, almost as living beings or as internalized deities. They even develop personalities: they quarrel, try to win control, or help us. They become fantastic. Yet they are not real; they are convenient names for a set of impulses and feelings, and these names are not very different in kind from medieval notions of little devils that sit on one's shoulders and hover about one's lips, or from the personification of impulses and sins as characters in Prudentius' *Psychomachia*. If one tries to generalize about psychic phenomena, rather than talk confessionally about one's own experiences, such *nomena* are the most economical way to classify and present the data. The ease with which these let us communicate quickly transforms them to *numina*.

Informal analyses of human nature slip naturally into fantasy. *Sir Gawain and the Green Knight* and MacDonald's *Phantastes* are both Christian evaluations of the human spirit that see a balance of good and evil in man. Both send their heroes into the realm of Faerie, and even conservative scholars have recognized the existence of parallels between Faerie (as these authors portray it) and the unconscious. Blake, however, is the pre-eminent producer of personal, semiformal analyses of human nature. He is not writing a textbook, but neither is he writing romances or epics in suggestive magic realms. He tells real stories, but his characters are also components of the mind. Blake does not parade them through the motions of the plot to a foregone conclusion. He is trying to see what the conclusion could be, and what the internal forces are, and how man might consciously contribute to the resurrection of the highest mental states. Blake sees human experience, its disharmony and inner strife, as the result of a fall. In *The Four Zoas*, he pictures the problems as being those relating to tyranny, constraint, and suppression rather than simply as sin: he observes that tyranny by one function of the mind (Urizen) causes Luvah and the others to lose their power to please, or to turn against their natural bent, or to sink totally into the waters of the unconscious. To describe the processes he was uncovering, and to give them an emotional truth, practically demands personification fantasy. Because he describes forces that are uncontrolled and unconscious, he cannot rationally analyze them. They are *un*conscious. The images and entities that rose to his command while composing mediate between his questing conscious and the unconscious: for him, fantasy was an utterly necessary means of communicating within himself, and equally necessary to him as writer trying to put across his theories of human nature.

Cosmological didacticism

Blake studies the human mind by turning it into a cosmos. Cosmological didacticism moves in the opposite direction.

> A mythological universe is a vision of reality in terms of human concerns and hopes and anxieties: it is not a primitive form of science. Unfortunately, human nature being what it is, man first acquires a mythological universe and then pretends as long as he can that it is also the actual universe. All mythological universes are by definition centered on man, therefore the actual universe was also assumed to be centered on man.[5]

The didacticism of cosmological literature has a different flavor from that of the moral sort. Cosmological literature does not bombard us with specific injunctions about personal behavior; it merely states what its author considers to be the truth about the structure of the world, including man's place in the system. Because man longs for assurance about his place, such a truth is naturally welcome. When such stories are sacred writ, they make no effort to convert the unbeliever; they do not even rely on logical coherence. Indeed, many creation myths are repetitive and contradictory in their detail. Fundamentally, however, they assert the importance of man's place in creation. Whether the works of cosmic literature are sacred accounts of creation and apocalypse or modern attempts to reinterpret the universe, almost all stress man's significance.

The first three chapters of Genesis are a well-known example of cosmological didacticism. They have been supremely successful at imparting assurance, not just to one religious tradition but to two. In the Jewish tradition, the first version of creation is more weighty. In the ritual repetitions, we experience creation as an exaltation of man. All that God makes is good, but at the apex stands man, his last and greatest achievement. Creating man in God's image, making him the darling of the universe: these exaltations of man are fantasy. The dreamers of this myth departed from the common reality they knew when they imagined humans brought into being without birth or mortal parents.

The celebration of man's creation is not just a process of exaltation but of refinement and selection. Man is the best of a succession of life forms. Following the Eden story, we see a further process of selection, as God winnows through his sinful creatures, trying to find a righteous strain. The rest of Genesis and many other parts of the Torah record this sifting process. Gradually, the field is narrowed to Abraham and his offspring. To them is given the Covenant, which must then expand and be transformed to accommodate a whole people. That select people is battered by misfortune, hammered by chance and neighbors and natural catastrophe, softened by corruption and cultural contamination, rehardened by purification and more trouble. It is given territory to reinforce its identity. Throughout this process, God interacts with man, sometimes even appearing to the patriarchs and addressing them directly, thus reinforcing the people's sense of specialness. An individual's sense of specialness is often projected in fantasy forms as his being the child of a god or of royalty. In Genesis, this fantasy of special birth is projected at a national level, and the stories involving the supernatural are woven to confirm this identity.

The Christian tradition found in Genesis a very different mythological message. Christ's re-establishment of contact with God made the racial/national myth irrelevant; his role as redeemer put more emphasis on man's fallibility than on man's exaltation. God's role is that of giver of the one taboo. The national history, which in the Jewish tradition records the refining of the good, becomes in the other a testimony to man's mindless repetition of his original failure in Eden. Genesis 1 encodes the belief in the specialness of man, and foreshadows the exaltation of some men in particular. The creation story in Genesis 2 embodies man's awareness of his own frustrating imperfections.

One need only glance at other creation myths to sense the vastly different possibilities for relating man to the universe. For some cultures, the world is heavy with its own implicit destruction: Snorri Sturluson's Old Icelandic account of creation tells of a world formed from a murdered giant. The forces of the universe are tenuously balanced between the frost giants and the gods. The extremes of fire and ice appear frequently in the stages of creation, and we come to see man's existence between these two destructive forces as marginal at best. The world is encircled by the ouroboric Midgard Serpent, who holds his tail in his mouth and thereby ensures temporary unity; but that image makes clear the potential for chaos should he let the tail go. Indeed the serpent does loosen his encircling grasp in the Norse apocalypse, the *Ragnarök*. Greek creation myths, in contrast, are mostly based on sexual union of primordial forces (Okeanos and Tethys, Gaia and Ouranos), and subsequent stories of early beginnings revolve about sexual and domestic feuds, both comic and tragic. Human actions recorded in Greek drama mirror this concern with domestic feuds as a principle for ordering reality. In sharp contrast is the creation story in the Brihadaranyaka Upanishad, where creation is the coming into existence and then into awareness of a "self". Wanting a companion, this self split into male and female, producing the human race. The female element transformed herself into each animal in turn, the male following suit, and in each form they bred their species. All creation is of the same substance as the creative spirit, and anyone who truly realizes this becomes the creator. In many Eastern religions, finding God is not a matter of relationship to an external deity but amounts to discovering this force within oneself.[6] Each of these creation myths encourages a view of man that gives him a defined relationship to the universe and an important place within the total framework.

Modern fantasists, aware as they are of the immeasurable eons of time that produced the universe we know, have mostly found an *ex nihilo* creation unimaginable. Calvino pictures the universe prior to the Big Bang, but all the personalities he describes seem to have existed before coming together at this one point, and his aim is not didactic so much as celebratory. In "Surface Tension", James Blish writes a creation story, not of our world and man but of a tiny aquatic creature made from human genetic material. Blish's story is didactic in that he apparently urges support of space exploration programs; he affirms the spiritual usefulness and impressiveness of heroic exploration, even if we know that every action seems nugatory in comparison to the infinite. Rather than clash with science on its own grounds, most recent fantasists avoid the issue of creation and deal mythically with a universe already in existence. C.S. Lewis and David Lindsay present such mythological interpretations of the universe, although fully aware of the scientific interpretations current when they were writing.

Lewis unfolds his cosmology in his planetary trilogy (*Out of the Silent Planet, Perelandra*, and *That Hideous Strength*). Each planet is ruled by an intelligence. Lewis adapts medieval and astrological lore, so he ignores the existence of planets beyond Saturn. The planetary rulers of Mars, Venus, Mercury, Jupiter, and Saturn are unfallen and unbesmirched by the sleazy associations they acquired as members of the Greek pantheon. Only Earth's ruler is evil – he is Lucifer, the fallen angel. The war in heaven and the binding of Satan have their counterpart in Lewis' cosmology. During that war, Lucifer nearly destroyed the surface of Mars before being bound in punishment to Earth's sublunary sphere. The cosmic equilibrium is threatened in the trilogy as man makes his way to the other planets, bearing his corruption with him.

Lewis weaves his new mythology in and out of traditional Christian myths. The ruler of the universe is Maleldil the Old, and Maleldil the Young took man's shape in order to redeem man. The hero, Ransom, sees a Martian water-dragon and later sees a bas-relief showing such a figure destroying the surface of Mars. Earthly iconography also associates Satan with the form of a dragon and with the water-monster, Leviathan. In *Perelandra*, Ransom discovers an unfallen paradise. An evil earthling scientist named Weston enters it as tempting serpent. Weston appears to be possessed by the Devil. In a semi-lucid moment, he moans: "They've taken off my head and put someone else's on me," that "someone" being one who heard with his own ears Christ's *Eloi eloi lama sabachthani*. In *That Hideous Strength*, the adversary is a research institute (NICE) whose Head turns out to be literally the head of a guillotined criminal apparently kept alive by machines, although the "life" later proves to be demonic rather than technological. When Merlin causes members of the institute to act out their true natures, the Head's nature is Satan's: it demands adoration and causes three institute officials to sacrifice one another to it while chanting "ouroborindra" – a word reminiscent of ouroboros, the serpent whose head eats its own tail. Lewis thus iconographically intermingles Satan, Weston (especially his head), serpent-dragon-leviathan-ouroboros, and The Head. Modern man places mistaken emphasis on the head, on learning rather than wisdom, on science and reason rather than religion and faith, and Lewis tries to drive home this mistake by associating head-imagery with traditional symbols of evil.[7]

Lewis offers us an odd mixture: his own cosmology, some slightly altered Christian myths, and a universe of the sort common in science fiction of the 1930s and 1940s. Clearly what interested Lewis was the chance to argue Christianity to an audience of technicians who would not have been particularly willing to accept his premises long enough to benefit from the message under most circumstances. Disguising the Christianity behind his invented cosmic history helps Lewis avoid instant rejection. After all, technicians read science fiction in part for its fantasy, and Lewis' imaginative detail is superb. By wrapping his didactic message in so colorful a package, Lewis made it more palatable. As he did in his *Narnia* chronicles, he takes theological doctrines which have gone dead for most westerners, strips them of their immediate connotations and contexts in order to evade our stock responses, and then makes their inner dynamic vivid again, attempting to reimpress us with the wonder of it all. How susceptible you are to this didacticism is a personal matter, but Lewis has a very good grasp of human psychology, especially its fears and desires. The comforts he offers to those who accept his mythic system are what many long for, and even those unwilling to give in to his arguments feel the powers of his persuasion.

The problems facing David Lindsay in *A Voyage to Arcturus* were more difficult than those occupying Lewis precisely because Lindsay was *not* working variations on a well-known mythic system, but instead was creating his own. Lewis had to overcome the handicap of preaching theology, but Lindsay has the double handicap of creating a fresh "religion" and of envisioning one so negative and terrible that readers would feel no urge to accept it. Only the brilliantly varied and original fantasy keeps readers so engaged with the story that there is any chance that they will be influenced by its message.

The hero Maskull travels to Tormance, planet to the double star Arcturus. We realize that it is not real science fiction when space travel is accomplished by means of a crystal torpedo fuelled with backrays, nor are the adventures on the planet, at first glance, sufficiently directed to seem like standard adventure. Rather, the repetitiveness of myth guides them; they are all variants on the same pattern. In each unit, Maskull enters a new region with some strikingly unearthly properties. He grows new sense organs that allow him different modes of perception. He interacts with the inhabitants and is frequently responsible, directly or indirectly, for their deaths. In each of his encounters, he falls under the sway of the local philosophy and then declares it an illusion when he has passed on to the next region, philosophy, and set of acquaintances. This paratactic, repetitive pattern establishes Maskull as trying and rejecting most philosophical approaches to the world as inadequate. Because he falls for most of them at first, so do we.

His questions become increasingly mythic as he goes on: Who rules this world? What is its nature? What moral principles should guide man? As he searches, we respond to the febrile clarity and hallucinatory vividness of the landscape: black trees with crystal leaves, red and purple sands hot enough to bake fish, water that varies in specific density, the valley in which matter becomes living creatures before Maskull's eyes, a lake that creates shapes and music when impelled by the player's thoughts, an underworld, a land where all matter is male or female and the two forces are violently inimical.

Lindsay shows us that his ultimately negative philosophy is inherent at all levels, microcosmic and macrocosmic; from the atomic level up, existence consists of a life force (represented in one mystic vision as fragmentary green sparks) and a debilitating and destructive power which envelops and degrades the sparks (depicted as white whirls). What Lindsay is doing is at first startling, for he knows perfectly well that no reader is going to abandon the periodic table and laws of physics and chemistry for sparks and vortices. Rather, we are in the realm of moral allegory or myth.

At the macrocosmic level are two deities, Krag and Crystalman. We see them mostly in their human forms, but gradually realize that they exist on a higher, divine plane.

> The spirit stream from Muspel flashed with complexity and variety. It was not below individuality, but above it. It was not the One, or the Many, but something else far beyond either. It approached Crystalman, and it entered his body – if that bright mist could be called a body. It passed right through him, and the passage caused him the most exquisite pleasure. *The Muspel-stream was Crystalman's food.* The stream emerged from the other side on to the sphere, in a double condition. Part of it reappeared intrinsically unaltered, but shivered into a million fragments. These were the green corpuscles. In passing through Crystalman they had escaped absorption by reason of their extreme minuteness. The other part of the stream had not escaped. Its fire had been abstracted, its cement was withdrawn, and, after being fouled and softened by the horrible sweetness of the host, it broke into individuals, which were the whirls of living will.[8]

The universal matter is cycled to feed Crystalman, the "devil", and the terms of this universe are such that the savior's main tool must be pain, a disadvantage which makes it all but impossible for Krag to win human converts. Yet he must try. Lindsay uses his mythology to propound his philosophy: anything that has ever given us pleasure in life – food, sex, sport, intellectual satisfactions, friends, love, social triumphs – is poisoned bait ensnaring our green spark. The purpose of Maskull's repeated adventures is clear. Before he can be expected to open his mind to so terrifyingly negative a philosophy he must see that all the other possibilities are worthless. He must perform his own winnowing and reject all standard interpretations of reality before there is any hope of his turning to this bleak answer. Like Lewis, Lindsay is fighting to win an audience and using fantasy as the enticement. As far as he is concerned, the scientific explanation of the universe, though all very well in its place, is trivial in its insensitivity to the meaning of life, and in its ignorance of the underlying clash of forces that define significant life.

For writers with didactic intentions, apocalyptic stories are a tempting form of fantasy. Pseudo-myth of Lindsay's sort is attractive, but one has to describe everything so pedantically that the audience may be put off by the preaching. A global disaster, whether it truly extinguishes all life or leaves a remnant to carry on, provides great scope for vivid images, excitement, moral lessons, and cosmology, especially if the apocalypse is caused by some agent other than man, and all these can be worked in with minimal preaching, if the author so desires.

Man's long history of sin makes the Biblical apocalypse necessary. So too, the destruction in William Miller's *A Canticle for Leibowitz* also grows out of the author's theories of human nature, and in that sense is moral rather than purely cosmological. In the course of his future history, which surveys approximately a thousand years, we see that our world, which bombed itself back into the Dark Ages, has gradually developed a new civilization, has reached the capacity for space travel and nuclear holocaust again, and it proceeds to destroy itself a second time with nuclear weapons. Not even the ever-visible reminders of the first fire deluge, the human mutants, can make man learn from his past mistakes: "The same, the same, everlastingly the same", muses a priest while hearing confession. "Even a woman with two heads could not contrive new ways of courting evil, but could only pursue a mindless mimicry of the Original."[9]

Miller draws a map of mankind's wrong turnings. In Part I, the new Dark Ages, we see the terrific pains the monks take to preserve any fragment of old learning, nonsense and sense alike, and we see too the peculiarity of humanity that it is not content to be ignorant, even though knowledge had once led to disaster. The next stage, the new Renaissance, shows the secularization of learning and the divorce between moral and intellectual thought. A scholar no longer feels called upon to react with a sense of personal responsibility to his ruler's evil policies, especially since that ruler funds the collegium and can disband it at will. The renaissance man has come to regard such political doings as "impersonal phenomena beyond his control like a flood, famine, or whirlwind" (p. 198). Man has learned to divorce himself from acts around him, to deny his personal moral responsiblity and complicity in the deeds of mankind. In Part III, the new Modern Age, complete secularity of outlook is again common. In line with his agnostic, human-oriented assumptions, Doctor Cors says that "pain is the only evil I know about. It's the only one I can fight" (p. 275). After a bombing, while dying half-buried under tons of stone, the abbot remembers his argument with Doctor Cors, and rehashes it semideliriously:

> Really, Doctor Cors, the evil to which even you should have referred was not suffering, but the unreasoning fear of suffering. *Metus doloris*. Take it together with its positive equivalent, the craving for worldly security, for Eden, and you might have your "root of evil," Doctor Cors. To minimize suffering and to maximize security were natural and proper ends of society and Caesar. But then

they became the only ends, somehow, and the only basis of law – a perversion. Inevitably, then, in seeking only them, we found only their opposites: maximum suffering and minimum security. (p. 305)

The abbot sums up Miller's revisionary doctrine in this same death-speech: "The trouble with the world is *me*. Try that on yourself, my dear Cors. Thee me Adam Man we. No 'worldly evil' except that which is introduced into the world by Man – me thee Adam us – with a little help from the father of lies. Blame anything, blame God even, but oh don't blame *me*" (pp. 305–06).

Like Vonnegut in *Cat's Cradle*, Miller traces the history of human stupidity. Whereas Vonnegut's story is mostly a despairing cry, Miller attempts to offer a solution and thus moves over from the literature of vision to that of revision. He presents his message of personal responsibility with a brilliant descriptive power. Horror radiates from the description of an atomic attack: "Before he [the abbot] had finished, a light was shining through the thick curtain of the confessional door. The light grew brighter and brighter until the booth was full of bright noon. The curtain began to smoke" (p. 302).

The horror is made stronger by thematic repetitions. In Part I, a novice during the Dark Ages was similarly, though not fatally, pinned under rocks, and found himself staring at a skull. The abbot of Part III also sees a skull when he is pinned by the cathedral rubble, and we know that it happens to be that very novice's skull. In the earlier age, had the rockfall proved fatal, the evil would merely have been an individual's pain; in the third age, the abbot's death is linked to the probable destruction of all life on earth. Buzzards feeding off human corpses (slain by fellow men) end Parts I and II; Part III ends with sharks feeding very poorly, most of their normal prey having been killed off by radiation. We do not know for sure whether they will survive or not, but we assume that land life is extinct. Even as his characters in the age corresponding to our own need not make the mistake a second time, we need not make it the first, and should not if we heal the divorce in our minds between moral judgment and public action. This is Miller's program for reform. The mental dissociation which we practice naturally is – to Miller – insane, but it can be unlearned.

To answer questions about the nature of the universe without using fantasy is practically impossible. Scientific answers excite a few scientists, but they fail to give most of mankind a sense of engagement with the universe. Yet without that engagement, there can be no lasting interest, no sense of purpose in life. Hence the prevalance of mythic outlooks, for these let one view the universe in terms that relate it to a human scale of values. Each mythic theory expresses its creators' views of man and offers man a framework in which to find his own significance. In creating and imposing these mythic systems of order, the originating cultures derive a sense of meaning. They create the universe afresh in their own image and naturally find therein their own significance. For readers who agree with their premises, this same gift of meaning is available.

When these explanations appear as sacred writ, the framework for experience is imposed on the audience as an absolute. No other possibility is acknowledged. When an author approaches questions about the nature of the cosmos in a non-scriptural context, he must rely heavily on persuasion. An audience born into a faith will accept its premises; an audience reading a modern didactic fantasy cannot be relied on to cede its own assumptions readily. To propagate a sense of meaning, the author must use the vivid power to make images which fantasy provides. These help keep the audience from rejecting the didactic message at the outset. Once well ensnared in the story and its values, readers will then proceed even if they disbelieve the author's premises, for the reward cosmic didacticism offers is a sense of man's significance.

A didactic author assumes that he knows the truth better than the reader. His job is to impart this truth and make it so compelling that the reader will reshape his life or beliefs to fit its dictates, or at least consider doing so. If converting the reader is the standard by which didactic literature should be judged, then naturally it fails much of the time, but that is true of non-literary didacticism too. One might say more fairly that didactic literature succeeds if it gains a serious hearing for its program. Its vivid images, if they work at all, can block or so modify our intellectual response that we will at least give an author a chance to speak. People who drive big American cars do not like the reproaches of conservationists, but they may listen as John Brunner unfolds his description of a world choking in its own pollution in *The Sheep Look Up*. One may recoil at Miller's dogmatic Catholicism in *Canticle*, but grant the problem and listen to his solution. His descriptions of atomic holocaust and of a world bombed into the Dark Ages are intriguing enough for us to keep reading. Not all such descriptions are fantastic: Vonnegut's firebombing of Dresden is not. Sinclair's sausage-making is not. They are just brilliantly vivid.

Fantasy in didactic literature has many functions. It may make the familiar strange (London of *1984*); or give an embodiment to ideas, in order that they may have a spokesman (Uncle Sam in *The Public Burning*). Or the fantasy may be a model concocted to make communication of complex data possible, as we saw for the various kinds of terms used to discuss the unconscious. Indeed, we see fantasy used in much the same way in atomic physics, where waves can be particles; where anti-matter can be brought into existence; and where the positron can be described as an electron moving backwards in time. To try to explain in words the meaning of the equations produced by subatomic studies, we need to resort to images which will help us handle their denial of cause and effect logic which makes everyday life possible. Such models – quarks, charm – are hypotheses; they may even prove to be mistaken as interpretations of the data. But for now they are what we need to make our facts assimilable. Fantasy provides the tool for creating such models, in science as in literature.

Didactic literature is often accused of being bad literature. It cannot afford serious ambiguity in its message without undercutting its own aims, yet we are used to ambiguity in life, to the frustration of not being able to extract a clear message or find the data for making a clear judgment. Didactic literature thus seems oversimple. Its characters, too, are often thin; were they complex, they would reintroduce ambiguity and might distract us from the ideas. When an author goes too far in presenting the ideas without fictional adornment, whether in the cause of religion or politics, we call the product propaganda rather than literature. To reject any literature with a message, as Collingwood and other aestheticians do, seems extreme, so long as entertainment remains one of its goals. *Canticle* is powerfully and explicitly didactic, but also enjoyable for its artistry and fantasy. Good didactic literature is a source of vivid fantasy, and hence of many rich literary experiences for readers. More than other kinds of literature, this literature of revision allows people to escape from their culture's imperfect systems of authority supposedly based on reason, and lets them experience other possibilities for ordering experience, whether religious or utopian. We of the western cultural tradition can ill afford to despise exposure to alternative styles of living: we need to reconsider our own too acutely.

6

Literature of disillusion: making reality unknowable

E.D. Hirsch, Jr defines philosophical perspectivism as "skepticism regarding the possibility of correct interpretation". He goes on:

> A perspective is a visual metaphor that stresses the differentness of an object when it is looked at from different standpoints. Under this metaphor come both of the chief varieties of modern hermeneutical skepticism – the psychological and the historical. The psychological version says that a text's meaning cannot be the same for me as it is for you because we look at the text from different subjective standpoints. The historical version proposes the same argument *a fortiori* for interpreters and authors who stand at different points in cultural time and space. Psychologism and historicism are thus quite interchangeable in the pattern of their skepticism and can be treated as a single phenomenon. Both stress that interpretation is relative to the interpreter, and thus imply that all interpretation must in the end be misinterpretation.[1]

Perspectivism or dogmatic relativism, as it is also known, affects interpretations of reality as well as those of literature. In addition to psychological and historical barriers, we have to admit that our senses are not reliable, so that what we absorb of our context may not be accurate. Similarly, what we try to say about it, and what others make of our words, will have little provable relation to reality. An author may wish to show us that we cannot know reality. He may wish thus to destroy our complacence and our blindness, to dis-illusion us. In a sense, perspectivist literature is an anti-form. Where other kinds of literature impose meaning on experience or encourage us to feel that some actions can be meaningful, perspectivist literature simply denies the validity of any such assurance, and implicitly makes any action on our part optional. We may abdicate from any responsibility toward the world, or we may act for the sake of activity, but neither stance has more meaning or virtue than the other.

Literature embodying this relativism defines itself by its general effect on its audience rather than by formal or internal similarities. The philosophies underlying perspectivist works vary, and the techniques for attacking the beliefs of the audience have little in common. In a few cases, the author's attack on the reader's assurance may even be unintended, the unconscious result of his own conflicting systems of value. Literatures of illusion, vision, and revision have stronger family similarities within each group, but the variety to be found in perspectivist literature is only to be expected of an anti-form. Its exemplars negate all the various positive approaches to reality. Brautigan's *The Hawkline Monster* attacks the systems of order that pervade adventure stories of both gothic and western sort; Robbe-Grillet's *In the Labyrinth* negates the heroic assumptions of most quest stories. Stanislaw Lem's *Solaris* undercuts the basic assumption of science fiction, namely the knowability of the cosmos. Aldiss' *Barefoot in the Head* is a kind of messianic story, yet it also attacks the messianic hope, and presents the kind of damnation that results when an individual can no longer rely on his senses for data.

Perspectivist literature, depending on your personal philosophy, smashes humanly desirable myths of meaning or liberates you from illusions. It achieves this separation of man from his basic assumptions in several ways. The first is to call attention to the limitations in the perspective of any one individual. We are taught how fallible our senses are through exposure to visions of reality that contradict the senses: dreams, psychotic experience, and drugs. Another is to call attention to the inadequacy of our means of communication, for without reliable communication we cannot escape the solipsistic prison of our individuality. Or an author can lay the blame for our warped perspectives on our membership in the human species, with all the culturally imposed assumptions which that brings. The author usually demonstrates these inescapable weaknesses to his protagonists and expects us to apply the message to ourselves and our own blindness. Another method is to attack the reader more directly with the weapons of exaggeration and caricature. The author creates worlds that are skewed, worlds we know to be distorted, but which are so cleverly twisted that we cannot say "*this* is an exaggeration, but *that* is true". Among these worlds are those of *The Good Soldier Schweik, Candide, Gravity's Rainbow*, Kafka's *The Trial*, and Laxness' *The Bell of Iceland*. The protagonist, often a stumblebum picaro, staggers through these skewed, hall-of-mirrors worlds unenlightened, but readers are made to feel the confusion of helplessness, the feebleness of their interpretive powers. The fifth way in which a reader can be robbed of assurance is by unresolved contradictions, where interpretation of reality clashes with another internal interpretation. This last differs from the other two in that it can be created unwittingly, and we do not always know from other evidence whether the effect is intentional or not. Swift batters our assurance in *Gulliver's Travels* by sending us contradictory messages, and we know this to be a game he was fond of playing, so can take it to be deliberate. Whether Twain did so with malice aforethought or not in *A Connecticut Yankee in King Arthur's Court* is more debatable, but the effect is the same. Its clash of values leaves us disturbed and unable to reach the release of a clear decision. We know we no longer discern right or wrong, that we cannot put a satisfying label on the actions. Didactic literature gives us the pleasure of applying such labels; perspectivist literature denies us that release.

One might wonder what the pleasures of uncertainty are. Why should we continue to read stories designed to frustrate us and to make us unsure and insecure? Escape literature flatters us and makes us feel strong. Expressive literature gives us the pleasures of emotional response to novelty, and assures us that our own interpretation of reality may be capable of being improved upon. Didactic literature pleases us with certitude and with assurance of our own importance in the universe. Such pleasure as there is to be had from perspectivist literature perhaps comes from our enjoyment in giving a name to the problem, even when we cannot find the solution.

Our inability to judge reality is not flattering. This literature tells us that our senses are too fallible, our judgment too crude, our suspension between conscious and unconscious too uncontrolled, and our creature limitations too severe for us to form a valid interpretation of life's data. Or rather, that those interpretations we persist in forming and using have nothing but personal relevance and local, cultural acceptability. They are our security blankets, imaginary bulwarks against the unorderable. To be told that valid interpretation is impossible also offers the option – or temptation – of surrender, for if relativist denials are correct, we are no longer obliged to try to identify right action or to attempt to determine any meaning in life. This literature of disillusion offers a powerful challenge to our mind-sets and outlooks; an ambiguous attack, since it can destroy our ikons, or can fulfill the highest function of literature, as Sartre saw it: remind us of our freedom.

The limits of individual perspective

A Chinaman of the T'ang Dynasty – and, by which definition, a philosopher – dreamed he was a butterfly, and from that moment he was never quite sure that he was not a butterfly dreaming it was a Chinese philosopher.[2]

The speaker of these lines goes on to exclaim, "Envy him; in his twofold security". Perhaps in comparison to Stoppard's Rosencrantz and Guildenstern, he is secure. His gentle, philosophical doubt does not much resemble their hysteric bewilderment. Stoppard inclines to view such enrichments of dull reality favorably. He and André Breton and other surrealists prefer any variation to the dullness of experience.

A man breaking his journey between one place and another at a third place of no name, character, population or significance, sees a unicorn cross his path and disappear. That in itself is startling, but there are precedents for mystical encounters of various kinds, or to be less extreme, a choice of persuasions to put it down to fancy; until – "My God," says a second man, "I must be dreaming, I thought I saw a unicorn." At which point, a dimension is added that makes the experience as alarming as it will ever be. A third witness, you understand, adds no further dimensions but only spreads it thinner, and a fourth thinner still, and the more witnesses there are the thinner it gets and the more reasonable it becomes until it is thin as reality, the name we give to the common experience. . . . "Look, look!" recites the crowd. "A horse with an arrow in its forehead! It must have been mistaken for a deer." (*Rosencrantz and Guildenstern are Dead*, p. 21)

Reality is thin, and we make the mistake of interpreting it as shallowly and imperceptively as we can. Stoppard's cheerful indifference to uncertainty is unusual. That valid interpretation and judgment are impossible upsets him not one whit. Most people, however, are not secure enough, or not desperate enough in their boredom with reality, to live happily with such uncertainty.

Dream is the commonest challenge to everyday reality. Literature relying on dreams can remind us of this loophole in our rationality, and challenge our casual assurance, particularly if the dream world asserts its own substantiality. That dream may have as much validity as real life was part of André Breton's *Manifestoes of Surrealism*; Carroll plays with the implications in *Through the Looking-glass*. Alice does not like the dreamworlds of Wonderland and Looking-glass Land because they contradict all the rules she has worked out by trial and error for dealing with experience in Victorian England. In her dream worlds, her body plays telescopic tricks on her; she cuts a cake, only to see the slices rejoin; shelf-goods in a store glide up out of reach; to get someplace, she must walk resolutely in the opposite direction. She meets the central mystery when she sees the Red King dreaming:

"He's dreaming now," said Tweedledee: "and what do you think he's dreaming about?"

Alice said "Nobody can guess that."

"Why, about *you!*" Tweedledee exclaimed, clapping his hands triumphantly. "And if he left off dreaming about you, where do you suppose you'd be?"

"Where I am now, of course," said Alice.

"Not you!" Tweedledee retorted contemptuously. "You'd be nowhere. Why you're only a sort of thing in his dream!"

"If that there King was to wake," added Tweedledum, "you'd go out – bang! – just like a candle!"

"I shouldn't!" Alice exclaimed indignantly. "Besides, if *I'm* only a sort of thing in his dream, what are *you*, I should like to know?"

"Ditto," said Tweedledum.

"Ditto, ditto!" cried Tweedledee.

He shouted this so loud that Alice couldn't help saying "Hush! You'll be waking him, I'm afraid, if you make so much noise."

"Well, it's no use *your* talking about waking him," said Tweedledum, "when you're only one of the things in his dream. You know very well you're not real."

"I *am* real!" said Alice, and began to cry.

"You won't make yourself a bit realler by crying," Tweedledee remarked: "there's nothing to cry about."

"If I wasn't real," Alice said – half-laughing through her tears, it all seemed so ridiculous – "I shouldn't be able to cry."

"I hope you don't suppose those are *real* tears?" Tweedledum interrupted in a tone of great contempt.

"I know they're talking nonsense," Alice thought to herself: "and it's foolish to cry about it."[3]

Alice clings to her long-standing assumptions because she sees no advantage to being the king's dream creature, but she is shaken, and can handle the argument only by tearfully denying it. She cannot see that the inhabitants of her dreamscapes are symbolically "real" as transformations of the authority figures who scold her and mold her. Nor is she aware that she, as Alice in Looking-glass Land, is a dream creature – her own. Nor is she aware that she is Lewis Carroll's creation. She is blind to several possible interpretations of her reality, but we know that her interpretation is not the only possible one. There is enough to disquiet us in Carroll's story that we can accept Alice's interpretation as uniquely valid only by giving in to her blind fear and urgency.

Medieval poets often use dreams to challenge our sense of reality. Dream poems offer them a chance to open the veiled eye of the flesh to clearer vision of the absolute. Dante speaks of spiritual and physical sleep as prelude to his entry into the forest in which he loses his way. Langland's narrator, Will, must fall asleep before he can see the structure of the Christian cosmos: the tall tower, the deep dungeon, and the fair field full of folk which lies between. The dreamer in *Pearl* enjoys a vision of heaven, and the lover of his rose in *The Romance of the Rose*. Most medieval dream literature is positive, for even a vision of hell assures us that there is order and justice for us once we escape the material world we think of as real. But some medieval poets could explore the negative, and use the dream frame to question whether reality can be known. In *The House of Fame*, Chaucer faces the possibility that his life as artist is insubstantial, even bad. He considers himself a love-poet, yet admits the foolishness and triviality of much of love's subject matter. Venus' temple lies in a wasteland, and the scenes depicted on its walls show futility as well as fame. As he also sees in his dream, human fame is arbitrary and often undeserved, thus making the sense of order represented by his beloved classical literature, by history, and by tradition, a dubious set of props on which to depend. The assurances made to him as an individual by Christianity are given no voice within the poem, thus creating a partial vacuum, which fosters the atmosphere of doubt and uncertainty.

The dream world he creates is not a patchwork of scenes from everyday life but is a literary world, one inhabited by the subjects of his favorite authors, especially the pagans. In much the same way, Alice's worlds are inhabited by the figures she knew from nursery rhymes. Alice can return to the everyday with relief and deny the Red King's dream power, but Chaucer cannot make such a move without denying the beauties of the literature he most values. He shows that he is aware that the world of artistic literary endeavor may indeed be a foolish dream, no more substantial than the visions that crowd our night hours – an unpalatable possibility to the father of English poetry – but his personal perspective leads him to question that valuation. The vivid but evanescent quality of dreams suggests an analogue to human literary production. With his dream frames, Chaucer explores alternative interpretations of reality, and tries, apparently without success, to determine what values in literature he could count on to be real. The implicit lesson to be found in *The House of Fame*, *The Parliament of Fowls*, and even *The Book of the Duchess*, is that there are no unambiguous answers, at least none that can be arrived at by means of reason and the senses.

We all dream. The convincing reality of such dreams while they are taking place does not trouble us afterwards, because the universality of the dream-process makes it unthreatening to our sense of reality. We label our unicorn a horse with an arrow in its forehead and forget it. Forms of consciousness which cannot be so readily dismissed as common disturb us far more. Various forms of mental disturbance produce waking dreams of such total conviction that our confidence in our senses can be destroyed. In Sartre's *Nausea*, waves of existential malaise are real while they last, and their reality seems an overwhelming truth. They usually reduce everything Roquentin sees to anesthetic meaninglessness, but occasionally they intensify perceived reality, which proves, if anything, less comforting to him. As he stares at a tree in a park, he notes:

> Existence had suddenly unveiled itself. It had lost the harmless look of an abstract category: it was the very paste of things, this root was kneaded into existence. Or rather the root, the park gates, the bench, the sparse grass, all that had vanished: the diversity of things, their individuality, were only an appearance, a veneer. This veneer had melted, leaving soft, monstrous masses, all in disorder – naked, in a frightful, obscene nakedness. . . . The chestnut tree pressed itself against my eyes. Green rust covered it half-way up; the bark, black and swollen, looked like boiled leather. . . . Knotty, inert, nameless, it fascinated me, filled my eyes, brought me back unceasingly to its own existence. In vain to repeat: "This is a root" – it didn't work any more. I saw clearly that you could not pass from its function as a root, as a breathing pump, *to that*, to this hard and compact skin of a sea lion, to this oily, callous, headstrong look. . . . Each of its qualities escaped it a little, flowed out of it, half solidified, almost became a thing. . . .[4]

Roquentin's psychic vision adds to what his eyes see. That tree and its surrounds occupy him for pages. It shoots up, it melts down, its roots writhe. He is inside it and outside it. His reality is very different from that of a casual passerby who might wonder why he was staring so fixedly. This, plus his descriptions of the town (so different from those that its inhabitants would recognize) plus his problems with interpreting his book's historical subject, are all ways in which Sartre challenges our ability to interpret reality meaningfully.

Some kinds of visionary worlds stemming from psychic aberration are so compelling that their creator loses the power to distinguish reality from illusion, and in literature these worlds can be made to play such tricks on the reader. Robert Coover's *The Universal Baseball Association, Inc., J. Henry Waugh, Prop.* explores such a psychic world and charts the steps by which it becomes more real than consensus reality. Ultimately, the story challenges *our* grasp of reality because the imagined members of an invented baseball league become characters in the fiction, and we forget that they are only the brainchildren of the fictional J. Henry Waugh. He plays the game with dice, and compiles ledgers on the play-by-play of each game, with extra material for pennant races. He tape-records interviews, writes obituaries and satires, composes ballads, analyzes the history of league politics, develops great baseball families through several generations, writes biographies and newspaper stories and scandals. The unsatisfactory nature of his dull job, the poor relationships he has with other people, and his increasing age all drive Waugh into the company of his created men. He shares their acute awareness of the impermanence of the flesh – most of the songs are about being forced to retire and about death. He enters their world of the locker room and of locker-room language, the taboo tongue that wards off the threatening world of women. He shares their ultimate equation of women and death. He also shares the intensity of awareness that the game-ritual gives to life. Winning matters desperately to him and them, although a man racing to step on a white mat on the ground is pointless *sub specie aeternitatis*, and such an act symbolically carried out as a roll of the dice is, for most people, yet further removed from significance. The accidental death of the perfect rookie pitcher threatens the balance of the game world and of Waugh's mind. He almost gives up the game and burns the records, but instead consciously commits himself to it by setting the dice down to the combination he wants in order to kill off the player whose brush-off pitch had killed the rookie. He plays God (J H[enry] W[aug]H), and must take responsibility for his creation. Or, to view it in another way, he has made a sacrifice, fed his myths blood, one of the surest ways of keeping myths alive and potent.

After one hundred more "seasons", Waugh has lost all consciousness of the outer world, and so do we, for the last chapter takes place entirely on the players' plane of action. As one of the players remarks, "God exists,

and He is a nut" – at one level, a locker-room comment, but also, to this
created world, a literal truth. And we have been taken in. Our sense of our
own consensus reality is not dimmed – we know that we are sitting in an
armchair reading a book – but the inner, fictional "real world", the story of
a fired accountant and his amusements, dissolves as we forget the
existence of Waugh and take his creations to be the characters of the
fiction. Thus are we shown how reality can disappear. Fantasy takes over
and we accept it, as he does, because it offers intensity, commitment, and
sensation. Insofar as we too wish to experience that intensity, we are
susceptible to his dreams, and we learn how shaky our sense of reality is
when we find that we have entered his created world and lost awareness of
the frame.

Dreams and psychosis create new models of reality. So do the chemical
reactions of psychoactive drugs. More clearly than the others, these show
us the peculiar unreliability of our senses, because we come to realize that
the everyday reality we trust to our senses for is only one set of chemical
reactions in our brains and that these can easily be altered to create new
data. William Burroughs explores such alternative visions in *Naked Lunch*.
To the reader sucked into this vortex, swirling bits of consensus reality
streak by, hardly distinguishable from the more blatant fantasies. At first,
we label as fragments of reality most of the references to policemen, but
even that little anchor is destroyed when the narrator describes his arrest
by two cops, his clever escape after killing them, and his subsequent
discovery (he thinks) that neither man is known to the City Narcotics
Squad. They too are probably just figments of the narrator's imagination.
When the plausible, repellent murder scene occurs, we accept it as real,
because the slimy motives, the implicit corruption, the offer of betrayal in
exchange for one last fix, the probing for the vein – all seem only too true.
When this scene proves to have been unreliable, we feel that nothing can
be counted on. Everything described is mere sensation, and New York
cops no more real – or unreal – than the orgiastic visions, torture dreams,
sanitarium nightmares, and pathetic questing for fixes. Drug literature
implies that our sense of reality is chemical. Change the chemistry and a
new reality ensues, one just as real to us as the old. Reality is a function of
our receptive senses and their physical, chemical condition. This is
disturbing perspectivism.

The inadequacies of communication

If we doubt our senses on some occasion, we would naturally ask
someone nearby for confirmation: "Do you smell something funny?"
"Could that have been a groan?" If the bystander's experience agrees with
ours, then we feel the experience to be as confirmed as we can make it.
But this confirmation relies on communication, and some literature

devotes itself to destroying our trust in our means of communication. This is relatively easy to do. Language is tautological. It cannot transliterate something like the color red. We may know scientifically that lightwaves of a given length are involved, but two people seeing a red sweater may not "see" the same color. When we realize that a phrase spoken one way is a sincere comment, but spoken in another way becomes ironic and a complete negation of the previous meaning, then we know that idea is a function of expression, and the words used are no clue to meaning. Synonymy is impossible according to many theorists, and if this be true, so in theory is explanation. Signs may be ambiguous. And language that has been strung out in shining strands of story, as we know all too well, is open to different interpretations.

In *The Castle of Crossed Destinies*, signs as a means of communicating are explored through Calvino's initial donnée: chance-met wayfarers, robbed mysteriously of the powers of speech, contrive to tell the tales of their lives by means of tarot cards. The first tale enchants us with its novelty. By the third or fourth, we see the trap. In the first, the card representing strength stood for a fierce brigand who robbed our hero. In another, it is the hero himself, crazed and destructive. Moreover, as Calvino lays the stories out as files of cards, he does so in a complex crossword puzzle array such that, if read downwards, the column forms one traveler's story, and if read upwards, the story of another. Backwards and forwards also supply life histories. Thus most cards are used by four different narrators, and each card has four different meanings, depending on its context. The major arcana are opulent fifteenth-century works of art, with gold leaf and loving, inventive detail, and they suggest the potential richness of the tales thus generated. But then again, the recognition of the functional elements used over and over remind us of the limitations of narrative patterns: vary it how you will, the hero monomyth, for instance, has rigid limits not readily overcome. One can shuffle cards and shift the placement of episodes only so often. Calvino goes on with an eighteenth-century deck to tell the stories of *Hamlet, Oedipus, Parsifal, Lear,* and *Faust,* and our belief in communicability through these signs crumbles as we realize that we do not recognize those stories from the rows of cards laid out. Both the narremes, the minimal narrative units, and their syntagmatic patterns lose their illusion of communicativeness. They lie there before our eyes, glorious, beautiful, intricate, but mute.

Limitations of *mythoi* (both plots and myths) for interpreting reality are explored by Ovid in his *Metamorphoses*. He follows the intertwined stories of change down their genealogical lines, much as Calvino follows the strings of cards. The story of Pygmalion, two generations later, becomes that of Myrrha, whose blood in turn flows through the veins of Adonis. Change after change is rung. Gods become animals, men become animals and plants, men become gods, and all beget upon each other future avatars of shifting form. When Ovid has run through all history, religions, philosophies, gods, men, beasts, cities and farms, the heroes of the past and of the present, he is left with nothing. They all resist capture, like quicksilver or like water flowing through the fingers. Each line peters out into nothingness. Nothing can be depended upon. Nothing stands firm. The ringing affirmations of recently deified Caesar sound ludicrous after the long build-up of other transformations. Hamlet, in Act V, scene i, is also made insecure by such an atomized and fluctuating world: he too wants to find permanence – in the idea of Caesar and of greatness, for instance. But if all things change shape, if Alexander's dust stops a beer barrel and Caesar's clay daubs a wall, where is any sense of lasting order? The world of infinite transformation is one in which nothing, no interpretation, can be trusted.

Nor can we find an objective prose style with which to relate our sense of any experience. Queneau's *Exercises in Style* narrates the same two banal incidents in ninety-nine styles. Each version remakes the episode so thoroughly in its own image that we hardly recognize it, and certainly cannot be sure that any description we might give would cover all the salient points. After all, some of the material is only in the minds of the onlookers. Each viewer absorbs part of the episode, embroiders part, adapts part to his or her own mind-set, and fails to take in other facets of the experience.

When we first read the version called "Dry Notation", we take it to be objective. We soon realize that objectivity is impossible, and that literary mimesis is as much imitation of styles as it is of external reality. A connoisseur of nineteenth-century fantasists will revel in "Dream", which starts:

> I had the impression that everything was misty and nacreous around me, with multifarious and indistinct apparitions, amongst whom however was one figure that stood out fairly clearly which was that of a young man whose too-long neck in itself seemed to proclaim the character at once cowardly and quarrelsome of the individual. The ribbon of his hat had been replaced by a piece of plaited string. Later he was having an argument with a person whom I couldn't see and then, as if suddenly afraid, he threw himself into the shadow of a corridor.[5]

"Noble" gives us an ironically Homeric account. It opens with undercut epic similes:

> At the hour when the rosy fingers of the dawn start to crack I climbed, rapid as a tongue of flame, into a bus, mighty of stature and with cow-like eyes, of the S-line of sinuous course. I noticed, with the precision and acuity of a Red Indian on the warpath, the presence of a young man whose neck was longer than that of the swift-footed giraffe, and whose felt hat was adorned with a plait like the hero of an exercise in style. Baleful Discord with breasts of soot came with her mouth reeking. . . . (p. 86)

After all the verbosities, "Haiku" is refreshing: "Summer S long neck / plait hat toes abuse retreat / station button friend" (p. 139). When we realize that distortion is unavoidable in the mind that observes, in the means of reporting, and in the mind that reads the report, we see that whatever final understanding emerges can hardly lay claim to validity as an interpretation or judgment of reality.

Signs can also be used to betray us deliberately. Nonsense in verse or story leads us to expect meaning, yet frustrates our attempts to extract it, at least in a conventional way. Carroll's *The Hunting of the Snark* is the best-known long nonsense poem in English. This agony in eight fits is Carroll's *Moby Dick* – the ocean quest for a mysterious creature. Like whales, snarks may be hunted for utilitarian reasons: "Fetch it home by all means – you may serve it with greens / And it's handy for striking a light."[6] But if it prove a boojum, it is far more dangerous than a normal snark, even as the White Whale apparently possesses malignant powers beyond the ordinary. But having said that this poem celebrates a hunt, one can only add that one member of the crew vanishes with the boojum. That is all there is of rational plot.

The baker's fate is certainly dramatic, but look at the ways in which nonsense frustrates our quest for meaning:

> Erect and sublime, for one moment of time.
>   In the next, that wild figure they saw
> (As if stung by a spasm) plunge into a chasm,
>   While they waited and listened in awe.
>
> "It's a Snark!" was the sound that first came to their ears,
>   And seemed almost too good to be true.
> Then followed a torrent of laughter and cheers:
>   Then the ominous words, "It's a Boo – " (pp. 86-7)

The inappropriate laughter and cheers undermine our sense that we understand the situation, as do most descriptions of emotion in the poem. One character goes insane with terror, for no comprehensible reason. Inappropriate words likewise foul up our sense of order:

> There was silence supreme! Not a shriek, not a scream,
>   Scarcely even a howl or a groan,
> As the man they called "Ho!" told his story of woe
>   In an antediluvian tone. (p. 55)

Inappropriate deeds and behavior also unsettle us. The baker is introduced as having forty-two boxes, each with his name on it. When he forgets them all on the beach, we learn that he has also forgotten his own name.

The thin thread of plot gives no meaning to the experiences described.

The random interactions of the characters suggest no lessons about life, and the lack of logical connections frustrates our natural expectations. We may well enjoy the sensation of floating in meaninglessness for a brief time. A fictive world that foils all expectations renews our awareness that we had expectations and reminds us of what those expectations were. Unless we enjoy frustration or feel no need to seek meaning, however, we are unlikely to revel in such nonsense for any length of time. We are more Rosencrantz and Guildenstern than Chinese philosopher of the T'ang dynasty. We want at least the semblance of meaning and order, the illusion that pattern is there. The principle on which nonsense works is even more clear when we look at nonsense words. The sounds, the cheeky but illusory suggestion of meaning – these please us for a short while. But with "Jabberwocky" Carroll shows how far one can go in the nonsense vein. Everyone knows "Twas brillig", but far fewer would be able to recite it if it were two, three, or four stanzas long. One stanza of teasing sounds is enough. Then we want at least a wisp of plot. Nonsense, whether in word or story, reminds us of our assumptions about reality and order, and denies those assumptions.

Our limitations as human animals

Some authors attribute our inescapable limitations to our species and its patterns of socialization rather than to the individual's senses or to the problems of communication. They present a new model of reality by means of nonhuman protagonists. Sometimes this technique serves simple humanitarian aims, in which case the work is usually expressive or didactic. Tolstoy's "Kholstomer" and Jack London's *Call of the Wild* show life from domestic animals' viewpoints. They display man's brutality and careless selfcenteredness. If we read in some heroic work that the hero rides his horse till it founders, we may not think twice about it, but "Kholstomer" lets us feel the full force of what that act means to the horse. He also lets us feel the castrator's knife from the horse's vantage. Ultimately, however, this gimmick for reversing perspective is too obvious and demands so much anthropomorphizing that we lose some of our faith in its insights.

Some nonhuman narrators take us further afield. Golding's *The Inheritors* and Saint-Exupéry's *The Little Prince* put us in touch with something that could be human but isn't. Because of the physical similarities to man, we assume many likenesses to ourselves. The differences that emerge are therefore more shocking.

Golding introduces us to the pre-logical, collective consciousness of the Neanderthal mind, and we learn to identify with Lok's intuitive modes of perceiving reality. What starts as a simple challenge to our understanding when we enter his pattern of perception becomes an exciting new view of social relationships and of the world. Then we see the enemy, Cro-

Magnon man, and realize our far closer kinship to him. The enemy has our logic and language, our noncollective, single (and lonely) consciousness, our tool-using skills, and our taste for intoxication. Golding chides us harshly for our exclusive belief in one mode of perception. He switches perspective in the last two chapters, and invites us to feel pain as he forces us to view the Neanderthal from a modern perspective. Lok, whom we knew and liked, who was male and had hands and feet and an attractive, developing personality, is presented from a vantage point that sees him as a creeping animal, an "it". We read of its forepaws and hindpaws. When we enter the thoughts of the Cro-Magnon people, we find that they have complex names like ours; fears and lusts; defined social relationships and sexual morality; artistic drives; a sense of humor. Above all, they have an incredibly blind arrogance and assurance that their culture is the only one possible.

The Little Prince challenges our adult values by showing how these values look to a "child" – not just a normal child, but one who has not been shaped by any of our socializing pressures. The little prince has never had to conform to an adult world. His candor, fearlessness, and concern with his own questions are all untrammeled by attitudes towards adults that would cause him to subordinate his needs to theirs. The man he confronts is in mortal danger; he works desperately on his downed airplane, measuring everything by his progress and his dwindling supply of water. He too thinks that his concerns matter, but he claims to retain some sense of a child's values too. Guided by the prince, we see the king and the tippler, the conceited man and the lamplighter, the business man and the geographer, and we appreciate this ruthlessly simple demonstration of the manner in which professional and adult concerns make us view entirely different things as real. To the geographer, an extinct volcano on the prince's planet is still important, but a living flower of the same size (the planet being very small) is of no significance, however beautiful it may be. The prince learns from a fox that one can find worthwhile relationships by taming and being tamed. "It is only with the heart that one can see rightly; what is essential is invisible to the eye."[7] But if the essential is invisible, it is also unprovable, non-objective. Because the little prince is nonhuman, he may know true reality better than we do. Unless we make an act of faith, however, and accept his message, we are left seeing only that there are different interpretations of what is real and important.

All these works show that our perspective is unreliable simply because we are humans living in human society. We are blinkered by cultural traditions to the point that we drastically limit what we perceive without being aware that we do so. Nonhuman narrators can be an effective gimmick for exposing us to this human failing.

Skewed worlds

An author can also attack the reader's assurance directly by trying to persuade us that our judgment is inadequate to the challenge of interpreting reality. In such narratives, the hero is relatively normal. His world, however, is twisted. When the distortion is slight, we cannot draw a line between fantasy and reality. *The Trial* and *The Good Soldier Schweik* are such caricatures. Other skewed worlds are more extreme. We see various kinds of grotesque worlds in Cervantes and Rabelais, in *Candide*, *Satyricon*, and Pynchon's worlds in *The Crying of Lot 49*, *V.*, and *Gravity's Rainbow*. Menippean satire is a natural mode for this attack. Another variation is a world in which supposedly mutually exclusive alternatives coexist, as they do in Robbe-Grillet's *The House of Assignation* or in Borges' "Tlön, Uqbar, Orbis Tertius" or in Coover's "The Babysitter". All of these works demand some recognition for their worlds as a kind of reality, for the worlds are not meant to be shrugged aside as some other planet (which is possible in science fiction) or as something apart from the realm we know. They are recognizable as our own world, and they pit their interpretation of reality against ours.

The shadowy tribunal that enters Joseph K.'s life brings a different focus to his world. Where once his work at the bank was precise, tolerably satisfying, and clearly established in his personal foreground, and where once his sexual needs were met by a conventionally minor liaison, he now drifts away into more disquieting attachments and finds himself unable to concentrate on work. He mishandles clients through abstraction and inattention, or through problems of language and communication. He cannot get his work done, and takes more time away from the bank than is proper. Although K. has heretofore led a correct life, he is now found inadequate. He has lost the ability to feel any emotions – surprise, determination to do something, attachment to other people. His former, frigid concerns and activities lack the vitality that would help him spiritually during his time of need. Yet he had once been satisfied with his life. Clearly his former interpretation of life's actuality was wanting.

Kafka is not satisfied with merely one such reversal of values. True, Joseph K. is weighed and found wanting. Nonetheless, we also side with K. against the shadowy accusation and shadowy legal machinery. K.'s situation speaks to the paranoia most readers can feel at least fleetingly. We know logically that the paranoid interpretation of reality is inaccurate – the world has better things to do with its time than think up ways of persecuting us – but emotionally, this interpretation attracts us because it relieves us of responsibility for our predicaments. We are thus teased into viewing K. two ways at the same time – as guilty malefactor and as persecuted victim. Because the world of his nightmare is so close to the real world of business and courts, we cannot separate them decisively, and we cannot stake out the realm of the real.

A stumblebum picaro like the good soldier Schweik inhabits a world whose relation to reality is much like that of K. It is caricature, but subtle enough that we shrug off parts as amusing exaggerations and accept the whole. Practically everything described could happen. If any element can be labeled unreal, it would be Schweik's indifference to physical torment and his lack of fear. Hospital treatments designed to cure malingerers leave him unmoved. So do lunatic asylum regimens, jail regimens, and army life itself. Unlike K., he starts by accepting guilt – any and all guilt, no matter how innocent he actually is – and cheerfully endures one interrogation after another, and awaits sentence calmly, however dire the probable punishment. Yet because the world of the army is insane, we identify with Schweik and wish him well in all his scrapes. Cumulatively, we know his adventures to be farce, but we cannot pin down the elements which keep the realistic detail from forming a far more tragic statement. The same technique makes Heller's *Catch-22* so teasing and frustrating. The line between real and fantasy is as smudged as the line representing the Front on a general's map: it wavers back and forth, is erased and redrawn daily.

Candide goes much further than the distortion of caricature; so do *Satyricon*, Lucian's *A True Story*, Pynchon's *The Crying of Lot 49*, and a multitude of other paratactic, episodic, and parodic quests and journeys. Lucian sails immediately into pure fantasy, whereas Voltaire relies more on improbables. The crude zest with which he revives "dead" characters upsets our biological as well as our literary expectations. Deprived of rational expectations, we are forced to cling far closer to the plot and to the primitive curiosity over what comes next, a mental stance consonant with a child's approach to literature and a child's inability to be sure what is real and what is meant to be understood as fantasy, and if fantasy, what sort of fantasy. This produces the odd effect of dual perspective: on the one hand, we do not take the story as a representation of reality seriously. Any serious thoughts we have will be directed toward philosophical, political, or allegorical extrapolation. On the other, we enjoy what comes at us naively, as a child does, and share as a dim memory the child's uncertainty about the reality, mixing this innocence with sophisticated laughter at the satires. Such a dual view means that we cannot lay out the text's world and label it. We respond to *Candide* in two very different ways simultaneously, each with its own inner sense of what these created worlds represent, and the two interpretations of reality resist any desire we might have to make them one and hence fixed. Instead of developing improbabilities as a linear sequence of adventures, Robbe-Grillet's *The House of Assignation* gives us alternative versions of a violent action, any or none of which may be true. All are presented circumstantially, and the expectations we bring to narrative would lead us to take them as real, yet they stubbornly remain mutually exclusive. Once we have struggled feebly to force the evidence to fit a logical pattern and once we have realized the impossibility of reconciling the contradictions, we are left without any means of labeling the action real. This skewed world shows us our limitations as judges.

Literature of unresolved contradictions

Literature can also challenge our ability to interpret reality by presenting a contradictory or confusing set of values which makes impossible any effort on our part to integrate the data and make it harmonious. Whereas Robbe-Grillet sets similar situations or actions supposedly imitating reality side by side and refuses to tell which one is true, Swift will set mutually exclusive ideas side by side and refuse to resolve the ambiguity. He batters our sense of our own judgment this way in *Gulliver's Travels*, *A Tale of a Tub*, and *An Argument against the Abolishing of Christianity*. Few authors do it as obviously and even maliciously as he. In many other instances, the clashing values reflect their own internal conflicts; author and audience alike get lost in the labyrinth of the undefinable, the unjudgeable, and the unprovable. Works in this last category – Twain's *Connecticut Yankee* and Carroll's "Jabberwocky" – cannot be identified as sharing a technique, because the confusion may not be consciously produced. Nonetheless, they affect readers in a manner which destroys their confidence in judging, and so will be discussed here, even if that effect is sometimes accidental.

Swift's blows at reader assurance are well known from such unresolvable critical quarrels as the hard and soft schools of interpreting *Gulliver's Travels* Book IV. Carroll's contradictory values are subtle enough to require more comment. His "Jabberwocky" upsets our sense of order in a novel fashion: the poem is wed to a picture, and the two clash. The picture is not, of course, by Carroll himself, but was approved by him enthusiastically, so he either did not feel the clash of values or accepted it. The poem celebrates the victory of a young man over a monster. At least, we assume (if we only hear the poem) that the hero is more than a lad. He behaves with adult decisiveness and has considerable skill with weapons. His father's calling him "son" and "boy" seem merely a parental mode of address, not an indication of age. The picture, however, shows a very small child, whose sword is so long and heavy that he clearly would be physically incapable of swinging it up into action, let alone controlling it or chopping off a monster's head. Moreover, that head, supposedly borne back by the hero, is nearly as tall from jaw to crown as the hero is from head to knee. He would be entirely unable to drag it, let alone galumph home with it. That the hero portrayed in the picture should slay such a monster with that sword is manifestly impossible, yet the poem celebrates that victory. For me, at least, the resulting literary experience is sinister and disturbing, not festive. The impossibilities involved force us to fight with the text, either to take it as an exaggerated fairy-tale story, or to treat it as sardonic or ludicrous. Yet we want to believe in the possibility of the hero's victory. We are left without grounds for choosing or affirming.

Mark Twain also shakes our assurance and clouds our vision in *A Connecticut Yankee in King Arthur's Court*. The confusion of values that undermines our ability to judge emerges only slowly in the story. Hank starts full of Yankee know-how and determination, and we share his scorn for the superstition and irrationality characteristic of Arthur and his subjects. As he recreates gunpowder, electricity, telegraphs, and printing, Hank seems justified in despising knighthood, chivalry, Merlin, the King, and the various knights and women, including Sandy. Yet upon returning to his own century, with its relative freedom from superstition and its rationality akin to his own, Hank is so miserable that he dies. To the end of his stay in Arthurian England, he robustly espoused his own principles, yet his actions and emotions brought him into conflict with them. He finds that Sandy, Arthur, and Lancelot have virtues that outweigh their ignorance and superstition. The technical tricks he had prided himself on – which had seemed to his audiences like magic – prove hideously destructive, more so than the native superstition, torture, and other practices which Hank so despised. The Boss's tyranny was merely more effectively tyrannical than that which it replaced. The story starts with loud affirmations of technology, and Hank never gives them up, yet his technology kills 25,000 knights and leaves Hank fatally entrapped by the mountain of corpses. When Twain undercuts the world of technology so drastically, we are left to try to untangle what values he really does expect us to draw from the story. All our data for judgment is destroyed by the end of the book. We are unable to work out what Twain meant us to think real and significant, and we find our own allegiances divided and conflicting.

Relativist literature explores, even revels in, the no man's land between the rational and the irrational. The tensions it generates are twofold. First, the attack, which is aimed at the assumptions by which we live, is akin to that made by negative expressive literature, but greatly magnified. Second, this literature rests defiantly upon a foundation of paradox. It denies the possibility of making valid judgments and interpretations, but such a conclusion can only be reached through the very process of rational judgment which it denies. This need not bother us if we wish to shrug it off. An axiom cannot be proven within its own system. Euclidian geometry is founded on unproven axioms. So is Christianity. But their axioms do not contradict their message. Most readers do not search literature for the basic axioms, and most narratives were not written with systematically articulate philosophies shining forth between each line. Readers are especially likely to miss this paradox because they will be trying to protect themselves from the destructiveness of the perspectivist message by cultivating indifference, ironic distance, fervid faith in some other value system, or allegiance to the "everyday". It is easy to dismiss the disquieting message of drug literature by rejecting drug use. Psychosis can be tossed aside as maladjustment. Dreams can be dismissed as not significantly challenging everyday reality.

Not everyone shares Stoppard's or Breton's boredom with the ordinary. For any of these reasons, readers miss the paradoxical fact that this is an emotional appeal masquerading as reason, but the paradox remains, an interesting characteristic of the form.

To yield to perspectivist literature, one must have already felt at least fleetingly that interpreting reality is impossible and that standards of value are unprovable and unimportant. To exchange one concept of reality for another, as most literature asks us to do, is not nearly as disturbing as the perspectivist demand that we give up all sense of reality whatever. Readers may prefer to respond with heated denial, as Alice does to the supposed primacy of the Red King's dream, rather than face the void. To keep the audience reading, an author working in this vein must create vivid enough problem worlds for us to enjoy the adventures or visions in their own right. If we enjoy the vision (or anti-vision), or even if we enjoy finding that someone else has also reached the conclusion that interpreting reality is impossible, we will not be bothered that this conclusion is itself unprovable. This fact points up an otherwise disguised quality of this literature of disillusion, however, namely that it is emotional literature. It makes its ultimate plea to our emotions, not our intellect, yet the terms used are almost always supposed to be logical, and the extraliterary support for the stance relies on such intellectual disciplines as philosophy, language theory, and biochemistry.

At the outset of Part II, I suggested that man concerns himself most with two kinds of reality – the personal and the cosmic. As a rule, his perspective on the cosmic is handed to him by his culture, and he thinks little about it. If cosmic reality happens to draw his attention, he may, like Qwfwq's deaf cousin, rejoice in exploring the atomic or stellar spaces. In literature, it is the other kind of reality, the personal, that matters most often. Man wants assurance of his nature, his role, and his significance. This craving expresses itself in stories, and to a degree satisfies itself there as well. In myths and stories, the stars may tell us of our importance, whether through astrology or galactic travel; the gods will answer when questioned, be it through oracles or computer print-out. Stories can encourage us to project such meanings and our enjoyment of them into the events of everyday life.

Literature offers us four basic approaches to reality, if it is concerned with the nature of reality at all: illusion, vision, revision, and disillusion. We agree to accept illusions and evade everyday reality when weary obligations sap the vitality of ordinary experience. The evasion we try may be frivolous, or nostalgic, or an attempt to quiet fears and frustrations. The worlds invoked by escape literature are not necessarily impossible, but close inspection makes plain that even were a similar situation to arise in real life, we would not enjoy it as much as we do in a book. Whether detective story or pastoral, the fictive world lacks the petty irritations inseparable from the world we know. However pleasant a mellow ramble in the countryside, we cannot escape the blackflies in blackfly season. Likewise, in the real world, murder mysteries would breed fear, suspicion, and misery (if one were a suspect) or frustration (if one were a detective).

Emotional and intellectual involvement called forth by literature of vision offers us a different way of achieving a sense of intensity. Whether our emotions remain fixed on the new reality or manage to transfer some of the concentration and vividness back to their own world will depend on the success of the work and on the mind-set of the reader. Most expressive literature, however, relies on some overlap between fictive and real worlds that will make that transition possible. That portion we think of as "real" in the story, we come to see through new eyes. Habit and the automatic filtering of consciousness are thus bypassed, and our alertness and sense of well-being are thereby increased.

The affirmation demanded by literature of revision is meant to change perceived relation to reality permanently. In this group of works, more than in the others, cosmic reality is important because religious issues are often at stake. "What is man?" is the lesser concern, compared to the craving which finishes the sentence "that Thou art mindful of him". Didactic literature makes more presumptuous claims than any of the other forms. In order to demand action, it must give us answers, not unproven hypotheses. To persuade us that they are indeed "answers" calls for emotional persuasion, and vivid images calculated to push us in the desired direction. Logic may adorn the surface arguments, and often does, but underneath, the enticement is aimed at a nonverbal, nonlogical level of our consciousness.

The same is true in the literature of disillusion. Its denial takes many forms: denial that what we think of as everyday and objective is the only reality, and assertion that others have equal validity; denial that we can develop a system of validation by checking our impressions with those of others; denial that language will let us communicate an interpretation. This negative stance gains its logical trimmings from modern science and philosophy. The objects we see as solids are, we know, illusions; instead of being a solid object, the desk top before me is mostly emptiness, with the occasional atom, and those atoms in turn dissolve into electrical charges. Theoretically, the philosophies that feed the negative stance are correct: language is tautological, our senses are fallible, and communication cannot be made precise. Nonetheless, we do manage to communicate for everyday purposes. As E.D. Hirsch points out (quoting Sir Karl Popper), dogmatic relativism "simply exaggerates a difficulty into an impossibility" (*The Aims of Interpretation*, p. 148). But be the theory what it may, authors and readers can *feel* that denial of interpretability is the only possible response, and for them, this literature reinforces their feelings and reassures them that others too have reached this conclusion. Some can even find comfort in the disengagement which it fosters, a sense that one has no responsibility to determine the real or pursue purposive action.

Throughout these various responses to reality, the authors show themselves interestingly unconcerned with drawing any line between the real and the unreal. Of course, authors do not tell themselves as they sit down to write that they wish to comment on reality, but their conscious aims will be affected by their attitudes towards reality. The literary result, as we have seen, is a widespread refusal by writers to limit their story matter to the purely material and empirically possible. Pure materiality is mindless. One cannot do anything with events and objects without interpreting them, or without responding emotionally to them. Interpretation without emotion tends toward science and is of relatively little interest to most readers. Emotions, some of which would attract readers, are not always readily extracted from the mundane and ordinary. To attract an audience, the author must keep in mind the need to sway emotions. These are more readily touched by images than by mere observation. The reasons for this, and the implications for writers, will be discussed in Part III. We have seen in Part II how fantasy is used and how its powers differ from those of mimesis. In Part III, we will focus on why an author would use it – what demands form makes on the author, what satisfactions for the artist it gives, and what desires of the audience the author can meet by using it. Overall, we can ask what human purposes it serves.

Part III

The functions of fantasy:
why use fantasy?

Introduction

Thanks to the Greek philosophers, Christianity, and the Enlightenment, we have no vocabulary for analyzing literary departures from reality. Myth, fable, fancy, fantasy, image, symbol, and metaphor – all the inherited terms – have specialized and sometimes negative connotations when applied to serious literature. Having acknowledged the existence of the problem, I have tried to start solving it, first with the inclusive, non-generic definition and then with a survey of the roles played by fantastic elements in each of three kinds of literature – traditional, realistic, and modern. Part II sketched the four significant, conscious responses to reality which are logically possible within an artistic framework: illusion, vision, revision, and disillusion. We have seen what both mimesis and fantasy, especially the latter, have contributed to these responses to reality. Part III is more narrowly concerned with fantasy and its functions – with the relationship between literary fantasy and the author who produces it; and with the human needs of the audience which it fulfills. Chapter seven will deal with the effects that literary form have on fantasy and those that fantasy has on form; these clarify some of the reasons that would motivate authors to use fantasy.

Chapter eight explores the relationship between literary fantasy and readers. Psychoanalytic theory – Freudian, Jungian, and Gestalt – suggest how some kinds of fantasy work on readers' minds. They suggest a definition of meaning, and shed light on our mental responses to the experience of meaning. We can also consider meaning, not from the standpoint of the mind receiving it, but from that of the structure imparting a sense of meaning. Literature is such a structure. So are religion and science. Examining the latter two and applying what we see to literature lets us build a model of how literature functions as a meaning-giving experience, and also lets us determine many of fantasy's roles in this process. For fantasy proves to be peculiarly important to the experience of meaning, even though western culture has traditionally been hostile and dismissive toward fantasy in most of its manifestations. Throughout this book, fantasy has been treated as an object. In the last chapter we will try to understand fantasy as a subject, different kinds of fantasy as the agents which act upon us, manipulate us, activate conscious and unconscious responses, and supply the meaning-structures which we seek. Instead of trying to net the butterfly and pin it on a board, we will observe it acting as a creative force in the relationship between man and literature. If we are lucky, we may even see this butterfly turning into a Chinese philosopher.

7

Fantasy as a function of form

In the first six chapters, I have discussed fantasy as if it existed on an invisible interface between author and audience. The author creates a delightful escape, or presents a new interpretation of reality, or enjoins obedience to that interpretation, or simply destroys the audience's assurance. Fantasy mediates between authorial intention and audience response; it creates much of the desired effect. But fantasy is not some form of energy which can traverse the void between two minds. A vehicle is necessary – the literary work. As I suggested in chapter one, the work itself can make formal demands which affect both the author and what he can hope to achieve with his creation.

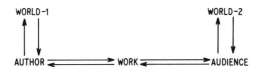

Figure 13

We often forget that the author⟷work relationship is reciprocal, not one way. True, the author brings a work into being, but that work, in the process of being created, makes formal demands which distort, modify, limit, and discipline the initial impulse. The structure of a sonnet affects the presentation of the author's emotion or idea. Many an analytic comment or expression of emotion has to be left out because it would take too many syllables, or because it would not adapt to the constraints of rhythm and rhyme. While prose fiction has no such obvious limitations, it is far from formless or undemanding. At times, these demands dictate the use of fantasy; at others, they more or less preclude it. They also affect the kinds of fantasy that can easily be called into service.

Audiences, too, respond to formal demands by bringing form-conditioned expectations to their encounter with the work. We can feel gratified when a fantasy we expect really does materialize in the story: let the hero kill a monster, and we will feel pleased. On the other hand, the author can disconcert, excite, or distress us by deliberately thwarting our expectations: let the monster kill a hero in a work not marked by the formal signals of tragedy or farce, and we will recoil in dismay.

The term "literary form" has many meanings, so "formal" demands of several kinds must be sought. One kind of form that generates clear expectations is what Northrop Frye calls *mythos*. He sees stories as following one of four *mythoi*: comic, tragic, romance, and ironic. The conventions of each require or reject the use of particular sorts of fantasy. The kind of fantasy, whether trivial or central, and the ways it can be introduced are further controlled by what Frye calls the five modes. I shall use *mythoi* and modes to explore formal demands from one possible perspective. From another, I shall use the parts of narrative as defined by Aristotle, Crane and others: *mythos*, *ethos*, and *dianoia*; or plot, character, and idea. If an author tells a character-oriented story, for instance, there is little room for fantasy, but a plot- or idea-oriented tale can use fantasy readily – and can abuse it easily as well. Finally, when trying to reconstruct an author's choices, one can approach form from yet another vantage, identifying the piece as lyric, dramatic, or narrative. Again, the limits of each of these "forms" set their mark on the responses to reality that a given work can convey.

If I have hitherto seemed to consider fantasy an invisible phenomenon which somehow flows from writer to reader, the present chapter should help to remedy that illusion. Fantasy is not bodiless; like a living creature, it is affected by the limitations of the particular body it inhabits. By approaching the functions imposed by form from these three angles, we should uncover the logic governing some major authorial uses of fantasy. By isolating some of the techniques used for dislocating us from reality, and by seeing the forms which foster them, I hope to shed light on the differences in the quality of fantasy. Why is so much fantasy incontrovertibly trivial? How do some manifestations of fantasy achieve potent resonance? What forms foster such excellence?

Fantasy, modes, and genres

Northrop Frye's great pattern of patterns, *Anatomy of Criticism*, has been said to possess an all-too-fearful symmetry. Anyone can think of exceptions to his rules; can carp at his changing bases for classification; can disagree on his use and conflicting reuse of terms. Despite the validity of such objections, Frye's patterns remain extremely helpful when one wishes to divide literature into categories. Each pattern does fit so many works so well. His system can help us understand why two similar works have such diverse effects on us as readers or can show us the underlying similarities in pieces superficially different.

To get most benefit from the four *mythoi*, one must avoid making two errors. First, a work embodying the comic *mythos* may be called comic but should not be confused with comedy since the latter term has too many meanings that are exclusively dramatic. The same stricture applies to tragedy and the tragic *mythos*. The second error is to assume that a work embodying the ironic *mythos* is an anti-romance. Frye fosters this notion by putting the four *mythoi* in a circle, with romance opposite ironic; but the ironic *mythos* seems to me able to negate any of the other *mythoi*, not just romance.

Frye offers, in his theory of modes, another pattern which helps differentiate works sharing the same *mythos*. If the hero is divine or semi-divine, the mode is myth; if he is "superior in *degree* to other men and to his environment, the hero is the typical hero of *romance*".[1] "If superior in degree to other men but not to his natural environment", the hero belongs to the high mimetic mode. If the hero is one of us, superior to neither men nor environment, he belongs to the low mimetic. If he is inferior to us, "so that we have the sense of looking down on a scene of bondage, frustration, or absurdity", the hero belongs to the ironic mode. Frye chooses only to discuss comic and tragic fictional modes, yet one can speak just as usefully of modal differentiation for works following romance or ironic *mythoi*. Granting this to be a cumbersome system cursed with overlapping terms, it is useful because the probability of overt fantasy is logically predictable within its categories. Readers should not look on the twenty permutations of *mythos* and mode as a grid to be memorized – it would make a cumbersome butterfly net indeed. Its usefulness lies in its ability to bring to our consciousness the elements often ignored in literature which provide a nourishing matrix for fantasy.

The probable presence of fantasy

MYTHOI	comic	romance	tragic	ironic
MODES				
mythic	yes	yes	yes	yes
romance	almost always	almost always	almost always	almost always
high mimetic	minor, if present	minor, if present	minor, if present	probably
low mimetic	minor, if present	no	no	probably
ironic	in caricature	in caricature	in caricature	probably

Simply put, mythic and romance modes practically demand fantastic elements because the hero is so superior in kind or degree to men and environment. It is his superiority that carries him beyond the realm of the realistic. Similarly, the ironic mode has a penchant for negating the other forms through caricature, satire, and distortion, all of which deliberately depart from mimesis. Rather than continue in this abstract vein, let me turn in more detail to works within the four *mythoi* and show the way that these patterns foster or discourage the use of fantasy, depending on their own formal demands and on the demands made by the modal levels.

The romance *mythos* is the one most immediately associated with fantasy. It flourishes in adventure tales from romances like *Yvain* and the *Faerie Queene* to science fiction. In its simplest form, the pattern shows the hero at equilibrium with society. Then he either leaves his security to seek adventure, or is victimized and ejected. In either case, he crosses the threshold into a special world that is characterized by magic or other non-rational, non-normal forces. The hero undergoes tests and trials, survives adventures, and finally emerges triumphant. Usually, he returns to his own world and reestablishes himself. If there is no actual return, he nonetheless reintegrates himself with society, typically as a leader.[2] Obviously it is possible to follow this pattern without using the supernatural; many B-grade adventure and cowboy films do so, and these constitute the low mimetic version of the *mythos*. But in such works, the special world has been so rationalized and normalized that the only original element remaining is danger. It is hardly special any more. In less displaced versions of the *mythos*, the special world embodies an interwoven nexus of images: land of the dead or spirits, tomb, womb, and "belly of the whale" (as Campbell calls it). Adventures bearing yet the faint aura of descent to the underworld abound; and either at the crossing of the thresholds in and out, or in some central adventure, images of death and rebirth are common. In initiation ritual, an analogue and prototype for this pattern, the initiate is finally reborn into society as an adult. In what I believe to be the ultimate source for the pattern, the archetypal sequence of unconscious images studied by Erich Neumann,[3] the special world corresponds to the unconscious regions of the mind. Hence, magic — fantastic, non-rational images, the language of the unconscious — is natural to it. Even in the modern world of reason and science, romances tend to use magic devices and fantasy monsters, although these are sometimes given a speciously scientific air: n-space drive and time warps replace magic carpets; technologies from other galaxies make possible immortality or time travel or telekinesis and teleportation. The *mythos* of romance formally fosters fantasy. The affinity may actually be organic (if Neumann is correct) or just traditional. In either case, the historical preponderance of fantasy in the romance form conditions the reader to expect it, and authors to provide it.

The kind of fantasy varies, however, not just with authorial taste, but with the mode of the piece. The hero's relative superiority or inferiority to mankind and to his environment encourages some kinds and discourages others. A few examples of each mode should show how mode and *mythos* interact to make clear formal demands.

A romance in the mythic mode figures a divine or semi-divine hero or characters. Many classical tales would qualify, such as the story of Persephone, or that of Psyche rewinning Eros. Both, incidentally, identify the special world as the underworld. E.T.A. Hoffmann's "The Golden Pot" and Heinlein's *Stranger in a Strange Land* are more recent fictions belonging to this category. Anselmus' gaining semi-divinity in "The Golden Pot" was not a foregone conclusion. He felt poetic stirrings, but he also felt lured by middle-class material rewards. On the one hand, he is sought by the bourgeois Veronica; on the other, by Serpentina, who frequently appears to him as a serpent in a tree and offers him new knowledge which he can grasp only if he goes against the bourgeois taboos. When he does accept her kind of knowledge, he becomes indeed "like the gods", for as poet, he is creator of new worlds. Apotheosis naturally demands fantasy.

So does a plot in which the hero appears with his divine powers fully developed, as does the hero in *Stranger in a Strange Land*. Mike not only controls his autonomic nervous system and bodily functions; he has telekinetic power, and can cause chemical reactions in his body to take place simply by "thinking" the molecules through the process. Fantasy cannot be avoided in the mythic mode. While nothing can guarantee good fantasy, the potential exists in this mode simply because it is suited to deal with issues important to man. A god or godlike hero can face or battle the limitations that most trouble man, such as the meaning of life and death and the possibilities of transcending the ordinary. Setting such a hero lesser tasks would be wasteful. Under slightly different circumstances, a mythic romance becomes a religious work and even the basis for a new religion.

A romance in the next lower mode (the romance mode) is also extremely hospitable to fantastic elements, since the hero is greatly superior to the rest of mankind. To this group belong the *Odyssey*, saints' lives, many medieval and renaissance romances like *Yvain* and *The Faerie Queene*, and their modern descendants like *Perelandra*. To prove the hero's superiority to other men, he almost has to be supplied with fantastic adversaries. Odysseus is more than mere man: he consorts with goddesses, he listens to the sirens' song without perishing, and he turns down immortality. Whether the rest of us would comport ourselves as he does will never be known because we will never face his adversaries, they being fantastic. This kind of tale can address itself to moral questions, and offer comments allegorically as well as directly. Romance in the romance mode is logically a fertile matrix for fantasy, and historically it has proved to be so.

A high mimetic hero does not require a fantastic background. Most detective stories belong in this class, and they would be destroyed by the addition of fantasy. Seriously fantastic adversaries which a normal human could not overcome would necessarily change the classification of the work. But fantasy is often present as background rather than as adversary. A high mimetic hero on another planet – Shevek in *The Dispossessed* – would fulfill such conditions. The low mimetic hero can pursue a romance pattern adventure, but he must not comport himself too spectacularly or he becomes high mimetic or even a romance mode hero. Tolkien's Bilbo and Frodo are borderline, but while Frodo eventually becomes high mimetic, Bilbo remains a low mimetic hero. Alejo Carpentier's *The Lost Steps* is a good example of low mimetic romance in an intellectual vein; Nevil Shute's *In the Wet* or *An Old Captivity* are good popular examples. What differentiates the intellectual romance from the popular in this instance is the author's concern with music and creativity, with culture and savagery, and his self-conscious reliance on *Don Quixote* and the *Odyssey* for comment on the adventures. Interestingly, *The Lost Steps* avoids departing from consensus reality by only the narrowest of margins. The story's material belongs to the realm of the nonprobable, but never actually strays into the impossible. Shute's novels, most of them low mimetic romances, show people struggling to do their jobs, struggling to make the world a better place, struggling to be decent and humane even during world wars. What sets some of his romances off from other good war stories is his unusual indulgence in occasional fantasy: reincarnation and dream-access to the future or past. Shute could have written just the same story without departures of this kind, and the fantasy elements in no way make his heroes superhuman. His beliefs drew him toward the fantasy implicit in the romance form, even when working in so thoroughly mimetic a vein.

Once we reach the ironic mode, we have passed beyond the world of realism. The picaro or trickster or stumblebum or any other type of anti-hero usually embodies some negative realistic qualities, but he interacts with a world that is a demonic caricature of the one we accept as real. We usually root for this central figure, and he may achieve an ironic imitation of success or of failure. But we also look down on him. He must not prove too capable, and his success should not be too admirable, nor should his world be too magical in its departures from consensus reality, or our sense of wonder would erase our condescension. Don Quixote is a beautifully refined version of such a hero. We look down on him because he is mad: we see the true underpinnings of his fantastic encounters, and enjoy the dramatic irony inherent in his every adventure. Without literally departing from reality, Cervantes' fiction achieves that effect because at one level the episodes are luminous projections of the Don's gently crazed mind.

As we can see from even so brief an exposition, the romance *mythos* calls for and encourages fantasy in the adventures that take place in the special world. The mode of the story modifies and limits the kind of fantasy that can be developed. Fantasy developed too thoroughly in the high or low mimetic modes would almost inevitably change the modes, unless the author were working very deliberately to yoke logically disparate elements. Authors drawn to the romance *mythos* are likely to be favorably inclined to fantasy, or at least to daydream heroism. Readers drawn to such works will know subliminally what kinds of adventures to expect. Many will feel uncomfortable, even cheated, if the expectations are left ungratified or if the fantasies seem inappropriate to the mode. Brunner's *The Shockwave Rider* is one such disquieting romance. The hero is high-mimetic, but the society he inhabits is not ordinary; it is so demonically invasive and so powerfully in control of all facets of life that his overwhelming success against the system is not plausible. Named Haflinger, he is obviously a halfling, one who is half at home in the computerized society and half a successful member of the utopian counterculture fighting that computer world. He proves to be master of both worlds in the best romance tradition. Indeed, he serves as a *deus ex machina analytica*, a god out of a computer, who destroys the computerized society's ability to keep data secret. Yet he lacks the trappings of divinity needed to sustain such a power-wielding role. He remains only high-mimetic. *Mythos*, mode, and fantasy seem slightly mismatched. Although this disharmony leaves us uneasy, the discomfort serves no apparent point. Brunner does not seem to be trying to achieve a new interpretation of reality, nor is he trying to force us into new perceptions of the world through our discomfort. He has simply violated the logic of this form, quite possibly unaware that, in doing so, he has trespassed against our formal expectations.

The ironic *mythos* is the other which logically encourages fantasy. Frye treats it as anti-romance, but I see it more generally as an anti-*mythos*, the obverse of any of the three patterns. It violates their expected logic, whether denying their interpretation of reality or presenting its own assertion of meaninglessness and negativity. Like the others, it can operate on all five modal levels, even on the lowest, ironic level, where it parodies itself.

In the mythic mode, you would find the classic myth of Prometheus or the contemporary account of a down-at-heels god, J. Henry Waugh (JHWH) in *The Universal Baseball Association, J. Henry Waugh, Prop.* In Coover's brilliant story, Waugh creates a baseball world. When the phenomenal player dies, Henry leads a friend to believe that his own illegitimate son has died. One hundred "seasons" later, God has withdrawn from his universe: we as readers are no longer aware of Henry; we only enter the world of his players. The two dead players have become the sacred progenitors of a dualistic myth. What places this novel in the ironic *mythos* is partly its attack on the reader's sanity. In the last chapter, we lose all awareness of Henry as creator, and we enter his world, even as he lost all sense of the outside world to enter his creation. The story also attacks its own mythic mode: Henry is god to his world, yet clearly he projects this massive fantasy world because of his inability to face his sexual problems and approaching death. He is mortal and has patent hangups, yet he is a god. The fantasy in this story is twofold: it is the product of Henry's mind, and we only grant that the tenuous reality we grant to any person's dreams, but then the psychological fantasy becomes a fantasy world claiming the reality of any fictional world, and we succumb to its claim.

The ironic *mythos* in the romance mode gives us various kinds of romances. The quest itself may be undercut, as in *The Hunting of the Snark*. The hero may be undercut, as in the Middle English travesty *The Jeaste of Syr Gawayne*, in which the hero, because he is Gawain, is not a stumblebum, but he behaves with most unGawain-like caddishness. In Barth's "Perseid" we see not a man becoming a hero but a hero becoming a man. In his "Bellerophoniad" we see a man who follows the monomyth perfectly, yet knows in his heart that he is an imitation and fraud. Perhaps one of the subtler examples of this class – ironic *mythos*, romance mode – is *Sir Gawain and the Green Knight* itself. The plot is perfect romance, the hero all but perfect. What makes this – for me and for some other critics – an ironic *mythos* rather than pure romance is the poet's handling of the ending and of King Arthur's court. The poet hints, ever so delicately, at its internal flaws, the weaknesses we know will cause its downfall. Morgan le Fay tests Gawain's chastity and troth, the two virtues which, when violated by Lancelot and Guinevere, will destroy the Round Table. At the very end, the irony tightens its hold on what is otherwise a normal romance, when Gawain returns to court. He sees his own sins and failings; the court refuses to take them seriously. While he is still staring with sick horror into the abyss that has opened at his feet, the courtiers do the equivalent of singing "For he's a jolly good fellow". (The shallow and imperceptive response in the sextet at the end of *Don Giovanni* similarly heightens the irony, as Kierkegaard pointed out.) Gawain is the hero who returns with the ultimate boon – knowledge that could lead to salvation for his civilization – but nobody really listens to his message.

In the high mimetic mode of the ironic *mythos*, we find parodies of tragedies: Barth's *Taliped* play in the middle of *Giles Goat-Boy* or Fielding's *Tom Thumb*. In the latter, the characters are all courtiers and royalty, the concern is the love of a great general for the princess, his grotesque death on his wedding-day, and the wholesale slaughter brought on by jealousies and disappointed court interests. This is standard fare for heroic drama of the seventeenth and eighteenth centuries. However, Tom Thumb is no ordinary general. He is thumb-sized and (according to gossip) boneless – a mere lump of gristle. The adoration lavished by court ladies on this phallic figure provides amusing lightweight fantasy in a setting usually confined to the idealizations of the high mimetic. Thumb's death is also light fantasy: he is eaten by a cow. Both fantastic twists are part of the author's ironic subversion of the high mimetic conventions of the plays of his day.

Modern writers enjoy the low mimetic mode of the ironic *mythos*: the concept of modern man as the little guy lost in the labyrinth produces such stories, particularly if the writer is self-conscious, and can invite an analytic stance as well as identification. Pynchon's *The Crying of Lot 49* is of this class, as are Stoppard's *Rosencrantz and Guildenstern are Dead* and Vonnegut's *Breakfast of Champions*. Fantasy is not a necessary component, but the low mimetic world, when presented in the ironic *mythos*, does not preclude departures from reality as it tends to do in other *mythoi*. In *Rosencrantz and Guildenstern are Dead*, the protagonists feel their status as playthings of an arbitrary power. (God? Stoppard?) When they are hidden in the three barrels, the power shuffles them as if they were peas under shells. And when it is time for them to accept their deaths, they evaporate. In *The Crying of Lot 49*, Oedipa Maas discovers – or thinks she discovers – a massive, centuries-old, silent conspiracy, an underground postal system, a valued means of communication in a world where authorized channels are taken up with junk mail. Struggling in the mysterious web, she tries to determine if the alternative reality is real or the product of her own paranoia. Pynchon does not make the mail system impossible – it contravenes no law of physics – but it is exceedingly improbable, and in that sense, it is fantasy in a mode usually free of fantasy. Vonnegut, too, plays with fantasy and ironic inversion in his otherwise quintessentially low mimetic world of *Breakfast of Champions*. Vonnegut enters his own story and talks with Kilgore Trout, a character he has created and used in his other books. Vonnegut mingles with the other characters, and reaches a new personal insight of what is sacred in life by listening to one of his created characters, while also highlighting the helplessness of man by playing around with his helpless created characters. He looks at the bartender, decides to make the phone ring, and then watches him go to answer the phone. Many of the funniest effects in this extraordinary book come about through the insertion of the fantastic into a low mimetic world of fast foods and car salesrooms.

The ironic mode of the ironic *mythos* must be so self-conscious of its own irony that it almost parodies itself, and fantasy is almost always present. Gay's *Beggar's Opera* and Brecht's *Threepenny Opera* carry out their ironic reversals (Macheath's reprieve and lavish pension) and achieve their effect without departing from the possible. Though it is not likely that a criminal on the scaffold would be pardoned and rewarded, it is feasible, and allegorically, Macheath's good fortune corresponds to that of many corrupt politicos whose well-paid sinecures reward them for crimes. However, we do find fantasy in another example of the ironic mode of the ironic *mythos*, Coover's *The Public Burning*. Some of his fantasy is shocking because he makes historical characters like Richard Nixon do things they never in fact did. The Rosenbergs' execution takes place in Times Square, in the presence of all the celebrities of the day, with Betty Crocker acting as hostess and the Marx brothers clowning on the scaffold. Uncle Sam moves among the guests, a nonhuman entity, an animated myth, an American deity, the local embodiment of Mammon. (As Frye notes, the modes are cyclic, the ironic shading into the mythic.) Uncle Sam buggers Nixon in the last scene, the accolade which promises him the presidency. Ultimately, most irony pulls us down below the level of existence that we accept as real. It drags us to a demonic realm of nightmares, and this demonism is as much fantasy as any higher divine realm, such as the realms of beauty and order to which romance aspires. Hence the penchant for fantasy in the ironic *mythos*.

In most of their modes, the comic and tragic *mythoi* do not lend themselves to major departures from reality. In the mythic, yes. Dante's *Paradiso* or the Gospel story of Christ's death; apotheosis and ascent; any dying god – such stories, because they deal with the divine, transcend the ordinary. Prospero's experiences with the world of spirits and Beowulf's with monsters to some extent fall within comic and tragic *mythoi* of the romance mode. Within the high and low mimetic modes, however, fantasy is usually superficial. The ghost of Hamlet's father, the witch-fed vision of Macbeth, are a kind of shorthand, an externalization of processes and convictions that could be entirely internal. They are useful gimmicks. They can be used to heighten human feelings, but the same story could be told without them. Fantasy as departure into the future is common in the low mimetic mode: utopias (comic) and dystopias (tragic) are a kind of fantasy, but only in the initial given that nothing like them exists today. The human emotions remain similar enough to our own that we can identify with the future-foreign views we are being invited to embrace. In the ironic mode, fantasy again becomes a possible tool. It is not necessary: *Volpone* and *Tartuffe* do not depart from consensus reality, however improbable they may be. But Book IV of *Gulliver's Travels*, an ironic work which attacks the comic *mythos*, uses fantasy to indict the topsy-turvy values of Gulliver, his home world, and the world of the Houyhnhnms. And in the tragic *mythos*, ironic mode, Kafka's *The Trial* and *Metamorphosis* show the push toward caricature and then into outright fantasy when Gregor becomes a bug.

Frye's *mythoi* remain awkward because we also use their names with other meanings. His modes, in recycling the term "romance" and "ironic", redouble the terminological tangle. Despite this weakness, the grid of possible literary combinations that the two create is impressively comprehensive. Doubtless some kinds of literature remain which are not represented. Some individual works may waver between two forms which seem discrete in Frye's abstract pattern. In general, though, he has given us a way to view literature, one of whose incidental benefits is clear insight into the elements of literary construction which encourage fantasy because of their inherent characteristics. As we can see from the grid, fantasy is not a superficial frill added to a mimetic framework. Both fantasy and mimesis are structural, and their relative strength and nature are generally predictable.

Fantasy and the parts of narrative

In "The Concept of Plot and the Plot of *Tom Jones*", R.S. Crane describes plot as having three components: action, character, and idea.[4] All are present, but their relative importance will vary in any given plot. So strong is the natural tendency to emphasize one at the expense of the other two that Crane can characterize most plots as plots of action, plots of character, and plots of idea. Fantasy can likewise be seen as fantasy of action, of character, or of idea. One of these three components supplies the means by which fantasy enters the plot. Usually, if not necessarily, a narrative that has an action-orientation will also have an action-based fantasy and a character-based fantasy naturally appears in a character-oriented plot. Though such correlation is not exact, it is common enough to permit a discussion of just three orientations of fantasy rather than a nine-part analysis of the permutations of fantasy and plot. Recognition of the natural affinities and limitations of each kind could save some authors grief or suggest to them new possibilities.

An action-orientated fantasy is one where the departure from reality generates the action. There are two common kinds, one simple but usually trivial in effect, the other capable of producing new insights and effects but difficult to sustain. The easy kind, the backbone of pulp fiction, is based on a given departure from the reality we accept, but once that departure is assimilated, the story remains an ordinary adventure, with no new insights or experiences. Space travel, another world, the scientific "miracle" or magic: all work equally well and are virtually interchangeable in such fantasies. As most readers realize, space-opera is horse-opera passed through a transformer. Asimov's *Fantastic Voyage* lets a miniaturized submarine and human crew travel through the bloodstream of a critically injured man, its mission being to attack and destroy the blood clot in his brain and then escape before the spell – pardon! the miniaturization process – wears off. The submarine is more than a little like Cinderella's coach if we ignore the scientific trimmings. Once the departure is accepted, however, the dynamics of the story are normal. In no significant way would they vary were the setting in dangerous caverns, or underwater – whether in the oceans of earth or the canals of Mars. The same pairings, sexual stereotypes, heroics and villainies emerge. Dirty work at the junction of two blood-vessels is as predictable as dirty work at the crossroads.

Carroll's Alice books are much more effective as action-based fantasy. As with *Fantastic Voyage*, the gimmick is a strange environment, but in Wonderland and Looking-glass Land, the newness of the landscape is better sustained, and it creates adventures and actions which threaten the protagonist's standards instead of just offering danger. Alice does little, but she observes and reacts and judges. Each situation is painfully new and threatening, in part because events do not seem to follow a logical sequence. We form few expectations, and enjoy wondering what will happen next. The uncertainty is part of her adventure, and of ours. As readers, we see parallels between her dream world and the oppressive world of her reality, but our superior sophistication and insight convey little better interpretation of what is happening. For us as readers, the endings are a final irony, in that Alice finds the adventures so disturbing that she welcomes return to the oppressive world of everyday reality. This action-based adventure forced her to face too many painfully new possibilities, most of them threatening. *Fantastic Voyage* bequeaths to us the cheerfulness brought on by an escapist happy ending. Alice's return gives no such cheer; the girl who chafes at the bullying from authorities, and who wins her way to being a queen, can only, upon return, bully her kittens – lovingly, to be sure, but bully them she does, taking an adult role and playing it for all it is worth. Many readers who sympathize with Alice the child find this projection of Alice the adult disconcerting, and for more reasons than one are sorry to see her relief at returning to everyday reality.

Works whose fantastic landscape similarly generate action are David Lindsay's *A Voyage to Arcturus* and George MacDonald's *Phantastes* and *Lilith*. In each, there is an idea-component as well, but it emerges at the end of the story as a philosophy which the characters could be expected to embrace only after their assumptions have been battered and shattered by the fantastic landscapes and by their adventures therein. The landscapes dictate the adventures. The protagonists perform acts they never could or would have performed on earth – murder, absorbing the soul of another, and dying while managing to preserve consciousness. These fantasies could not be transposed to other worlds without altering their essential effect.

In all these works, the fantastic worlds generate the action. All are well-sustained efforts. The Asimov creation, however excellent it is in conception, has no new insights to offer us, and his special world is merely a backdrop for formulaic adventures, whereas the fantastic worlds created by Carroll, Lindsay, and MacDonald could not be transferred into any other world without destroying the story. The world *is* the action, and, therefore, the fantasy. C.S. Lewis talks about fantasy as gimmick and fantasy as new experience when he criticizes one kind of science fiction in which the author leaps forward into an imagined future when planetary, sidereal, or even galactic travel has become common. Against this huge backcloth he then proceeds to develop an ordinary love-story, spy-story, wreck-story, or crime-story. This seems to me tasteless. Whatever in a work of art is not used, is doing harm. The faintly imagined, and sometimes strictly unimaginable, scene and properties, only blur the real theme and distract us from any interest it might have had.[5]

He goes on to praise Wells' *First Men in the Moon* for "the first glimpse of the unveiled airless sky, the lunar landscape, the lunar levity, the incomparable solitude, then the growing terror, finally the overwhelming approach of the lunar night – it is for these things that the story (especially in its original and shorter form) exists".[6] Writers find it all too easy to introduce some wrinkle to reality which gives us the temporary fantasy of a new setting, but few can sustain the effort and fewer can challenge the assumptions either of the protagonist or of the reader in a fundamental way. Here is one aesthetic element which leads to triviality or rich effectiveness, depending on the author's tactics.

Fantasy based on character is relatively rare and exceedingly difficult to sustain. Perspectivist fantasy is the backbone of this group, and all the comments I made about nonhuman narrators apply here. Golding's *The Inheritors* is a good character-based fantasy. Entering a Neanderthal mind is startling and liberating. We learn what living within a strictly intuitive mind might be like. We share a collective consciousness and group identity; we struggle with what we would call rational concepts when no words exist for expressing them. The switch in perspective at the end, when we enter the Cro-Magnon mind, is painful, for we realize that *we* are the enemy. The Cro-Magnon mind and our own are essentially the same, and ours is the outlook which views the erstwhile protagonist as a beast.

A somewhat different kind of character fantasy but one that also uses a switch at the end is seen in Zamiatin's *We* and Orwell's *1984*. You might say that the stories start as political idea-fantasies which shift to character-fantasies. To drive their messages home, both authors want us to live through the breaking of a mind, so we experience and identify with the rebel-heroes in their rebellion, and then come to feel their total capitulation and love for the oppressive government.

Character-based fantasy is difficult to create and sustain. Adams' *Watership Down* starts with an attempt to enter rabbits' minds, but quickly lets the lapine vocabulary – owsla, sifflay, hraka – substitute for real strangeness, while the plot degenerates into the adventures of animals with human brains. These rabbits can communicate with a gull and can carry out forays that depend on careful timing and co-ordinated tactics. Men, dogs, and foxes take on new, lapine values, but these are very predictable. The novelty and strangeness which entering a rabbit's mind should entail quickly disappears. The fantasy of this adventure is literally only skin deep;

the minds and characters of these furry humans are but little touched by newness or originality. Rather than spin the material beyond its limits, an author might better create a short character fantasy. Borges' "Deutsches Requiem" lets us enter the mind of a Nazi who tortured Jews. That attitude is as alien to some readers as is a rabbit's, but Borges manages to maintain the full impact of his creation because he does not stretch it so far that the character comes to seem ordinary.

Fantasy based on idea can sometimes be distinguished from action-based fantasy only with difficulty, for the two blend very readily. Multiplication of humans as Bokanovsky twins is so important an idea in *Brave New World* that it generates the most memorable features of the new world and much of the action. By contrast, cloning in Clarke's *Imperial Earth* is incidental, an idea which allows an interesting emotional gesture, but which changes the action very little. In a good idea-fantasy, the importance of the idea is not just itself, but the implications for humanity. Gogol's "The Nose" illustrates some of the qualities of good idea-fantasy. If we start with the statement that a man's nose has disappeared, we hardly know what should come next. No plot is implicit in the idea. Yet the story becomes rich in suggestive meanings. The emotions which Gogol distinguishes – the social insecurities far in excess of facial disfiguration – plus the nose's phallic overtones raise the idea beyond a "let's pretend" ploy to the status of informing idea.

In the realms of the expressive and symbolic, idea-fantasies are readily identifiable. Borges' *ficciones* are clear examples of intense idea-fantasies. The idea of a lottery pervades, shapes, creates the world of "The Lottery in Babylon"; the idea of a library does the same for the world of "The Library of Babel". Action is practically nonexistent. The ideas of these fantastic worlds are the stories' *raison d'être*.

Many ideas need only minimal development. Like cartoons, they exert most impact when trenchant. Too great a length can trivialize even a good idea. What mars so much popular fantasy is either the author's inability to gauge the proper dimensions of his creation or his failure to enter far enough into the fantasy. For an action-based fantasy to escape the banal, the fantasy must affect the plot and characters in ways which would not readily be duplicated by other settings. Perhaps the greatest weakness of science fiction is that good ideas are so plentiful that writers have not felt pressed to develop them lovingly and imaginatively. But the good material is there, be it science, politics, philosophy, or psychology, man's future, man's nature, man's happiness, or man's failings. Some of these topics can be better approached through some form of fantasy than through realism, because a realistic treatment lets readers rely too lazily on their own standards and cultural assumptions. Fantasy helps liberate both author and audience from such sloth.

Fantasy in lyric, drama, and beyond

Although narrative fantasy is my main concern, a brief look at the formal demands of lyric and drama (especially the latter) may be in order. Insofar as a work has a story line, it can use any of the kinds of fantasy available to prose narration: "The Rime of the Ancient Mariner", "Caliban upon Setebos", and "Lycidas" are obvious examples of action-, character-, and idea-based poems with action-, character-, and idea-based fantasies. If the term lyric is narrowly defined to mean the expression of emotion, then the possibilities of action fantasy fade, but the other two remain. In lyric poetry, however, fantasy enters most easily in the symbols and metaphors.

Drama presents more complex problems. Some kinds of fantasy are not easily reduced to a physical stage, human actors, and a three-hour time span. A romance, for instance, with its special world and a time lapse of several years (to show the growth of the hero) does not translate easily into the dramatic medium. The very human limitations of the actors prevent them from giving convincing imitations of the greater-than-human heroes of the romance mode. Moreover, mimetically presenting the supernatural on stage is difficult. Machines for special effects exist, and have a long stage history, from the *deus ex machina* of the Greek theatre to the Peter Pan flyings of this century. However, our reaction to such an event in the theatre is not purely literary or emotional. We enjoy it for its novelty and expend our energy in trying to figure out how the effect is achieved, or in congratulating ourselves for spotting the mechanics. We feel little wonder, and such a special effect does not cause us to question our assumptions about reality. Moreover, the marvels which can be presented are limited. A hero like Beowulf might just be plausible on stage, but Grendel would be considerably less so. Even with flyings, Superman would not carry conviction. Science fiction has a minimal stage history; its materials transcend the limits of stage mimesis.

If, however, you jettison some of the mimetic assumptions we tend to bring to the theatre and accept symbolic drama, then some of these limiting considerations disappear. Symbolic fantasy is present in the scenic metaphor of Beckett's plays. The tree in *Waiting for Godot* is not realistic. In non-western drama, one finds nonrealistic representation: in Kabuki drama, animistic deities interact with mortals. In ballet, the narratives display firebirds and mouse kings as readily as princes and gypsies. Opera, too, especially in modern productions, uses scenic metaphor rather than realistic settings. Some operas even parade the overtly nonrealistic: *The Magic Flute* traditionally has beasts dancing to the flute, and a monster. In Bergman's movie of *The Magic Flute*, the moviemaker's awareness of the limits of stage mimesis shows itself in his sight gags: the presentation of Prince Tamino's monster flaunts the fact that it is only a man with a huge papier mâché head. When realism is not possible, one can emphasize the artifice of the representation, accept such a monster-man as a conventional symbol, and discard the mimetic assumptions that bind most drama. There will still be actions and plots not suited to drama – representation of a long journey is difficult – but some limits are superable.

Film suffers far less than stage drama from the limitations of mimesis. Super-heroes still tend to be merely life-sized physically, but their deeds can be made as nonhuman as the budget will allow. Film can present journeys better, for it is not limited to stage sets for indicating the shifting landscape. Moreover, it can produce amazing special effects or seek the fantastic through animation. Fantastic films are most likely to fall short in much the same way that science fiction does: the special effects are so rich that they lessen the need for developing idea or character. Action dominates, and the fantasy is too often merely a gimmick. This weakness is not necessary or inherent. Film can do much with fantasy. Cocteau's *Beauty and the Beast* explores character and psychology. *The Wizard of Oz* has a subtextual concern with the making of movies (metafilm) that does not appear in Baum's story but that lends a good deal of depth and humor to the cinematic presentation of the story. But the movie of *The Hobbit*, to take a single example, reduces to nothingness such elements of character and idea as were present in Tolkien's narrative, itself already notably action-oriented. The result is a silly vulgarization in which the child-sized hobbit becomes a most implausible strength-hero, heaving boulders as big as himself.

Film naturally emphasizes action because it is a visual medium; we can see action, but character and idea have to be presented through such action. Far too many films, especially American films, accept this natural tendency as a law of nature. Film is also limited by its customary three- or four-hour length. This limit is impoverishing, but, undeniably, film has potential strengths for both realistic and fantastic narrative.

Degree of dislocation and techniques for introducing it

Fantasy challenges our assumptions about many important issues: the nature of the universe and man's place therein; mortality, morality, corporeal limitation, space/time limitation, physical confinement to one sex and one body. These major issues differ in the degree to which they impinge on our everyday life and hence seem important. Galactic travel at speeds faster than light is relatively unimportant. It is merely travel, even though faster than we can imagine. Although n-space drive would overthrow our laws of physics, we are unshaken and our assumptions untouched by reading about it. After all, the aerodynamics of an airplane are incomprehensible to the man on the street, so a spaceship does not represent a new mystery. We are told that space is curved and finite; both notions defy ordinary imagination. Subatomic physics offers more troublesome concepts than interstellar travel, and so our assumptions about the universe – which for many of us are ill defined anyway – are not bothered by the fantasy. A fantasy concerning immortality, however, is more "important" even though personal, because its truth could change our own lives. Hence the importance of religious myth.

How can one distinguish between the important and the unimportant in fantasy? If we look at n-space drive, or many another science-fiction gimmick, we see that there is a simple substitution of a functional unit. Much shallowly developed idea-fantasy and action-fantasy is of this sort. Death-rays replace guns. Simultaneous transmission of matter (*Star Trek*'s "Beam me aboard, Scotty") replaces ordinary transportation. Tasting dragon's blood to learn bird language is more effective (especially for Sigurd) than hours in a language lab. All of these fantasies replace common functions (killing, traveling, and learning a language) with a fantastic version of the same process, but the function remains the same. Such substitutions can be simple or complex, but they rarely present fundamental alterations in assumption or perspective.

The power of the fantasy increases if it offers us something genuinely new and compelling. The limitations of our own corporeality can be abolished or the ground rules changed to give us new experiences. A ring that renders the wearer invisible changes the limits in one direction, as Tolkien saw in *The Hobbit*. Rebirth (as an adult, with full memory extending back beyond "death") is a new experience in Philip José Farmer's Riverworld series. Gregor Samsa's awakening as a monstrous bug represents another shift in corporeal image. Transformation of sex is another, seen in Heinlein's *I Will Fear No Evil* and Le Guin's *The Left Hand of Darkness*.

Insofar as a reader responds imaginatively to such fantasy, it has an edge over a more ordinary functional equivalent, but the importance of the fantasy still depends heavily on how the author develops his idea. If the author looks at all the implications and ramifications, then he may be able to go beyond gimmickry. In "The Sword in the Stone" section of *The Once and Future King*, T.H. White's turning Wart into various animals is only half-developed. The adventures themselves are self-contained and pleasing, but their implications are not made explicit. Wart himself hardly ever makes the connection between the displays of various kinds of power and his own troubles as king, so any connections to be made have to be made by the reader. Kafka too uses a shift to animal form but goes far beyond White in developing the implications as he follows Gregor's fate. The detailed presentation of the reactions of Gregor and his family over a period of time is a far more impressive and moving use of the idea of transformation than are Wart's brief adventures as ant or goose, intriguing and pleasant though those may be.

Besides substituting a function or transgressing one of a narrow group of standard assumptions, an author can reach a new kind of reality by manipulating language. Joyce does it in *Finnegans Wake*. Aldiss does it in *Barefoot in the Head*, a tale of Europe after a war waged with psychoactive drugs, where air and water bring new poisonings at any time, and most inhabitants live with chemically changed realities. Usually such linguistic fantasy is simply introduced to flesh out the author's central fantasy. Almost any new world uses a bit of linguistic fantasy for local color: Adams' rabbit world, Burroughs' drug world, and Joyce's unconscious rely on their languages to give them substance. The more elaborate the world, the more a new language is needed, and this creative technique incidentally makes readers feel that they are members of a select group, one that shares a private language not generally known to the public. But there is a limit. Beyond a certain point, the more difficult and elaborate the linguistic fantasy is, the more the audience will resent the difficulty it imposes, unless they feel certain that the result will repay their effort. Some readers were deterred by the linguistic fantasy of Russell Hoban's *Riddley Walker*. Straying too far from reality in the linguistic realm can damage our ability to explore the new world.

Many kinds of fantasy are a combination of these three means of dislocation: substitution, transgression against fixed limits, and linguistic manipulation. Awareness of the three lets us distinguish among superficially similar fantasies. Adams' rabbits are a simple substitution of one species for another. Their insights offer no contradiction of consensus reality. We see man, tractors, cats, and farms from a different vantage-point, but lapine and human perspectives are not mutually exclusive. *Barefoot in the Head* offers a more demanding vision. We may wish to deny its shifting realities by calling it drug-insanity, but the logic of the vision and the linguistic effects used to put it across leave us with few weapons to defend our own vision. If we grant the possibility of a psychoactive drug war, Aldiss' scenario seems all too possible. Plain substitution is stronger, "deeper", when reinforced by linguistic manipulation. As a story, Burgess' *Clockwork Orange* is substitution of a future society for the present one, but the invented vocabulary, its mixture of Russian-derived words and cockney rhyming slang, give power to the vision. In our own language, words have largely lost their primitive naming-magic. In a new world, with strange names, we feel the shadow of that original mythico-magical relationship between object, name, and namer.

In this chapter I have tried to discuss some of the relationships between fantasy and form. To an author, these observations may seem irrelevant, for one who creates is presumably responding to an inner vision of the world being created. But seeing the demands which form can make on fantasy lets us as readers better understand various authors' successes and failures. Seeing these demands also allows us to understand the existing literary map a bit better: where fantasy is distributed through romance, comic, tragic, and ironic works; why it is concentrated in some modes while virtually absent from others; and why its appearance in dramatic forms is so erratic. By testing the limiting factors in the relationships between form and fantasy, we also come to see more clearly how and why so much fantasy is "cheap". By contrasting action-, character-, and idea-based fantasies, we can see the attractions and difficulties of each, the easy ways out, and the techniques by which the fantasy creation can be expanded and developed until it really challenges readers with a new vision.

Most literature tries to wring from its audience an intense commitment, a focusing of the conscious mind, the intellect, and the emotions. Such focus and intensity are hard for us to maintain. To evoke them, an author often uses novelty, suspense, and identification. In fantasy literature, where the stories are not known in advance to the audience, novelty is more easily achieved than in traditional literature. But the fantasy will not remain of interest for a second or third reading unless there is something more than simple newness. The author must create some kind of new intellectual opening of the mind or some powerful sensation. Fantasy challenges us with perspectives we do not usually entertain. It takes some security to give up one's standard assumptions and try out new ones. Novelty helps startle and entice us to take that step. Belief is not really a factor. We know that what we read is not true in certain gross ways: no man turns into a beetle overnight. But successful fantasy persuades us to consider the situation as if it were possible. Or it persuades us to wish that the violation of consensus reality could take place. Or it suggests to us that a rich experience awaits us if we recognize the metaphoric ways in which the substitution or contradiction *is* true on a nonliteral level.

8

The problem of meaning and the power of fantasy

Why read fantasy? What does a reader gain from nonrealistic plots and strange images? What does a fantastic image mean? By what mechanisms does it give readers a sense of meaning? And is such meaning delusory? These are questions to be explored in this final chapter.

Basically, I am concerned with the interaction between readers and literature, and with the many roles played by fantasy in this complex relationship. I shall start with a consideration of man's omnipresent need for meaning, and what such meaning seems to consist of. After presenting the argument that our sense of meaning is essentially a matter of feeling and emotion – i.e. not rational or objective – I shall go on to explore some of the psychological forces that trigger this feeling. Various schools of psychoanalytic theory are helpful here, and each one – Freudian, Jungian, and Gestalt – sheds light on different ways in which fantasy can induce a sense of meaning. Freudian thought helps explain latent fantasy; the Jungian approach attempts to make sense of certain more overt or patent fantasies, the so-called archetypal images; Gestalt theory is particularly useful when we ask what makes some literary fantasies work or not, giving us a sense of the synergistic relationship possible between images or parts of images.

After culling what seems useful to literary study from these psycho-analytic theories, I will turn from their focus on the internal (i.e. the reader's) part of the meaning-experience to its external components. Myth is generally considered a powerful stimulus to the human feeling of meaning. Using the myth of Medusa, Perseus, and Pegasus as an example, I will try to suggest some of the elements that would have made it work on the feelings of the original audience (if not on those of later Greek philosophers). Comparing the myth to John Barth's recension of the story in *Chimera*, we can identify some of the techniques by which literature appeals to man's teleological cravings.

Some of the techniques in both the myth and Barth's fiction parallel those operative in the realms of religion and science. Consequently, I will go on to consider the ways in which the external structures provided by religion and science can induce a sense of meaning. Many of these ways have important parallels in the relationship between text and reader.

Both the internal mental responses and the external stimuli that trigger them are relevant to any sort of literature, not just to works that rely heavily on the fantastic. I am discussing them primarily in terms of fantasy, however, because the meaning mechanisms in mimetic texts are so often disguised and displaced that they are difficult to isolate and discuss. But before we plunge into these investigations, we need a working definition of meaning and its role in human consciousness.

Man as teleological animal

> Tiger got to hunt,
> Bird got to fly;
> Man got to sit and wonder, "Why, why, why?"
> Tiger got to sleep,
> Bird got to land;
> Man got to tell himself he understand.[1]

In this calypso, Vonnegut's last line pinpoints mankind's problem. Our need for a sense of meaning is so overwhelming that we must find ways to assure ourselves that we understand, whether we do or not. Later in the same book, Vonnegut invites us to relish the unresponsiveness of the cosmos and of God to this desire:

> And God created every living creature that now moveth, and one was man. . . .
> God leaned close . . . as man sat up, looked around, and spoke. Man blinked.
> "What is the *purpose* of all this?" he asked politely.
> "Everything must have a purpose?" asked God.
> "Certainly," said man.
> "Then I leave it to you to think of one for all this," said God. (p. 177)

Vonnegut makes us acutely aware that the meaning structures we have relied on in the past are lies. Religion, science, systems of social order, and economic and materialistic values – all are lies. He upholds religion as a useful lie, but treats the others as useless, even dangerous. Since we still need to feel that we understand, and the old structures can no longer be accepted, what can replace them?

The question of where to go if old meaning-structures are now empty leads us back to a more basic problem: what is meaning? Meaning seems to be any system of values that causes phenomena to seem related according to a set of rules, and, preferably, that makes them seem relevant to human concerns. John Gardner's dragon attributes this power of giving meaning-as-relatedness to poetry: the bard whom Grendel so admires provides

> an illusion of reality – puts together all their facts with a gluey whine of connectedness. Mere tripe, believe me. Mere sleight-of-wits. He knows no more than they do about total reality – less, if anything: works with the same old clutter of atoms, the givens of his time and place and tongue. But he spins it all together with harp runs and hoots, and they think what they think is alive, think Heaven loves them.[2]

Such a meaning-system, the "gluey whine of connectedness", does not objectively exist. It operates only as we perceive, or rather, as we project it. Meaning is subjective, and our sense of meaning is a feeling which the individual can experience. Aniela Jaffé, a Jungian, calls meaning the myth of consciousness.[3] This felicitous definition reminds us that we project meaning onto the cosmos, however much we think of meaning as something outside of us and objectively extant. Yet even if meaning is not "real", not independent of our perceptions, and even if we know this, we still seem to need it if we are to cope with everyday life and maintain our sanity.

Without a minimal system of values, we would be unable to deal with the flood of data reaching our senses. As Ornstein, Huxley, and others insist, our consciousness is a filter that removes as much as 90 per cent of the stimuli impinging on it, and it must have a grid of values for deciding what to include or exclude.[4] Without a way to distinguish between threatening and harmless or significant and trivial, we would always be poised for emergency action. No sanity would survive such perpetual tension. A minimal meaning system allows one to seek pleasure and avoid pain, lets one survive, do what is necessary to perpetuate the species, submit to some disciplines and delay some gratifications in order to ensure these basic purposes in life.

Such a minimal system of meaning is reachable through pragmatic reasoning and through experience. But larger frames of meaning, though by definition they must be experienced to matter, cannot be reached through formal logic or normal reasoning. Mystic experience, although intensely meaningful, is ineffable. Religions, being a jumble of beliefs, behavior codes, and mythic stories, are not free from logical contradictions. Neither is science. In attempting to be logical, scientists have had to exclude all values like good and bad, and limit their grid to consistency and predictability, but even in the greatly narrowed field remaining, contradictions and inconsistencies exist at the edges of their map. Given the limits put on knowability by Heisenberg and on consistency by Goedel, science cannot be expected to produce anything more than relative and limited systems of meaning. Nor can philosophy. Having recognized moral values as non-logical, the philosopher can at best find value in the act of making decisions in the face of total freedom.

Ultimately, the sense of meaning is a subjective feeling.

The ease with which man has found larger frames of meaning – systems that gave him some sense of significance as an individual, some individual purpose, absolute values – has varied historically with changes in culture. In a traditional, religious society, with its unchallenged religious mythology, both internal feeling and external systems for evoking it were less fettered than they are in modern western society. In the Middle Ages, for instance, religious authority was compelling, and science was not yet a challenge to its mythology. Christianity provided assurances about death, promises of a future life, mental disciplines to handle fear and guilt, rituals and rules to be observed, and the goal of salvation, which could satisfy man's teleological imagination. Not only were the physical and moral worlds made coherent by religion, the social and economic worlds also fitted the structure, and these gave everyone an inherited place in the social system, so that few had to make meaning for themselves.

Meaning seems to have been easier to feel then than now. Encouraged by the social climate (as well as by physical conditions – bad food, poor medicine), religious visions were common. Such projections of the unconscious mind can establish lifelong value-structures for the individual. Even in written form, visions like those of Dame Julian of Norwich were popular, and so was the literary device of dream-vision in poetry. *The Romance of the Rose*, *The House of Fame*, *Piers Plowman*, and *Pearl* are only a few of the many literary "visions", all able to use the intersection of external system and internal experience for their power and effect. Medieval and Renaissance paintings likewise attest to the power of visions – of Christ and heaven, or of devils and hell. St Anthony's demons were part of his unconscious self, but through his visions these unconscious elements became accessible to him. Besides visions to make meaning experiential, there were festivities that could help people get access to unconscious projections of meaning. Mikhail Bakhtin and Harvey Cox both argue that such feasts, although nominally religious, were often intoxicating and psychologically liberating.[5] There were also ceremonies of initiation, such as confirmation, knighthood, and investiture, which should have reinforced the individual's sense of progress and development. For the most part, these ceremonies no longer exist, or persist only in attenuated and atrophied forms.

Our access to meaning in this century is much more restricted. As Albert Levi, Colin Wilson, Abraham Maslow, and other twentieth-century thinkers in other disciplines have insisted, the men and women who lack externally imposed meaning structures and who do not impose them on themselves are likely to lose their grip on life.[6] Boredom and depression weaken their will to live, since nothing matters. Anxieties petrify; repression makes large tracts of the mind unavailable; life appears one-dimensional; and the visible world seems made up of entirely dead matter. Such individuals will be cut off from any experience of the numinous – whether the numinous is considered a projection of one's own unconscious or an independent force. This is indeed how twentieth-century western man is said to be. Twentieth-century writers have explored these depressed states of mind: Barbusse (The Inferno), Camus (The Stranger), and Sartre (Nausea) offer famous depictions of such mentalities. Many modern writers deal with characters who have lost their sense of meaning and are struggling to find authenticity: Pynchon's The Crying of Lot 49, Coover's The Origins of the Brunists, and Vonnegut's Sirens of Titan feature such protagonists.

I take it to be fundamental that man is a teleological animal. Pure survival will satisfy his need for a goal and significance, but when that aim is met the need for further purpose persists, and with that goes a craving for a sense of meaning.

Latent fantasy content

Before trying to navigate the Scylla and Charybdis of Freud and Jung, a brief defense is in order. Useful comments on the psychology of reading and on the psychological basis for literary fantasy are not easy to make. A Freudian interpretation of a story's component fantasies will not entirely agree with a Jungian reading, and both will differ from readings based on other schools of psychoanalytic thought, and all of these readings will seem at odds with the surface events of the narrative. Exponents of each of these psychoanalytic approaches tend to consider all other approaches invalid: a Freudian accepts a Jungian interpretation no more willingly than a Christian missionary accepts the religious pronouncements of the local shaman. To someone outside the factional disputes, however, the interpretations do not seem so mutually exclusive, particularly after one penetrates the preferred metaphors of each terminology. From such an outside perspective, each approach seems to offer a part of the total picture rather than an exclusive truth. No one approach applies for all readers or to all kinds of fantasy, but each will shed light on some. When I express reservations about an approach, I am concerned to establish limits of applicability, not to belittle the entire theory, for I am convinced that psychoanalytic theory can help us understand fantasy, even though its terminology and factional disputes interfere with our applying it readily to literature.

I have hitherto said little about latent fantasy content in literature because it does not depart from consensus reality in the same sense that a story featuring a dragon does. Indeed, the latent fantasy content may be the same for a piece of science fiction and a George Eliot novel, which makes it quite different from other types discussed in this book. To overlook it, however, would deprive us of some part of the picture of how fantasies in literature can work on us, creating a sense of meaning.

One obstacle to discussing the latent fantasy is the specialized language needed to present the argument. Terms like castration anxieties, oral engulfment, and anal fixation arouse acute hostility in many readers. The other obstacle is the disputability of this mode of interpretation. Non-psychologists dismiss Freud all too readily – but more damagingly, so do experts from other schools of psychology. Because such intradisciplinary quarrels seem to me to exaggerate superficial differences while masking fundamental similarities, they need not prevent our using the various psychological approaches as tools for literary study, and I shall ignore such disputes.

Norman Holland's *The Dynamics of Literary Response* lays out some of the relationships between Freudian theory and literature.[7] I cannot summarize his detailed arguments here, but would like to list the stages of latent fantasy he describes, and will mention texts relevant to each.

Holland lists seven phases of development which an individual must go through: oral, anal, urethral, phallic, oedipal, latent, and genital. These may overlap, and imperfect mastery of any one phase affects a child's success in mastering the others. Holland argues that unresolved conflicts and anxieties from such infantile phases are one kind of psychological content embodied in literature. Authors project their own anxieties into their stories as a means of handling their own subconscious tensions, and readers enjoy literature in part because it plays with these sensitive issues in a way that keeps them from seeming too threatening. Such sublimation is one of the recognized functions of fiction, as Robert Scholes observes at the outset of *Structural Fabulation*:

> As sublimation, fiction is a way of turning our concerns into satisfying shape, a way of relieving anxiety, of making life bearable. Sometimes this function of fiction is called a dirty and degrading word: "escapism." But it is not exactly that, any more than sleep is an escape from being awake, or a dream is an escape from not being in a dream, from being wherever we are when we are asleep and not dreaming. Sleep and dreaming are aspects of life which are important because they are necessary for our functioning as waking beings. A healthy person sleeps and dreams in order to awake refreshed. As sublimation, fiction takes our worst fears and tames them by organizing them in a form charged with meaning and value.[8]

The first phase, the oral, according to Holland and others, leaves residual images of oceanic oneness with the world (a positive effect) but also images of eating and of being eaten, engulfed, overwhelmed, confined, and buried. Poe's stories about being walled up or buried alive, and David Lindsay's *A Voyage to Arcturus* play with such images. In the latter, the hero's first experience is a sense of oneness with creation. He, Maskull, then survives several crises in which peculiar emotions all but overwhelm him: strange music from the earth-harp nearly kills him; a "passion storm" practically blows his emotional fuses; and a mad woman almost succeeds in absorbing his soul and taking over his body. He has a vision of all created life being the food eaten and digested by a disgusting god. Maskull's final adventure is a plunge through oceanic feelings of oneness, nothingness, and then dissolution of the ego into death. These are only some of the latent images from the oral stage embedded in the plot of *Voyage*. On one occasion, the underlying oral anxiety reaches the surface of the plot: Maskull's "sexual" adventure with a devouring female force takes the form of a kiss on her "gash-like" mouth. The forcefulness and inappropriateness of this orality in what should be a genital venture strongly suggest authorial obsession. With evidence like this, Holland and other Freudian critics seem justified in labeling some literature "oral". For the most part, this psychic substratum remains submerged. The tensions and anxieties played on are subliminal. Although many readers are made vaguely uneasy by Maskull's adventures, they are unable to say why. The images are usually not naively concerned with mouths, but they are censored modifications of these early anxieties. Those readers with oral-stage anxieties, however, are likely to find the story peculiarly compelling. Their response will be more intense than usual, and the tale will seem meaningful on more than just the philosophical level.

The anal phase of development characterizes another kind of literature. Its connection to a kind of prim, precise, repressed character was traced by Freud; its intertwined linkages to greed, money, and worldly goods have been expounded by Norman O. Brown; its characteristic functions of hoarding and expelling are discussed by Erik Erikson; and its emphasis on smells (putrid or etherially lovely) and on filth and corruption are widely recognized.[9] Sometimes a scatological theme will surface directly in a story, as with the frequent reference to excrement in Swift's writings. More commonly, this set of anxieties manifests itself indirectly through themes of gold and riches, or through extreme sensory images. Jonson's *Volpone* and Chaucer's *Summoner's Tale* are based on greed, and part of their aura derives from anal images: the fox's corpse, friars in the devil's anus, farts, and the like. *Sly Fox*, Larry Gelbart's modernization of *Volpone*, appropriately stresses anal matters even more heavily than the original. Holland puts Mann's *Death in Venice* in this group because of its obsession with fetor and corruption, and in the etherial group he puts some of Gerard Manley Hopkins' poems.

Holland separates urethral conflicts from anal and treats them as an independent stage. He associates this stage with images of flood and drowning, and with their opposite, fire. Psychically, he links this stage to the character who drifts aimlessly, flows with random current, as well as to one who experiences "restless urgency, or discomfort, as, for example, 'burning ambition'". He offers Kerouac's *On the Road* as an example, and one might add Stendhal's *The Red and the Black*.

The phallic phase is not primarily concerned with sex as such but with exploration, with risking oneself adventurously, and with aggression. At this stage, a child learns through trial and error the powers and limitations of the body. Plots influenced by these anxieties involve body imagery, fears of injuries and mutilations, and physical experiences that try the body to its limits. Holland links to this phase stories involving magic and the occult, ghost stories, omnipotence fantasies, stories of telepathy and telekinesis, primal scene fantasies, and plots based on all kinds of watching, peeping, and spying. Many sorts of tales belong in this group, from swashbuckling tales of derring-do to the painstaking psychological dissection of the peeping protagonist of Barbusse's *Inferno*.

The oedipal stage naturally concerns conflicts with parents, problems of identifying with them, fearing them, losing and finding them, killing them, loving and hating them. Family romances – rediscovering a lost parent or finding one's real parents – belong here. We can see oedipal tensions being caressed into relaxation in Mary Stewart's stories about Merlin (*The Crystal Cave, The Hollow Hills, The Last Enchantment*). More disturbing in their treatment of oedipal fantasies are *The Metamorphosis, Giles Goat-Boy,* and *Breakfast of Champions*.

The latency stage, and even more the genital, seem somewhat different from the other categories Holland discusses. In the literature reflecting concern with the earlier stages, the anxieties are latent. The stories are censored distortions of the actual tension. One can read *Breakfast of Champions* without consciously noticing the miserable background music of oedipal anxieties, though its presence is obvious if called to your attention. But the stories Holland identifies with the latency and genital stages deal with their psychological tensions directly, with little or no transformation, disguise, displacement, or management of fantasy material. The fictions of latency are mostly read by children passing through that stage, and the tales concern conflicts between children and adults, problems of understanding and getting along. *Heidi*, or Kate Seredy's children's stories, are examples. Likewise, the distortions and fantasy-management of pornography (the stories reflecting the anxieties of the genital stage) are minimal. The anxieties surface directly, and the stories function more to reassure the reader of attractiveness and potency than to disguise sexual content.

Psychoanalytic criticism has gotten a bad name, in part through applying such schemes too rigidly. Holland himself tends to interpret all night scenes as primal scene fantasies, ignoring the fact that twelve hours out of the twenty-four are dark, and some actions take place at night that are unrelated to sexual anxieties. However, his categories are useful because they help us see that a particular piece of literature might appeal to a particular reader if its latent fantasies match the reader's anxieties. Manipulation is one of the keys to meaning in literature. When literature successfully (i.e. pleasurably) manipulates a nexus of repressed anxieties, the result will probably involve both an arousal of tension and then a release. The anxieties themselves feed our sense of engagement with the work we are reading. They intensify our responses and make us feel that the work signifies something to us, although what, exactly, may remain hidden. More than one developmental stage may be invoked by the latent fantasies of a complex book. *Gravity's Rainbow* has a strong anal component in its imagery,[10] but we note too that its quest, like most quest stories, has phallic overtones; we also see the explicitly oedipal fantasies of Slothrop regarding his father, and the oral images of dissolving into sky and sea that grace the end of Slothrop's story. All these can work on a reader's sense of meaning, some more strongly than others, and they can also contribute to another level of meaning – Pynchon's philosophical message about western man's fear of death and the obsession with lethal technology that has become man's perilous defense mechanism.

A work in which the latent fantasy is crude and relatively undisguised may just seem silly to someone without major repressed anxieties on the subject, or the fantasies may be too threatening to face if the reader does suffer from such worries. Instead of assuaging tension, the fantasy material may aggravate it. However, if the artist is skillful, he can carry most readers beyond such obstacles to enjoyment. Thus it is with Pynchon's exuberant scatology in *Gravity's Rainbow*. A few critics cannot tolerate it; a few seem puzzled and indifferent, but most recover from their initial recoil, and become fascinated and pleased by what Pynchon does with his startling material. Fantasy is not a simple phenomenon and does not work the same way for all readers.

Patent fantastic images

Literature possesses more ways of influencing readers than the latent fantasy content discussed by Freud and Holland. Jung and his followers called attention to the power which "archetypal" images can exercise over the audience. Of particular interest is the argument that these images form a sequence, and while a literary work may simply emphasize one, we often find echoes of the entire sequence. This sequence parallels the basic units of the romance and even the tragic *mythoi*, and hence suggests itself as a psychological source for these major plot patterns. I want next to examine this sequence of images as it is expounded by Erich Neumann in *The Origins and History of Consciousness*, and then look at the latter part of a similar pattern promulgated by Lord Raglan. Raglan's sequence goes beyond Neumann's into the latter end of a hero's life, towards death, and also helps move us from psychoanalytic theory toward literature. Then, I wish to examine another set of images found in cosmological myth. These, though less complex than the Neumann series, shed some light on comic and ironic *mythoi*. Though doubtless it is impossible to develop a grid that could represent all permutations of reader and text, adding a Jungian perspective to a Freudian lets us identify more of the reasons that would drive an author to depart from consensus reality and more of the reasons an audience would welcome this departure, despite the contradiction to experience that it represents.

The hero monomyth is Joseph Campbell's term for the pattern he analyzed in *The Hero with a Thousand Faces*, which appeared almost simultaneously with Erich Neumann's *The Origins and History of Consciousness*.[11] Neumann's version of the pattern is based on Jungian archetypes and on myth and individual psychology. He sees the hero story as a reflection of the pattern of archetypal images which guides the unconscious development of the individual's psyche. Campbell, also influenced by Jung, collects his evidence from myth, legend, folktale, and literature, and presents his hero monomyth with more attention than Neumann to applications in literature and narrative. Lord Raglan, working earlier than the others, tabulated heroic legends in order to separate the shared pattern from the surface differences. While his twenty-two point story is rarely found in perfect form and is presented without any explanation for its existence, it agrees in many features with those of Campbell and Neumann, and it has the advantage of going further in the life cycle than they do. Other versions of the pattern appear in other fields: Vladimir Propp analyzes its functional units in Russian folktales, while Mircea Eliade shows its imagery in initiation ritual. In *The Educated Imagination*, Northrop Frye states:

> This story of the loss and regaining of identity is, I think, the framework of all literature. Inside it comes the story of the hero with a thousand faces, as one critic calls him, whose adventures, death, disappearance and marriage or resurrection are the focal points of what later became romance and tragedy and satire and comedy in fiction, and the emotional moods that take their place in such forms as the lyric, which normally doesn't tell a story."[12]

Frye may go too far in treating this pattern as the framework for *all* literature, for it does not account well for works that deal with the world beyond the individual, with society and the universe at large; for them we need the cosmological myth as well. But certainly Frye, Campbell, Neumann, Raglan and others have made us conscious of the single most pervasive literary plot in western literature.

The image embodying the earliest of Neumann's stages is the ouroboros, the serpent with its tail in its mouth. Implicit in the image are the ideas of a never-ending round, an encircling comfort, a complete entity uniting all opposites. At the personal level, they correspond to the child in the womb and to some early experiences of being nursed. To this stage, according to Neumann, belong a number of literary images, both realistic and fantastic: paradisal and pastoral worlds are linked to this archetype, as are also moments of ecstasy when the hero feels sensorily joined to his world by an oceanic sensation of oneness. All three express this earliest experience of meaning.

The fact that the snake has its tail in its mouth warns us of the flaw in this paradise: the serpent can let go and unwind. The womb and childhood offer no permanency. With the opening comes the recogniton of opposites and strife. The next stage is the dim awareness that consciousness and unconsciousness exist, and that the unconscious is the more powerful. The ego slips into it helplessly and has no control while enfolded there. The unconscious offers the attraction of letting go, but also the threat of annihilation. The image Neumann identifies with this stage is the "great mother". She is the unconscious. The Magna Mater cults of the Celts and Mediterranean peoples offer versions of this figure. She tends to be hard on her young lovers (immature ego figures like Tammuz, Adonis, Acteon, corn gods, and kings for the year), for she annihilates many of them. Whereas Freudians interpret the images of sexual congress with this mother-image in terms of the child's tangled relations to his own mother and his fantasies about her, Neumann interprets them as metaphors for entering the unconscious, and translates the threat of castration as the threat of being overcome by the unconscious forces. In Neumann's scheme, there is essentially no physical dimension to these images: castration and incest are bodiless terms. While Freud and Jung or Neumann might see their interpretations as entirely different, there are parallels between mother and unconscious for the infant, and our picture of the unconscious is clearly colored by mother-fantasies. Moreover, different readers may well respond according to either identification, depending on their individual experience.

The third stage is the ego's assertion of itself and its learning to identify with the conscious. Moreover, the ego gains enough control to push the unconscious away at times, to keep it from irrupting into consciousness. Neumann identifies the cosmogonic myths of separating the world parents as the embodiment of this psychic development: sky from earth and light from darkness represent consciousness and unconsciousness. These three stages, taken together, represent the first surge of development, and in literature correspond to the initial equilibrium of the hero and the gains he has made before setting off on his main adventure, or the early adventures that he undergoes before the main one. The next stages represent the heroic adventure itself.

What Neumann calls the birth of the hero seems better described by Campbell's term, call to adventure, since it alludes more to spiritual than to physical birth. The minimal gains in strength and consciousness so far are not enough to satisfy the ego. Furthermore, the unconscious, now being repressed, can make its demands felt yet not be answered directly. Accordingly, the ego needs further control over this repressed material. To this struggle, Neumann attributes a constellation of archetypal images which he gathers under the heading of the slaying of the mother and the father. Within these adventures come all sorts of monster fights, ordeals, and enlightenments. Whereas to Freud the slaying expresses repressed hostility toward the physical parents, Neumann sees the struggles as taking place within the unconscious and involving the ego in trying to gain control of various threatening aspects of the unconscious. This struggle with forces located in the unconscious is the basis for heroic adventure in literature. In Campbell's scheme, some of the staple adventures are meeting with the goddess (*Wife of Bath's Tale*, Rider Haggard's *She*), woman as temptress (*Sir Gawain and the Green Knight* has both), atonement with the father (gruesomely distorted in *1984*; used straight in *Out of the Silent Planet*), apotheosis (*2001*, *Children of Dune*, "The Golden Pot"), and winning the ultimate boon, whether the boon be treasure or knowledge (McIntyre's *Dreamsnake*, Le Guin's *The Left Hand of Darkness*). Neumann treats knowledge and treasure, the latter broadly interpreted as anything or anyone of value, as the chief aim of the adventures. After winning the treasure and freeing a captive, the hero is transformed to a higher and more knowledgeable state.

Campbell then describes the hero as returning from the special world of the adventures to his own world and becoming integrated into society, usually as a leader. The hero has gained mastery of two worlds, his own and the special world of his adventure. He wins the freedom to live in a manner that is better, higher, and fuller than that of his fellows. Within Neumann's scheme, the ego gains such control of the unconscious forces that it can resolve some of its anxieties, and rescue positive energy from the unconscious (free the captive, win the treasure). The ego's centering in the conscious is firmer than ever before, but the ego also has gained more control of the unconscious as well.

Both Neumann and Campbell deal rather sketchily with stories that go beyond the heroic first half of life, but Lord Raglan's twenty-two point composite pattern is particularly strong on the latter half of a heroic figure's life. Beyond winning his kingdom, wife, and enjoying success, he follows this path:

14 For a time he reigns uneventfully, and
15 Prescribes laws, but
16 Later he loses favour with the gods and/or his subjects, and
17 Is driven from the throne and city, after which
18 He meets with a mysterious death,
19 Often at the top of a hill.
20 His children, if any, do not succeed him.
21 His body is not buried, but nevertheless
22 He has one or more holy sepulchres.[13]

Out of a possible twenty-two points, Oedipus scores twenty-one, Perseus eighteen, Moses twenty, Arthur nineteen, Robin Hood thirteen, Sigurd eleven, and so on. From this set of standard episodes, we get a sense of the traditions that shaped such fantasies as the once and future existence of Arthur, the bodily assumption into the Perelandran third heaven of the hero in Lewis' *That Hideous Strength*, the strange death and transformation of Maskull in *A Voyage to Arcturus*, the mysterious disappearance of Giles Goat-Boy, and the later legends of Odysseus' voyage to the west. Lord Raglan defines his story units far more restrictively than do Campbell or Neumann, but both Neumann and Campbell do less well with the end of the hero's life. They slide away from the monomyth proper to talk of apocalypse and cosmic destruction rather than the death of hero or ego.

If we accept Lord Raglan's extension, recognizing that its terms are far more literary than psychological, we can stretch the hero monomyth to cover a life from birth to death. We have then a pattern that can embrace any sort of story focused on a hero. The story may cover the entire life of the central figure or any portion of it. Some monomyth stories concentrate on early stages: the Grimm "Hansel and Gretel" deals with the tensions and fears of the phase which Neumann calls separating the world parents. Some stories explore later developments: shamanistic or mystic transformation rather than heroic (*Dune Messiah*); the Raglan fall from fortune and mysterious death (Barth's "Perseid" and "Bellerophoniad"). Most of these stories use a condensed form of the total pattern, but direct their emphasis to a single stage or image within the sequence.

With this pattern, whether monomyth or Raglan *vita*, we have a strong tradition of situations, creatures, and beings that cluster about the hero in his adventures. Monsters and goddess-like women are the most readily recognizable. Neumann supplies a logic for the images by linking them to the development of a maturing ego, and thereby gives a reason for the sequence. That monomyth stories relate to "growing up" is generally obvious, even to someone who rejects Jungian terms and assumptions, but Neumann puts this obvious relationship on a more rigorous basis.

As Frye implies – although he does not develop the idea in detail – the hero monomyth encompasses not just romance, but tragedy as well. The sorrows of the hero who refuses the call to adventure, or who gets trapped in the special world and never finds his way out, constitute one form of tragedy. Hamlet stumbles into a world of horror and never wins his way through to the other side. Lear lands himself in a mad world and only partly escapes. Romance and tragedy, because they usually focus on a single person, best fit the monomyth. Satiric comedy, however, such as we find in *The Alchemist*, *The Misanthrope*, and Stoppard's *Dirty Linen*, or sentimental comedy like *Oklahoma*, or farce such as we find in P.G. Wodehouse novels, give us a paradigm for actions that does not coincide well with the monomyth. In comedy, our concern is more with society than with the individual. Young lovers may play roles of nominal importance, but they are often so stereotyped that we do not take them or their problems seriously. What matters is the re-establishment of social order. Those individuals who really stand out are the villains, and the comic plot calls for society to expel, circumvent, or convert them, or, in the case of *Dirty Linen*, to recognize its own hypocrisy and stop seeking scapegoats. Removing the threat posed by such figures creates our sense that the ending is happy, and so does a new equilibrium represented by the lovers' marriage. Because society, not a hero, is the focus of our emotions, many comedies belong rather with cosmological patterns of fantasy than with the hero monomyth, and it is these I would like to discuss next.

If we turn from the I to the not-I and look beyond man toward the universe, we find this other system of patent fantasy images embodied in what I am calling the cosmological cycle, consisting of creation, the world of time and history, and apocalypse. Much of the cycle has traditionally been the province of religion, since creation without a creating intelligence is difficult to narrate. However, the stories can focus on any part of the cycle. In this kind of story, we find a strong drive to view the world as object, analytically and descriptively. In the hero monomyth, the world is hardly noticed, let alone studied objectively; it is a sketchy backdrop against which the hero performs his valorous deeds. Furthermore, the hero himself draws admiration, not skeptical, impartial scrutiny. In the cosmological mode, even the protagonist is just a phenomenon to be observed, a part of the cosmos like any other. In religious exemplars of the mode, the objectivity is modified by teleological theories of man's purpose and favored status, but fiction of the eighteenth, nineteenth, and twentieth centuries increasingly presents man scientifically, as an object.

Relatively few works portray the whole of the cosmological cycle. The Bible and Márquez' *One Hundred Years of Solitude* operate on a grand scale, and Calvino's *Cosmicomics* and Günther Grass' *The Flounder* only slightly less so, but most works simply assume the beginning or do not care how things came into being, and focus on the middle or final stages. Stories of the world take many forms: realistic novels, comedies, and utopias, many ironic and satiric works, worlds of Sisyphean torment, and dystopias. Many of the Icelandic family sagas belong to this group. So do gloomy moral visions of man's corruption and stupidity like Miller's *Canticle for Leibowitz* and panoramic visions of large movements like *War and Peace*. Although many such books have a nominal protagonist, his development is less important than the careful analysis of social problems. When tragedy appears in this cycle, it tends to be social tragedy: the near destruction of the world in Brunner's *The Sheep Look Up*, and the total destruction described in Shute's *On the Beach*, are tragic manifestations of the cosmological pattern, and they belong to the apocalyptic end of its spectrum.

Sometimes the two mythic patterns – heroic and cosmological – are so mingled that one cannot relegate a novel to one or the other category. The hero of Le Guin's *The Dispossessed* is a high mimetic hero in a romance *mythos*, but his personal development has little significance if it is not seen in relation to the disguised version of our world and in relation to the threatened utopia from which he comes. Brautigan's *In Watermelon Sugar* concerns both the nameless narrator and the iDEATH community. The inextricability of the two patterns is made clearer in the latter if you accept the reading that iDEATH is a psychic landscape, a projection of the narrator's inner space.

The cosmological and heroic patterns share an organic metaphor – the life-pattern of birth, growth, and death – and with this pattern, they share a set of images. Paradise is associated with the beginning of both cycles. The world of time and history in the cosmological cycle and the special world of the monomyth adventure can be similar, and tend to be if the author's vision leans toward the demonic. The hero's birth may be part of a larger creation – as it is in some myths and legends – and his disappearance may be equated with a more general destruction.

Having surveyed these sequences of images, we can readily see how they might contribute to readers' sense of meaning. The theory of archetypes has not won a wide following, but according to that hypothesis, the archetypal patterns within our minds can be activated when we are exposed to images or stories that embody some of the characteristics of the unknowable inner patterns. This is one way that Neumann's images might affect readers, but there are others not dependent on archetypal theory. Many of these images embody the same anxiety-provoking material that appears in Holland's Freudian phases, so anxiety manipulation is often just as relevant here. That the images occur in a sequence means that any one image, B, will possess predictable relationships to A and C, and will thus be part of a meaning-structure. The commonness of the images will influence us through repetition, and that repetition in literature, rite, and dream reminds us that the images are important to mankind, even if we do not know exactly what mechanism makes them so. Yet another way the images impart meaning is to invite emulation or offer compensation. If the reader is growing up, the developmental pattern of images may offer a model for inner and outer development. Or if the reader is weak in some aspect of personality, identifying with a hero who is strong may both temporarily supply the lack and give the reader something to strive for. The compensation may also be less for an individual's failure than for something lacking in society. Our culture, for instance, deprecates individuality, let alone eccentricity, and bestows the kudos of success on life patterns that are almost exclusively materialistic and bourgeois. Readers may turn to hero monomyth tales out of despair over their sense that modern lives are unimportant and uninteresting. Such a discontent is often dismissed as immature, but can genuinely reflect non-material aspirations and standards which are not met by current homogeneous patterns of bourgeois life. Whether the reader is heartened or made yet more depressed upon returning to real life will be a matter of individual psychology.

For readers who prefer fictions based on the cosmic rather than on the hero monomyth images, meaning comes in a different form. Creation, the world of time and history, and apocalypse invite an observer's stance, so the meanings available are those offered in any process of observation: identification of the unknown, fitting what is observed into a pattern, explaining a new phenomenon, and accumulating data. Stories of creation and apocalypse are partly significant because they explain how we got here and where we are headed, and partly because they lay out patterns to tie loose ends into symmetries, or give us the sense of fitting into a design. Hero monomyth stories adapt the world to our desires as individuals; cosmic fantasies help fit individuals to the world.

Synergistic interaction between images

Images can give or at least intensify our sense of meaning in a literary piece if they work together rather than in isolation. When an author can bring them into a synergistic whole, the result is greater than the sum of the parts. Gestalt therapeutic theory, as applied by Frederick S. Perls, gives us a way of viewing such interrelationships between fantasy images. Its contribution is limited and elementary compared to those of the approaches inspired by Freud and Jung, and like those it is not designed for literature at all, but for dreams. Nonetheless, its insights can help us understand why some fantastic stories are so powerful, while others remain Grade B adventures.

According to Perls, all the things in a dream, be they people, objects, or parts of the landscape, are part of the dreamer.[14] They, as well as the dream "I", represent parts of the dreamer's personality, and in therapy sessions the dreamer can be asked what they mean. A man who dreams of himself in a desert can be told to "be the desert", and can then be asked "What does the desert feel?" He can give answers which gradually bring into focus the conflicts underlying the dream. To a degree, the fantasy content of literature can be treated like the fantasy in dreams. The hero monomyth's images turn up over and over in dreams. Anne Wilson, in *Traditional Romance and Tale*,[15] recognizes a relationship between medieval romances and dreams, and comes to feel that if a hero is cast out from home by a wicked uncle, for instance, this is not just bad luck or oedipal struggle. Rather, the hero needs to leave his childhood environment and needs to prove himself; the means that bring about the desired end are irrelevant compared to the results, and sometimes they may even represent the hero's unconscious desires. Wilson treats the romances as dreams. We can expect the same underlying unity of emotional content in a good fantasy that we would find in a dream. We cannot ask the author "What does that landscape feel?" But we can sometimes sense such a feeling, even as we can sense the fittingness of the hero's chief adversary, or the unsuitability of that adversary. When there is no underlying relationship between hero and landscape or hero and adversary, no synergy, we have the usual uninspired adventure story, but when an emotional tension or logic exists, as it does in dreams, the fantasy of the story is more alive and more effective.

Grettir's Saga is an example of a work with such an underlying dream-like logic, and this helps explain why the folktale material used by the author is so much better than the similar monster fights in most of the Icelandic sagas of legendary times. Grettir is a strength-hero, the kind of fighter who has a place in a frontier society but not in a settled, civilized culture. He is a professional hero, the sort who figures in American westerns or in some Celtic and Icelandic stories. As long as the settlement sees itself as a small, struggling circle of light surrounded by a hostile darkness inhabited by monsters (be they Indians, outlaws, dragons, revenants, or trolls), he will be accepted because he fights those monsters; nobody will care if his life is irregular, his morals elastic, and his violence excessive. Once that circle of light is regarded as large and the darkness seen as banished to distant corners and crannies, then this strong, assertive, ill-controlled man becomes a menace to society rather than an asset. Grettir enters life when society is already too settled. For a while, his exploits are a mixture of vicious juvenile cruelty and heroism, and we realize that he does not altogether understand the difference. He has not grown up and learned to harness his energies for the good of society. Interestingly, his first adventures with berserks, a bear, and a mound-dweller seem to retain elements of initiation ritual.[16] It is as if Grettir were being sent again and again into the sort of ordeal that usually accomplishes the integration into society which he so needs.

When integration into society becomes impossible thanks to enmity, bad luck, and outlawry, Grettir encounters Glam. This revenant lives much as Grettir will in his days as outlaw, preying on outlying farms, taking sheep, and using his superior strength against his fellows. Glam was transformed from shepherd to spook after being bested and killed by another spook. Grettir, had he lost their fight, might have been transformed in like fashion, but even in victory he becomes more and more like Glam, thanks to the curse which Glam put on him. This monster represents something like Grettir's future or society's view of Grettir, and as such is not just a random opponent. For Grettir to have fought a dragon at this stage in his career would have been meaningless, but this monster, Glam, is really a projection of Grettir's own inner being, a kind of shadow. Anyone viewing the story as dream would recognize the semi-identity of the two figures, and would see the encounter as having a significance beyond a mere wrestling contest. There is an emotional unity binding the two.

Sometimes the underlying psychological unity is obviously present: Kafka's fantasies are not random, and no one would liken them to Grade B Westerns. E.T.A. Hoffmann and Isak Dinesen's gothic stories may not dangle obvious psychological solutions at us, but we usually sense the existence of a logic that links protagonist to antagonist or to the mysteries he encounters. Odysseus' adversaries and helpers are, many of them, women and goddesses. The story has been seen as a study of the tensions created by his patriarchal values (father, son, culture, sky gods) and the demands made on him by the Mediterranean world in which worship of the Goddess was not forgotten. In MacDonald's *Phantastes*, Anodos' encounters with various forms of the feminine suggest the working out of some of his unconscious problems. Our interpretation of precisely what the emotional logic is may vary, but most readers sense the presence of such a unifying force in these works.

Brautigan's *In Watermelon Sugar* is an excellent example of a work with a mysterious underlying emotional logic. Even readers who can make nothing of the story tend to feel that they are missing something, not just that the narrative has no meaning. Such puzzlement is understandable. The story's surface logic is so dreamily disjunct that readers can quite reasonably differ in their interpretation of what the tale is about. It takes place in iDEATH, a small communal group living within a larger, more or less pastoral society. The name iDEATH suggests death of the ego, but whether as regression (neurotic) or as advance to a higher psychic state is part of the interpretive difficulty. The reader's theories of mental health and attitudes toward the ego will thus affect any interpretation. Within this curiously passive pastoral society, the nameless narrator is struggling with writer's block. In this sterile period of his life, two crises take place. His former lover Margaret commits suicide, and a small band of dissidents – all loud, drunk, lewd, and rude – commit suicide. Outside the iDEATH region are endless ruins, apparently of a past civilization, and both Margaret and inBOIL's gang of dissidents were attracted to the artefacts of this former society. Our only other clue to the past and its meaning is the fast-fading memory of the tigers. Once there were singing, talking tigers. They ate people and so were hunted into extinction, but some of the inhabitants, inBOIL included, regret their passing, for with their extinction went the last vestiges of danger, excitement, community solidarity in hunting them, and also the wild beauty of the tigers' song. The tigers had killed the narrator's parents when he was a boy and were thus responsible for his having moved to iDEATH.

A world in which the ego is "dead" would naturally have no room for tigers or for adventure, danger, and wild beauty. inBOIL in particular seems to wish to reject iDEATH because it has killed the tigers. He despises the low-keyed communal life as regressive, and he himself behaves aggressively and violently. If the entire world of iDEATH is seen as a gestalt, an exploded psyche, the expulsion of these unconscious forces releases the narrator from his writer's block. The account of the actions which we have just read, *In Watermelon Sugar*, turns out to be his book. Somehow, by rooting out the longing for material possessions and for ego-building excitement, the non-egotistical being finds it possible to be creative. Readers may disagree with Brautigan's theories of creativity and the possibility of combining it with low ego-drive. Whether one agrees or not, however, one can sense that the narrator's adversaries are not random, however difficult they are to explain in simple terms. One senses that they are part of the narrator, or at least embody his problems, even as Pauline, an anima figure, embodies a nourishing and supportive part of his mind, and as the tigers embody a part of his unconscious which has not been available to him since childhood. In this unusual fantasy, free from many of the confines of ordinary probability and plot, the author's own psyche is responsible to an unusual degree for the details of the story, and this may account for the underlying psychological synergy.

When such unity is missing, much of a work's inner tension goes slack, and it loses most of its ability to communicate meaning. Monsters seem mechanical and villains vapid. If synergy is achieved and if the reader responds to it, a sense of meaningfulness will result. We may not be able to translate that coherence into didactic or logical statements. We may only notice it in terms of our more intense involvement with the tale, but such interaction of images – fantastic or mimetic – contributes a sense of meaning, and its absence is one of the more obvious signs of artistic mediocrity.

Meaning in mythological images

Having discussed some of the ways literature imposes meaning on the reader, let us turn to some examples to see what more we can deduce. We have so far considered manipulation of repressed anxieties, the echoing of archetypal stages of development (whatever the actual mechanism), imitative and compensatory experiences, the enjoyments of an objective stance, and the effects of imagistic synergy. However, the ways in which literature imparts a sense of meaning are far from exhausted, so let us try to identify other contributing factors by looking at a mythological story. Myth is often deemed to have more meaning than ordinary narrative, and modern literary use of old mythological stories seems to be based on the hope that using such stories may intensify or deepen the work's ability to impart meaning.[17] Comparison of the Medusa, Perseus, and Pegasus myth with John Barth's rendition of the story will disclose more about meaning-structures in general, and about mythological meaning in particular.

This early episode in Perseus' life is a standard mythic fantasy. Within the framework of the Greek culture, a wide range of associations attached to its mythical figures, particularly to Medusa. She is a still-potent remnant of pre-olympian matriarchal powers, the Erinys side of the Great Mother, whose mask-face on household utensils glares "*at* you if you are doing wrong, breaking your word, robbing your neighbor, meeting him in battle; *for* you if you are doing right".[18] She is the evil eye incarnate, just as her constellation, *Caput Medusae*, includes the baleful, malignly winking star, Algol.[19] She was inducted into the olympian world in the usual way: Poseidon lay with her, presumably in his horse aspect, since Pegasus is the offspring of this union. She was provided with parents: Phorkys, a sea god, and Ceto, a sea monster. Her functional existence as a head without body is thought to derive from her presence as a ceremonial mask, but was rationalized by inventing the myth of her beheading. The two other gorgons, who have no functional existence apart from Medusa, nonetheless serve her by making her part of a female triad, which fits her into a familiar cult pattern seen also in the Horae, Charites, Semnae, Moirae, Graiae and others.

As these elements gradually coalesced into a narrative, we get the story known to classical audiences of Perseus, son of Danae and Zeus, who could decapitate the monster because he had the help of both Hermes and Athene. Athene then mounted the head on her aegis and used it to strike terror into her enemies in battle. But what does Medusa *mean*? Why should the beautiful Pegasus be *her* offspring? (In archaic sculpture, Pegasus is simply her child and they are shown together, the terrifying Medusa with a little horse under her arm. Hesiod makes Pegasus the miraculous creature of Medusa's blood, for he springs from her headless body, along with the hero Chrysaor or "Golden Sword".) Why should Pegasus' hoof strike a mountainside and produce the Hippocrene spring so sacred to the muses? What logic binds these together? How should the images affect us?

Medusa, as a terrible female who petrifies men, belongs to a family of images which Freud associates with fantasies about the human mother and Jung with the unconscious. More specifically, Freud links the Medusa-head with the genitals of the mother, whose lack of penis confirms castration fears. "To decapitate = to castrate. The terror of Medusa is thus a terror of castration that is linked to the sight of something."[20] But this touches only the negative elements in the story. The Jungian approach encompasses the positive aspects of the myth as well. In Neumann's terms, the ego (Perseus) allies itself with wisdom and conscious intellection (Athene) and suppresses the unconscious (literally puts Medusa's head in a bag). This part of the myth reflects the first step of development taken by an individual in childhood. The ego/hero goes on to fight the sea monster (ultimately another manifestation of the unconscious), and this time the ego manages to rescue from the unconscious some helpful and creative elements, symbolized by Andromede. This much of the legend seems relatively straightforward, but what of Pegasus? In most recensions of the myth Perseus does not benefit from this divine steed; Bellerophon will be the hero to ride the winged horse. One could argue that Pegasus' disappearance meant that Perseus had lost something by killing Medusa and suppressing that part of the unconscious associated with her. Also possible is the interpretation that something wonderful has been released by his conquest of that part of the unconscious represented by this image of the terrible mother. Insofar as the landscape of the story is an interior landscape, the something would be still within Perseus, within the individual. Before Perseus' action, it did not exist, or did not have freedom. Neumann interprets the ascent of Pegasus as the freeing of the libido from the Great Mother and its transformation into a force for heroic, spiritual, and creative endeavors.

The flying horse has many overtones: nobility and mobility, something magic and nonmaterial. It is also strength, a libidinal animal force. It is beauty born of violence and horror. In early versions of the myth, there is no evidence that Pegasus was a winged steed, just divine. Freud's map of the mind gives us little expectation of such beauty, but he would also associate this soaring image with phallic omnipotence fantasies and see it as celebrating the inception of phallic awareness and the birth of "Golden Sword". This may be true for some readers, but Pegasus seems more than just that. His bringing one of the springs of the muses into being suggests a definite link to artistic creativity. He is also linked to heroic activity, for he aids Bellerophon against the chimera. His being a flying animal makes him a dream come true and suggests ties to the spiritual aspirations of man. The horse appears to be related to what is best in man. To invoke this quality of spirit, the Greeks turned to a fantasy image, but they did not feel this to be a constraint, for they considered fantasy the natural way of expressing something nonmaterial. "Meaning" needed to be less explicit than we would like because the fantasy mode was the norm. Someone within the tradition, hearing the story, could react to it on any of several levels of sophistication. It is adventure. Or it is semi-allegorical: the gods can help you dispose of "monsters". You can recognize that the monsters may be inside you rather than something along the road. These manifestations of fantasy both derive some of their meaning from, and give a sense of meaning by, belonging to an established system of values. The gods mentioned in the story are known. Medusa's having lain with Poseidon links her to values beyond her own. For Pegasus to be descended from this union and to be associated with the muses give him a value-saturated context. Each story invests the next with a sense of meaning. Each generation of numinous creatures, indeed each new begetting, helps spread the numinous into our world, and imparts the glow of significance. Pegasus is yet one more irruption of the eternal into time.

When Barth picks up this set of images in the "Perseid" and the "Bellerophoniad", the fantasy figures change meaning. Barth's audience does not automatically react to them as part of living religious and cultural context. Although most of his audience will remember that Perseus killed Medusa and rescued Andromede, and will associate Bellerophon with Pegasus, the audience's grasp of details beyond those will be weak. Watching Barth transform old symbols is a lesson in how *meaning* functions in literature. His Medusa is not a monster; she is a beautiful woman transformed by hardhearted Athene because Poseidon took possession of her within the sacred precincts of Athene's temple. For us, a monster is relatively meaningless, but we react positively to a victim of unfairness or harshness who only wants to love and be loved. Medusa becomes a Cinderella figure made ugly by a jealous stepmother. She is rewarded with eternal life for herself and Perseus as constellations when he risks petrifaction by looking at her. To modern sensibilities, the underdog has a claim on our feelings. Such is the difference between our times and the classical era that we take the anti-hero and anti-monster seriously, and respond more readily to them than to their straight counterparts.

Barth's Perseus is also transformed. He is no longer the fair-haired golden-skinned hero, but a has-been. He is bored and his marriage is on the rocks. The aging of his athletic body depresses him, and bouts of impotence rob him of his confidence. Yet despite being mired in middle-aged woes, Perseus finds a new heroism in accepting his mortal limitations and in risking petrifaction to gaze on the woman who has loved him. He gives up his claim to hero-hood, and redefines himself as human. It is not his relationship to the gods (Zeus being his father) that matters to us, but his mortality, yet because the tale mentions his traditional semidivinity, we are made more acutely aware of Perseus' mortality and humanity. No mere mortal could have highlighted the human condition as well as he can.

When Barth turns to Pegasus, we find the soaring creature likewise displaced downward. He represents Bellerophon's sexual abilities, for Pegasus flies lower and lower until the fateful day when Bellerophon cannot get "Peg" up at all – in the stableyard that morning or in the bedroom that night. In Barth's eyes, we respond with less feeling to a comment on man's spirit or on his creative fire than we do to comments on his sexual potency. Indeed, a recurring concern in these stories is Barth's own struggles with writer's block – creative impotence – but he feels that we will respond better if the problem is cast in sexual terms. His equating sexual pleasure with Pegasus shows just how high sex rates on our scale of values. Indeed, sex has acquired a new sacrality, not because of its tie to the generation of new life, but because of its being one of the few activities capable of creating intense engagement with the present, a kind of concentrated consciousness.

Barth's fantastic symbols work for his audience because the symbols have an interconnecting set of values. Not gods and a known mythology, but rather a series of problems that characterize our *Zeitgeist*: modern man's sense of alienation and existential angst, the individual's sense of insignificance and helplessness. Lacking religion, many people acutely feel the limitations of mortality, and our culture's stress on youth creates extra problems for the aging. Significance accrues to the monsters and fantastic creatures because they are made over in the images of our problems. Once Barth manages to yoke them to these problems, he need only invoke selected troubles, and the rest of the troubles that belong to this cultural nexus will lend their weight to the fantasy images, intensifying our sense of their meaning. Our own angst gives them weight. In addition, therefore, to readers' personal reactions to the fantasies, patent and latent, we also see meaning growing out of systems of meaning, out of cultural nexes of values.

Systems of meaning need not be mythological. We see Borges inventing them in his *ficciones*. He chooses a fantasy image which has no ready-made frame of values – the library, for example. To this, he explicitly attaches a number of philosophical and theological issues concerning the nature of the universe and man's search for meaning. He builds a framework of significance for his image, and chooses a subject which, for his readers, has enough resonances that they can supply some of the meanings for themselves. Calvino and most authors who create intellectual fantasies use similar techniques.

Those who prefer to create emotional fantasies work in a slightly different way to lend significance to their fantasy creations. Significance here usually comes from intensity. Kafka, above all, but also romantics like Poe, E.T.A. Hoffmann, and later practitioners of their tradition like Isak Dinesen, occasionally achieve powerful results. The emotions are almost always negative: fear, humiliation, guilt, or frustration at a mystery that will not let itself be resolved. Sometimes wonder is also present – wonder at the unearthly landscape of Lem's *Solaris* or Lewis' *Perelandra* – but the wonder is usually subordinate to other emotions or to intellectual fantasies. Of course, intellectual fantasies use emotions too: in *Chimera*, Barth relies on emotions of failure and fear besetting the middle-aged man of the twentieth century, but reading Barth is very different from reading Kafka. The point of "The Burrow" is to feel, to be engulfed by the burrower's fears and anxieties, whereas in *Chimera* we follow the heroes through their anxiety out to solutions. Barth wants solutions to their emotional problems and to his own problems as a writer of fiction, but there are no solutions to the burrower's problems, and none thinkable for Gregor Samsa or for the hunger artist or for Joseph K. They can only suffer, and we can only respond to their guilt and anxiety, and to some extent enjoy the voyeuristic sensations of looking on at their crucifixions.

Besides the various sorts of meaning determinable through Freudian and Jungian theory, we also see the synergy that works through associations in the Medusa, Perseus, and Pegasus story: beauty is shown emerging from horror and violence; the muses' spring is brought into being by an imaginary creature who combines the spiritual and the libidinal, a combination important in poetry. We also see how a traditional cultural network gives value, and see how an author can integrate the original mythological values (or some of them) with a modern network to get quite different resonances than would be available in a story without the mythological component.

There is an elegant efficiency to fantasies. Like dream images, they can condense several problems or ideas. They distance and depersonalize such psychological problems as one's relationship with one's mother. The very condensation of fantasy images, their ability to resonate with the different emotional needs in the members of the audience, gives fantasy a power and effectiveness that are different from anything achievable by mimesis alone.

Literature as a meaning-giving experience

Examining the mythological story has disclosed more elements that contribute a sense of meaning. We can find yet more through analogy if we consider the meaning-giving structures of religion and science, our culture's two most important institutions for imposing meaning.

Religions induce a sense of meaning in several ways. First there is imitation: according to Mircea Eliade, one can imitate the actions performed by the gods and heroes of sacred time and achieve identity with them (see chapter two). Whether as Polynesian fisher or Catholic priest, the participant receives a sense of the numinous which transforms personal actions into something filled with meaning. In literature, we can read about such imitation and find reaffirmation of values already held; traditional literature from the classical and medieval periods encourages our sense of meaning in this fashion. We may also emulate more directly, as much didactic and monomyth literature invites us to do: a pattern deemed so acceptable that we wish to recreate it in our own lives proves its meaningfulness.

Second, religion shapes values by enjoining ritual obedience to complex laws. The obedience itself can seem meaningful, if only because one feels pleased when one resists a tempting act of transgression. Even breaking the laws can be handled by ritual penances, whose completion creates a welcome sense of relief at again belonging to the community. Such religious obedience possesses only faint parallels in literature, but some similar mental effects are caused by generic conventions: we submit to some kinds of unpleasantness (a sense of inferiority, or horror) in order to enjoy the relief. We also get some pleasure from seeing how the story itself submits to the conventions and manages to be new without departing from old and well-worn paths. Whenever an expressive or didactic work puts forward a view of reality we do not share, we submit to this new view, to its rules and assumptions, at least long enough to understand what it has to offer.

Another element in religion that reinforces the structures of meaning is repetition. Rituals are repeated on a daily or yearly basis. Traditional religious myths are told over and over. Likewise, repetition in literature helps activate our sense of meaningfulness. The most obvious repetitions are generic – hero monomyth and comic literature are very predictable – but repetitions within a story may also work in this fashion. Edmund Leach and Lévi-Strauss identify redundancy as one of the characteristics of myth, the repeated situations working cumulatively to enforce values. Odysseus' dealing with one female force after another makes us focus on the clash between patriarchal and matriarchal values. The repeated embodiments of the feminine in *Phantastes* and the repeated initiation-ritual adventures of Grettir highlight the protagonists' psychological problems and rouse reader concerns and anxieties that intensify our response. Even very limited repetitions, such as the two rudderless boats, two savagely jealous mothers-in-law, and two sexual assaults in Chaucer's *Man of Law's Tale* direct attention to the saintliness of the heroine, to sex, and to the place of sex in the life of someone who is trying to lead the perfect Christian life. And finally, in religion, we find meaning given to life through the offering of a goal, whether it be paradise, or achieving unity with the One, or winning liberation from the wheel of life. In secular religions, the goal may be the creation of utopia for one's descendants. Although there is little direct equivalent to these goals in literature, writers of didactic fiction frequently urge such a sense of purpose on us.

If we turn from religion to science, we find other ways of imparting meaning, and these too have literary parallels. Most we have already seen in the discussion of the cosmic image sequence, for its objective stance encourages the same system of values, but we have also seen parallels in mythic thought as well. The key concept is the system or network of established relationships. In science, this has been built up through the labors of many individuals, and much of the activity valued by scientists consists of fitting more phenomena into the network. Systems of value work for mimetic and fantastic literature alike. Realistic literature certainly invites us to put what we have read into our mental systematization of human behavior and nature. Fantasy images, if they are in any way traditional, invite our connecting them to the tradition: Medusa grows in power for having relations with such known numina as Poseidon. A dragon gains strength to the degree that we can see physical kinship with other famous dragons, or even with dinosaurs. Make the dragon untraditional – give it eight legs, some feathers, and no ability to breathe fire – and we will lack associations for it. We may even resent its being called a dragon. An author can deliberately seek effects by rupturing expectations, but he cannot expect readers to receive the sort of feeling of meaning that a network can confer.

Part of the value imparted by systems is the power of naming. Naming, in a scientific context, officially fits a phenomenon into the network of known relationships; it gives one a sense of mental control over that phenomenon. Similarly, reducing masses of data to a simple equation gives a sense of control and relief. In this respect, the scientist is the descendant of the wizard or shaman, to whom naming was also a form of power and spells were a way of controlling Nature. The powerful sense of meaning given by being able to name or understand a phenomenon, even if the knowledge gives us no physical control over it, is beautifully demonstrated in Crichton's *The Andromeda Strain* and Wells' "The Star": in the one, the global catastrophe has narrowly been averted, and in the other disaster still looms, but scientists in both become cheerful and excited, despite all peril, when they manage to understand part of the enigma. This sense of release that comes when the unknown converts to the known, and chaos turns into cosmos, is echoed in fiction. We see it in expressive and relativist fiction, where a reality foreign to our own comes into focus for us when an author names and describes it. We may know in theory that reality is unknowable, for instance, but Robbe-Grillet makes us feel this abstraction more personally when we grapple with *The House of Assignation*. As critical readers, we may enjoy a similar rush of meaning when we identify the genre of an unusual work, when we find a way to fit it into our mental framework.

Finally, science gives its practitioners a sense of meaning when they gather data. Anything new is grist for the mill. Literary novelty may be valued for other reasons, such as suspense, but when the novelty concerns human behavior in mimetic works, we are indeed collecting data and attempting to accumulate a detailed picture of human nature. Ultimately, we will reduce the data to rules of thumb, truisms, in fact, to a network, but at first we may simply collect it because it is new.

All the value systems of science come down to established networks of relationships, and these are as important to literary meaning as to any other. When we notice relationships among things, and between ourselves and the things we observe, then we will feel some sense of meaning. A biologist will view man as an organism, see his similarities to other species, understand his position in evolutionary, ecological, and anatomical systems. This set of relationships gives one kind of meaning. The nonscientist, to whom these classifications are not familiar networks, will see meaning in different systems of values, such as the aesthetic, the social, the moral, or the professional. Some readers get pleasurably excited when they recognize the influence of one text on another; others consider that knowledge pointless, but find a text meaningful if it affects them emotionally. Both feelings of meaning come from systems of value.

Through these and other kinds of structures, man nourishes his sense of meaning. Fantasy is so important to this cycle of creation and consumption because most of the networks of relationships are not scientific, but are moral, aesthetic, social, or personal. Laboratory verifiability does nothing to validate such values. Fantasy allows a dream-like overdetermination and condensation. The language of science (and, by extension, of realism) can achieve no such effect, for its whole thrust is to rely on a technical vocabulary in which a word stands for one universally acknowledged referent and no more. It aims to be unambiguous. Fantasy instead aims for richness, and often achieves a plethora of meanings. This polysemousness of fantasy is its crucial difference from realism as a way of projecting meaning.

Literature, fantastic or mimetic, is unlike religion, say, in that it helps us develop our sense of meaning whether we agree with the author's values or not. In literature of vision, for instance, we are encouraged to develop a strong emotional response to what we think of as reality. Not only is the narrative's alternative interpretation of reality likely to be vividly projected, it is often expressive of shock and anguish. If we fight such interpretations and assert our own, we will have to muster an emotional force capable of matching the original. If, instead, we accede to the new reality, we may acquire some of the proverbial enthusiasm of the convert. Barthelme's *Snow White*, an expressive reaction to reality, tells us we live in a mindless nightmare. Vonnegut cries that we are idiotic contributors to the history of human stupidity. In *Grendel*, Gardner tells us obliquely that no war, not even defending democracy in Vietnam, is heroic, and that heroic literature is nothing but lies. If our sense of reality has agreed with that of the author, we will not experience the sense of meaning that comes from conversion, but that of pleasure at eloquence, and at finding our interpretation ratified.

Didactic literature presses us hard to formulate our own values. It presents a coherent set of values and an implicit or explicit sense of meaning. Anyone who agrees, or who is persuaded to agree, with Miller's *Canticle for Leibowitz* will enjoy a sense of meaning. Anyone who disagrees and rejects Miller's solution must in fairness do it on grounds other than gut reaction or prejudice against Catholicism, for Miller's arguments are logical and powerfully constructed. Either way, the reader's own meaning system is activated and tested.

Escape literature, the literature of illusion, does less than the others to help us interpret reality, but even its many forms can give some experience of meaning. Pastoral writing invites sensory awareness, and helps us relate to reality through pure physical response. The comic and the farcical challenge standard pieties, and teach us to laugh at, if not to reject, our culture's sacred cows. Values are thus introduced, however lightheartedly. Even heroic fantasy sometimes exposes us to seriously-meant value systems. Few readers of Tolkien would accept his aristocratic values if they understood their implications. Aragorn is best because he is descended from a long line of kings and elves; those of lesser descent have fewer noble qualities, and there is no place in the power structure for a bright and ambitious nobody. Yet even after such readers comprehended that their inadequate ancestry would condemn them to menial or minor status, some Tolkien addicts would still accept a one-way ticket to Middle Earth. Tolkien offers readers experience in the feeling of devoting one's life to an unambiguously good cause, and the readers most gripped by this experience almost resemble early Christians in their craving for a beautiful ordering of experience, even if it is non-rational. Read in this passionate way, such heroic literature ceases to be casual escapism, and becomes something more deeply subversive.[21] Heinlein's *Stranger in a Strange Land* is a pleasant escape for most readers; assimilated passionately by the Manson clan, its values were twisted into one of the motive forces behind the Sharon Tate murders.[22]

Even those readers who do not succumb completely to the spells cast by Tolkien or Heinlein can experience the aristocratic values of the one or the sexual values of the other, at least for the time spent in reading (and rereading) these lengthy narratives. When such readers are no longer under the immediate power of the story, they may carry a lingering sensitivity to the values. The values of many heroic fantasies would crumble under logical analysis, but few people willingly destroy sensations that give them pleasure, and escape literature not only gives us pleasure but reminds us that a pleasurable system of values may have its own validity as a way of reacting to reality.

The literature of dogmatic relativism is difficult to classify in terms of how it gives a sense of meaning. Its whole aim is to destroy prior meaning systems and inculcate disillusion. Whether the result is despair or freedom is up to us. *Naked Lunch, The Castle of Crossed Destinies*, and *Exercises in Style* show us the falseness of our assurances. But however negative the author's intention may be, this literature does force us to consider the problem of meaning simply by challenging our assumptions.

As I stated at the outset of this study, fantasy is not adequately defined as a genre. Fantasy and mimesis seem more usefully viewed as the twin impulses behind the creation of literature. At times, I have tried to deal with them apart from each other, but they are tightly intertwined and not readily separated. Their powers overlap, but are also often complementary and sometimes synergistic, rather than competitive. Insofar as literature gives its readers a sense of meaning, both are almost always involved. Mimetic techniques can be used with no significant admixture of fantasy, but that approach to creating literature has certain inherent limitations (as argued in chapter two), and has ceased to be our principal literary mode. Mimesis still demonstrates its power when an author's chief concerns are social interaction and human behavior. Mimesis excels at establishing the relationships between people and the likenesses between the fictive world and our own. Mirror-like, such similarities draw our attention, and persuade us that the issues at stake in the story are relevant to us individually. Fantasy serves many other functions, but perhaps five are most important. It provides the novelty that circumvents automatic responses and cracks the crust of *habitude*. Fantasy also encourages intensity of engagement, whether through novelty or through psychological manipulation. In addition, fantasy provides meaning-systems to which we can try relating our selves, our feelings, and our data. In other words, it asserts relationship. Fantasy also encourages the condensation of images which allows it to affect its readers at many levels and in so many different ways. And it helps us envision possibilities that transcend the purely material world which we accept as quotidian reality.

Novelty, intensity, relationship, condensation, and transcendence of the material and the materialistic: without these qualities, literature would only be able to affect our sense of meaning in limited, rational ways – and ultimately, meaning is not a rational matter. Reason can only deal with the material universe, and few people get enough intensity or assurance from that to find scientific truth an entirely satisfactory frame of meaning. If meaning is the myth of consciousness, it naturally has some mythic qualities.

Writers can still limit their art to the mimetic; they can choose to accept the minimal system of meaning available to realistic fiction, and may do so because they feel that any claims to larger frames of meaning are false. But many modern writers have found the realm of material reality insufficient, and so have invented or rediscovered the numerous ways in which fantasy's complex power over our imaginations can be exploited.

Returning to the use of fantasy is no failure. Abandoning it for realism was an interesting development, and a logical concomitant to the growth of western rationalism. But we need not – indeed cannot – follow that path indefinitely. The rediscovery of fantasy should be cause for optimism, and good reason to alter our critical vocabulary. Like the right hemisphere of our brains, and like woman in a culture where the standard of definition is man, fantasy has been the silent partner, ever since Plato and Aristotle promoted mimesis in their critical statements. Even when richly and imaginatively used (as it is by Plato), fantasy has received little critical attention. Many benefits should accrue from filling the gap rent in western consciousness by Greek intellectual distaste for both the traditional mythology and for faddish attempts to rationalize it. When one represses painful emotions, one loses the ability to feel anything, pleasure as well as pain, and repressing consciousness of fantasy has exacted a considerable toll. Acknowledging the fantastic impulse in all its manifestations, from the trivial to the transcendent, should loosen some of the repressive bonds constricting twentieth-century writers.

As Pegasus, liberated, leaps toward the heavens, one of his hooves strikes the barren rock. The Hippocrene spring, sacred to the muses, bubbles forth.

Notes

Chapter 1   Critical approaches to fantasy

1 Alain Robbe-Grillet, *For a New Novel: Essays on Fiction*, orig. French, 1963; trans. Richard Howard (New York: Grove Press, 1965), p. 147.
2 The passage from Tasso's *Discourses* is cited by Wimsatt and Brooks in *Literary Criticism: A Short History* (London: Routledge & Kegan Paul, 1957), p. 166. Hobbes' comment appears in his "Answer to Davenant's Preface to *Gondibert*", in *Critical Essays of the Seventeenth Century*, ed. J. E. Spingarn, 3 vols (1908-9; Bloomington: Indiana University Press, 1957), II, 61-2. In chapter two of *Leviathan* (1651), Hobbes suggests that those who read romances and identify with their heroes suffer a loss of self; extreme cases like that of Don Quixote or latter day Star Trek addicts lend support to his argument. For Granville's opinions, see *Literary Criticism*, pp. 166-67. David Hume's animadversions appear in *A Treatise of Human Nature*, ed. L. A. Selby-Bigge (Oxford: Clarendon Press, 1888), pp. 10, 123.
3 *Hard Times*, eds George Ford and Sylvère Monod (New York: W.W. Norton, 1966), p. 5. Among the forces of fancy, Dickens musters a pub named Pegasus.
4 J. F. Webb discusses Bede's introduction of marvels as an accepted form of ornamentation in his *Lives of the Saints* (Harmondsworth: Penguin, 1965), p. 25.
5 M.H. Abrams, *The Mirror and the Lamp: Romantic Theory and the Critical Tradition* (1953; New York: W.W. Norton, 1958), p. 6.
6 C. S. Lewis, "On Three Ways of Writing for Children", in *Of Other Worlds: Essays and Stories*, ed. Walter Hooper (1966; New York: Harcourt Brace Jovanovich, 1975), pp. 29-30.
7 Louis Vax, *L'art et la littérature fantastiques* (Paris: Presses Universitaires de France, 1960), ch. 1.
8 Brian Attebery, *The Fantasy Tradition in American Literature: From Irving to Le Guin* (Bloomington: Indiana University Press, 1980), quotation from Irwin on Attebery's p. 1.
9 Eric S. Rabkin, *The Fantastic in Literature* (Princeton: Princeton University Press, 1976), p. 8.
10 Tzvetan Todorov, *The Fantastic: A Structural Approach to Literary Genre*,

orig. French, 1970; trans. Richard Howard (Cleveland: Press of Case Western Reserve University, 1973), p. 33. See also Christine Brooke-Rose, *A Rhetoric of the Unreal: Studies in Narrative and Structure, especially of the Fantastic* (Cambridge: Cambridge University Press, 1981).

11 Harold Bloom, *Agon: Towards a Theory of Revisionism* (New York and Oxford: Oxford University Press, 1982), p. 206.

12 W. R. Irwin, *The Game of the Impossible: A Rhetoric of Fantasy* (Urbana: University of Illinois Press, 1976), p. 9.

13 Marcel Schneider, *La littérature fantastique en France* (Paris: Fayard, 1964), my translation. This and the following quotations come from pp. 8-9.

14 Ann Swinfen, *In Defence of Fantasy: A Study of the Genre in English and American Literature since 1945* (London: Routledge & Kegan Paul, 1984).

15 Darko Suvin, *Metamorphoses of Science Fiction: On the Poetics and History of a Genre* (New Haven: Yale University Press, 1979), pp. 7-8.

16 J.R.R. Tolkien, "On Fairy-Stories", in *The Tolkien Reader* (New York: Ballantine, 1966), pp. 54-5.

17 Rosemary Jackson, *Fantasy: The Literature of Subversion* (London: Methuen, 1981), pp. 3-4.

18 For other overviews of recent theories of fantasy, see the early chapters of Rosemary Jackson and Christine Brooke-Rose. As second-generation theorists, they provide detailed analyses of their predecessors.

19 Robert Scholes, *Structural Fabulation: An Essay on Fiction of the Future* (Notre Dame: University of Notre Dame Press, 1975), p. 7.

20 Christopher Caudwell, *Illusion and Reality: A Study of the Sources of Poetry* (New York: International Publishers, 1937), ch. 1.

21 "Creative Writers and Day-Dreaming", (1908[1907]), in *The Standard Edition of the Complete Psychological Works of Sigmund Freud*, vol. ix (London: Hogarth Press, 1959), especially p. 153.

22 Georges Poulet, "Phenomenology of Reading", *New Literary History*, 1 (1969), 53–68.

23 Albert W. Levi, *Literature, Philosophy, and the Imagination* (Bloomington: Indiana University Press, 1962), especially ch. 3, "The Teleological Imagination".

Chapter 2   Historical perspectives on fantasy and realism

1 Northrop Frye, *The Secular Scripture: A Study of the Structure of Romance* (Cambridge: Harvard University Press, 1976), p. 14.

2 Mircea Eliade, *The Myth of the Eternal Return or Cosmos and History*, orig. French, 1949; Bollingen Series 46 (Princeton: Princeton University Press, 1971), pp. 3, 5.

3 Gabriel Josipovici, *The World and the Book: A Study of Modern Fiction* (Stanford: Stanford University Press, 1971), p. 27.

4 E. H. Gombrich, *The Story of Art*, 12th edn (London: Phaidon, 1972), pp. 35–6.

5 See my "The Thematic Design of *Grettis saga*", *Journal of English and Germanic Philology*, 73 (1974), 469–86.

6 Emile Zola, "The Experimental Novel", in *The Experimental Novel and Other Essays*, orig. French, 1880 (New York: Cassel, 1893).

7 Victor Shklovsky, "Art as Technique", in *Russian Formalist Criticism: Four Essays*, trans. Lee T. Lemon and Marion J. Reis, Regents Critics Series (Lincoln: University of Nebraska Press, 1965), p. 12.

8 See Werner Heisenberg, *The Physicist's Conception of Nature*, orig. German,

1955; trans. Arnold J. Pomerans (New York: Harcourt, Brace & Company, 1958), pp. 8–31, especially pp. 23–4; see also Hannah Arendt, *The Human Condition* (Chicago: University of Chicago Press, 1958), pp. 261–68.

9 This is implied by Jungian theories of the animus, anima, and shadow; when we project these qualities onto others, we often misinterpret the real person. See Jung's "Anima and Animus", in *Two Essays on Analytical Psychology* (New York: Meridian, 1956), pp. 198–223.

10 C. S. Lewis, "The Weight of Glory", in *The Weight of Glory and other Addresses* (1949; New York: Macmillan, 1980), p. 19.

11 Robert Scholes, *Structural Fabulation: An Essay on Fiction of the Future* (Notre Dame: University of Notre Dame Press, 1975), p. 1.

12 For various and somewhat contradictory definitions of premodernism, modernism, and post-modernism, see John Barth, "The Literature of Replenishment: Post Modernist Fiction", *Atlantic*, 245 (January 1980), 65–71; Gerald Graff, "The Myth of the Postmodernist Breakthrough", *Triquarterly*, 26 (1973), 383–417. Philip Stevick, "Scheherazade runs out of plots, goes on talking; the king, puzzled, listens: an essay on new fiction", *Triquarterly*, 26 (1973), 332–62; and James M. Mellard, *The Exploded Form: The Modernist Novel in America* (Urbana: University of Illinois Press, 1980), esp. pp. 14–22, 127–41.

13 Gabriel Josipovici, *The Lessons of Modernism* (Totowa: Rowman & Littlefield, 1977), pp. 110–11.

Chapter 3   Literature of illusion: invitations to escape reality

1 Eric S. Rabkin, *The Fantastic in Literature* (Princeton: Princeton University Press, 1976), p. 73.

2 Frederick C. Crews, *The Pooh Perplex* (1963; New York: E. P. Dutton, 1965); and "Hell at Pooh Corner", originally in *Punch*, reprinted in *Golfing for Cats* by Alan Coren (London: Robson Books, 1975), pp. 32–5, especially p. 34.

3 Joseph Wechsberg, *Sweet and Sour* (Boston: Houghton Mifflin, l948), p. 27.

4 C. S. Lewis praises such traditional, transpersonal fantasy and condemns the sort with personal and local wishfulfillment that one finds in "Girls' Books" and "Boys' Books" or women's magazines. He says that these offer only flattery and encourage a diseased outlook. See *Of Other Worlds: Essays and Stories*, ed. Walter Hooper (1966; New York: Harcourt Brace Jovanovich, 1975), especially pp. 29–30.

5 Bruno Bettelheim, *The Uses of Enchantment: The Meaning and Importance of Fairy Tales* (New York: Knopf, 1976), and a synopsis entitled "The Uses of Enchantment" in *The New Yorker*, 8 December 1975. For a discussion of the positive values of daydreaming, see Jerome L. Singer, *Daydreaming: An Introduction to the Experimental Study of Inner Experience* (New York: Random House, 1966).

6 "On Fairy-Stories", in *The Tolkien Reader* (New York: Ballantine, 1966), pp. 60–1 of the section entitled "Tree and Leaf".

7 D. H. Monro, *Argument of Laughter* (Carlton: Melbourne University Press, 1951).

8 Arthur Koestler, *The Act of Creation* (1964; New York: Dell, 1967), p. 47. Koestler's theory of laughter is set forth at greater length in *Insight and Outlook: An Inquiry into the Common Foundations of Science, Art, and Social Ethics* (1949; Lincoln: University of Nebraska Press, n.d.).

9 Immanuel Kant, *Critique of Judgement*, trans. J. H. Bernard (New York: Hafner Publishing Company, 1951), p. 177.

10 J.Y.T. Greig, *The Psychology of Laughter and Comedy* (London: Allen & Unwin, 1923).
11 P. G. Wodehouse, *Leave it to Psmith* (New York: A. L. Burt, 1923, 1924), pp. 265–66.
12 P.G. Wodehouse, *The Mating Season* (New York: Didier Publishers, 1949), pp. 8–9.
13 Nikolai Gogol, *The Diary of a Madman and Other Stories*, trans. Andrew R. MacAndrew (New York: New American Library, 1960), p. 46.

Chapter 4   Literature of vision: introducing new realities

1 *The Doors of Perception* and *Heaven and Hell* (originally 1954 and 1956 respectively; published in one volume by Penguin in 1959). See especially the opening pages of *Heaven and Hell* and its first two appendices for discussions of consciousness as a reducing valve, and of the biological and chemical stimuli that lessen its effectiveness, thereby causing it to let through more of the material usually suppressed.
2 Kurt Vonnegut, *Breakfast of Champions* (New York: Delta, 1973), p. 24.
3 Norman Mailer, *The Naked and the Dead* (New York: Signet, 1948), p. 99.
4 For a more elaborate analysis of the relationship between the *Odyssey* and *Breakfast of Champions*, see my "Kurt Vonnegut and the Myths and Symbols of Meaning", *Texas Studies in Literature and Language*, 24 (Winter 1982), 429–47.
5 John Gardner, *Grendel* (1971; New York: Alfred A. Knopf, 1979), pp. 35–6.
6 J. L. Borges, *Labyrinths: Selected Stories and Other Writings*, translated by various hands, eds Donald A. Yates and James E. Irby (New York: New Directions, 1964), p. 35.
7 Tom Stoppard, *Rosencrantz and Guildenstern are Dead* (New York: Grove Press, 1967), p. 27 (ellipses in the original).
8 Italo Calvino, *Cosmicomics*, orig. Italian, 1965; trans. William Weaver (New York: Harcourt Brace Jovanovich, 1968), p. 16. I have discussed the originality of these stories from somewhat different perspectives in two articles: "Science and Imagination in Calvino's *Cosmicomics*", *Mosaic*, 15 (December 1982), 47–58, and "Italo Calvino's Cosmic Comedy: Mythography for the Scientific Age", *Papers on Language and Literature* 20.1 (Winter 1984), 80–95.

Chapter 5 Literature of revision: programs for improving reality

1 Upton Sinclair, *The Jungle* (1905; New York: New American Library, n.d.), p. 136.
2 Matthew Hodgart, *Satire*, World University Library (New York and Toronto: McGraw-Hill, 1969), p. 12.
3 Ronald Paulson, *The Fictions of Satire* (Baltimore: The Johns Hopkins Press, 1967), p. 9.
4 Kurt Vonnegut, *Player Piano* (1952; New York: Avon, 1970), pp. 299–300.
5 Northrop Frye, *The Secular Scripture: A Study of the Structure of Romance* (Cambridge: Harvard University Press, 1976), p. 14.
6 Joseph Campbell, *Myths to Live By* (1972; New York: Bantam, 1973), p. 79.
7 For a more detailed discussion of Lewis, see my "C. S. Lewis' Trilogy: A Cosmic Romance", *Modern Fiction Studies*, 20 (1974–5), 505–17.
8 David Lindsay, *A Voyage to Arcturus* (1920; New York: Bantam, 1968), p. 285.

9 Walter M. Miller, *A Canticle for Leibowitz* (1959; New York: Bantam, 1976), p. 301.

Chapter 6   Literature of disillusion: making reality unknowable

1 E.D. Hirsch, Jr., *The Aims of Interpretation* (Chicago: University of Chicago Press, 1976), p. 27.
2 Tom Stoppard, *Rosencrantz and Guildenstern are Dead* (New York: Grove Press, 1967), p. 60.
3 Lewis Carroll, *The Annotated Alice*, ed. Martin Gardner (New York: Clarkson N. Potter, Inc., 1960), pp. 238–40. The original dates of the Alice books are 1865 and 1871.
4 Jean-Paul Sartre, *Nausea*, orig. French, 1938; trans. Lloyd Alexander (New York: New Directions, 1964), pp. 127–28, 129–30.
5 Raymond Queneau, *Exercises in Style*, orig. French, 1947; trans. Barbara Wright (New York: New Directions, 1981), p. 27.
6 Lewis Carroll, *The Annotated Snark*, ed. Martin Gardner (New York: Simon & Schuster, 1962), p. 56. The original date was 1876.
7 Antoine de Saint-Exupéry, *The Little Prince*, orig. French, 1943; trans. Katherine Woods (New York: Harcourt Brace Jovanovich, 1971), p. 87.

Chapter 7   Fantasy as a function of form

1 Northrop Frye, *Anatomy of Criticism* (Princeton: Princeton University Press, 1957). This and the following quotations come from pp. 33–4.
2 See Joseph Campbell, *The Hero with a Thousand Faces*, 2nd edn, Bollingen Series 17 (Princeton: Princeton University Press, 1968), and my "Romance: A Perdurable Pattern", *College English*, 36 (1974), 129–46.
3 Erich Neumann, *The Origins and History of Consciousness*, orig. German, 1949; trans. R. F. C. Hull, Bollingen Series 42 (Princeton: Princeton University Press, 1970).
4 R. S. Crane, "The Concept of Plot and the Plot of *Tom Jones*", in *Critics and Criticism*, ed. R.S. Crane (Chicago: University of Chicago Press, 1952), pp. 616–47.
5 C. S. Lewis, *Of Other Worlds: Essays and Stories*, ed. Walter Hooper (New York: Harcourt Brace Jovanovich, 1966), p. 61.
6 ibid., p. 64.

Chapter 8   The problem of meaning and the power of fantasy

1 Kurt Vonnegut, *Cat's Cradle* (1963; New York: Dell, 1970), p. 124.
2 John Gardner, *Grendel* (1971; New York: Alfred A. Knopf, 1979), p. 65.
3 Aniela Jaffé, *The Myth of Meaning: Jung and the Expansion of Consciousness*, orig. German, 1967; trans. R. F. C. Hull (1971; Harmondsworth: Penguin, 1975).
4 Robert E. Ornstein, *The Psychology of Consciousness* (San Francisco: W. H. Freeman & Co., 1972); Aldous Huxley, *The Doors of Perception* and *Heaven and Hell* (1954, 1956; Penguin edn, 1959). See also *The Nature of Human Consciousness: A Book of Readings*, ed. Robert E. Ornstein (San Francisco: W. H. Freeman & Co., 1973).
5 Mikhail Bakhtin, *Rabelais and his World*, orig. Russian, 1965; trans. Hélène

Iswolsky (Cambridge: MIT Press, 1968); and Harvey Cox, *The Feast of Fools: A Theological Essay on Festivity and Fantasy* (Cambridge: Harvard University Press, 1969).

6 Albert W. Levi, *Literature, Philosophy, and the Imagination* (Bloomington: Indiana University Press, 1962); Colin Wilson, *Beyond the Outsider: The Philosophy of the Future* (Boston: Houghton Mifflin, 1965); and Abraham H. Maslow, *Religions, Values, and Peak Experiences* (Columbus: Ohio State University Press, 1964) and *The Farther Reaches of Human Nature* (1971; Harmondsworth: Penguin, 1976).

7 *The Dynamics of Literary Response* (1968; New York: W. W. Norton, 1975), especially pp. 3–62.

8 *Structural Fabulation* (Notre Dame: University of Notre Dame Press, 1975), p. 5.

9 Freud, "Character and Anal Eroticism", in *The Standard Edition of the Complete Psychological Works of Sigmund Freud*, vol. ix (London: Hogarth Press, 1959), pp. 167–77; Norman O. Brown, *Life against Death: The Psychoanalytic Meaning of History* (Middletown: Wesleyan University Press, 1959); Erik H. Erikson, *Childhood and Society*, 2nd edn (New York: W. W. Norton, 1963).

10 Lawrence C. Wolfley, "Repression's Rainbow: The Presence of Norman O. Brown in Pynchon's Big Novel", *PMLA*, 92 (1977), 873–89.

11 Joseph Campbell, *The Hero with a Thousand Faces*, orig. 1949; 2nd edn, Bollingen Series 17 (Princeton: Princeton University Press, 1968); Erich Neumann, *The Origins and History of Consciousness*, orig. German, 1949; trans. R. F. C. Hull, Bollingen Series 42 (Princeton: Princeton University Press, 1970). See also Lord Raglan, *The Hero: A Study in Tradition, Myth, and Drama* (London: Methuen, 1936).

12 Northrop Frye, *The Educated Imagination* (Bloomington: Indiana University Press, 1971), p. 55.

13 Raglan, op.cit., p. 180.

14 Frederick S. Perls, *Gestalt Therapy Verbatim*, compiled and edited by John O. Stevens (1969; New York: Bantam, 1971).

15 Anne Wilson, *Traditional Romance and Tale: How Stories Mean* (Ipswich, GB: D. S. Brewer, 1976).

16 A. Margaret Arent, "The Heroic Pattern: Old Germanic Helmets, *Beowulf*, and *Grettis saga*", in *Old Norse Literature and Mythology*, ed. Edgar C. Polomé (Austin: University of Texas Press, 1969), pp. 130–99. Mary Danielli, "Initiation Ceremonial from Norse Literature", *Folk-Lore*, 56 (1945), 229–45.

17 For theoretical discussions of myth reused in modern literature, see John J. White, *Mythology in the Modern Novel: A Study of Prefigurative Techniques* (Princeton: Princeton University Press, 1971); William Righter, *Myth and Literature* (London: Routledge & Kegan Paul, 1975); and Eric Gould, *Mythical Intentions in Modern Literature* (Princeton: Princeton University Press, 1981).

18 Jane Ellen Harrison, *Prolegomena to the Study of Greek Religion* (1903; London: Merlin Press, 1962), p. 188.

19 Jerome Y. Lettvin offers some unusual suggestions for the origin of the myth and the physical form its characters take in his analysis of the winking star in *Caput Medusae*. He suggests the octopus as ultimate source for the snaky head of the Gorgon. See "The Gorgon's Eye", *Technology Review*, 80 (December 1977), 74–83.

20 Freud discusses Medusa (though not Pegasus) in "Medusa's Head", in *The Complete Psychological Works of Sigmund Freud*, xviii, pp. 273–74; Neumann analyzes the Perseus story as paradigm for the hero myth in *The Origins and History of Consciousness*, pp. 213–19.

21 For the subversive qualities of fantasy in general, see Rosemary Jackson, *Fantasy: The Literature of Subversion* (London: Methuen, 1981).

22 Ed Sanders, *The Family* (1971; London: Rupert Hart-Davis, 1972). *Stranger in a Strange Land* greatly influenced Manson, but in fairness to Heinlein, we should note that Manson's favorite reading was the Bible (Sanders, p. 30).

Index

)